THE
MYSTIC
HAND

ALSO BY JOHAN VAN OVERTVELDT

The Chicago School

Bernanke's Test

The End of the Euro

A Giant Reborn

THE
MYSTIC
HAND

How Central Banks Shaped the
21st Century Global Economy

JOHAN VAN OVERTVELDT
WITH STIJN ROCHER

A B2 BOOK

AGATE

CHICAGO

First printed in January 2022

Printed in the United States

Library of Congress Cataloging-in-Publication Data

Names: van Overtveldt, Johan, author.
Title: The mystic hand / Johan Van Overtveldt, with the collaboration of Stijn Rocher
Description: Chicago : B2, [2022] | Includes bibliographical references. |
    Summary: "From a leading European figure in finance and economics, a
    look at the once and future role of central bankers-the pivotal players
    in shaping the global economy"-- Provided by publisher.
Identifiers: LCCN 2021022486 (print) | LCCN 2021022487 (ebook) | ISBN
    9781572843066 (hardcover) | ISBN 9781572848566 (ebook)
Subjects: LCSH: Banks and banking, Central. | Monetary policy. | Economic
    policy.
Classification: LCC HG1811 .O93 2022 (print) | LCC HG1811 (ebook) | DDC
    332.1/12--dc23
LC record available at https://lccn.loc.gov/2021022486
LC ebook record available at https://lccn.loc.gov/2021022487

10 9 8 7 6 5 4 3 2 1   22 23 24 25

B2 is an imprint of Agate Publishing. Agate books are available in bulk at discount prices. Single copies are available prepaid direct from the publisher.

AgatePublishing.com

More information can be found at TheMysticHand.com

This book is dedicated to the memory of Milton Friedman (1912–2006) and Paul Volcker (1927–2019), towering figures in the fields of monetary economics and central bank policies.

"There have been three great inventions since the beginning of time: fire, the wheel, and central banking."[1]
—Will Rogers, American humorist

"Since I've become a central banker, I've learned to mumble with great incoherence. If I seem unduly clear to you, you must have misunderstood what I said."[2]
—Alan Greenspan, chairman of the Federal Reserve Board, 1987–2006

"There are very few people who really understand what is going on."[3]
—Isabel Schnabel, executive board member of the European Central Bank

Contents

Introduction

CENTRAL BANK POLICIES HAVE ALWAYS HAD A HUGE IMPACT on private sector developments, public finances, and government policies—and not always for the better. My years of government service confirmed to me what economists like Raghuram Rajan have been saying for some time: when central bankers say they'll do "whatever it takes" or, on occasion, that they can "do even more," politicians have little impetus to enact structural reforms, reduce spending, and optimize revenue. Moreover, by taking on risky assets, central banks can incur losses that could hamper their capital and reduce their capacity to pay dividends, which directly affects the budget of their nation or region. Last, their policies on exchange rates play a significant role in ratcheting up trade tensions.

In short, since the 2007–2009 global financial crisis, central bankers have become pivotal players *par excellence* in economic and financial matters, and the immediate and bold actions they have taken in response to the COVID-19 pandemic have further expanded their domination. Their hand, so to speak, is felt everywhere, more so than ever before in human history. And that hand is surrounded by a lot of mystique.

During the April 2017 spring meeting of the International Monetary Fund (IMF) in Washington, DC, Christine Lagarde, the IMF's managing director, hosted an informal dinner meeting on the state of play within the euro area. Europe's monetary union was still recovering from the global financial crisis that had brought the union to the brink of collapse. In those days, concern was mounting at the IMF that the much-needed completion of the European monetary union infrastructure wasn't moving along as expected or necessary. As Belgium's minister of finance, I was among Lagarde's guests. On my way to the elevator in the IMF's main building on Nineteenth Street and Pennsylvania Avenue, I ran into another guest, Mario Draghi. Draghi is an old hand in monetary affairs who in 2011 succeeded Jean-Claude Trichet as the third president of the European Central Bank (ECB). (In late 2019, Lagarde succeeded Draghi as the fourth president.)

Although Draghi was rarely absent from the Eurogroup meetings of the euro-area ministers of finance that I attended in my capacity as Belgium's minister of finance from 2014 to 2018, this was my first real opportunity for a *tete à tete* with this brilliant banker, economist, and skilled political operator—one with a more-than-superficial Machiavellian touch. Draghi had serious credentials: he earned his PhD in economics at MIT; taught economics at the University of Florence; gained private-sector experience as the vice chairman of investment bank Goldman Sachs International; and served many roles in the public sector, including governor of the Bank of Italy, president of the ECB, and chairman of the Financial Stability Board. In February 2021, he became prime minister of an Italy engrossed in a full-blown crisis. I had no doubt that Draghi had almost singlehandedly saved Europe's monetary union from a chaotic implosion when, in July 2012, he made a "whatever it takes" speech in London that dramatically turned the tables on the euro crisis.

At the time of Lagarde's dinner, Draghi's ECB was still in the midst of its first asset purchase program—better known as *quantitative easing (QE)*—intended to calm financial markets, boost the European Union economy, and lift its inflation rate to closer to 2 percent in the aftermath of the 2007–2009 global financial crisis. As part of the same exercise, ECB moved to negative policy rates in June 2014—a bold and controversial move.

The conversation Draghi and I began in the elevator continued through the aperitif at Lagarde's dinner. I explained that I understood and greatly appreciated the actions the ECB had undertaken to first fight the financial crisis and then to save the euro area from extinction.[1] But wasn't it time, I suggested, to start turning the policy wheel? Did a 2 percent inflation target still make sense? Weren't the positive macroeconomic effects of the ECB policies melting away? Was the ECB running the risk of perpetual bubbles? Wasn't the fallout of his moves a subtle but very real assault on the savings held by ordinary citizens? Weren't very low and even negative policy rates set by the ECB becoming a heavy burden to carry for banks and other financial institutions, not to mention insurance companies and pension funds? In short: weren't the "unintended consequences" of the ECB's ultra-accommodative monetary policy eclipsing the positive effects of those policies?

Calmly, but decidedly, Draghi rejected my suggestions. "My responsibility," he argued, "is to take care of price stability within the euro area. This means getting inflation below but close to 2 percent and keeping inflation expectations anchored there. We're not yet there at all. If the policies we need in order to get to that statutory obligation of the ECB necessitate banks and financial institutions to adjust their business models, well, so be it. I'm not responsible for the bottom line of the banks' profit and loss account."

Draghi paused for a few seconds, gazed sternly into my eyes, and slowly but emphatically fired off a warning: "Everybody, and certainly you politicians, has to realize that we, the central bankers, cannot do everything. We create breathing space for you guys to act. Now play your part, too, and accelerate structural reforms. You better get at it soon. We're not magicians."

Draghi's sharp remark made me recall an in-between-meetings conversation I'd had with Benoît Cœuré, a brilliant French public servant (an *énarque*, a graduate of the top-level École Nationale) who was a member of the ECB's executive committee from 2012 to 2019. I encountered Cœuré in early 2016 at a Eurogroup meeting in Brussels. At that time, the ECB was a year and a half into its first quantitative easing program. I asked Cœuré to tell me what, in his opinion, were the limits of the program.

After he was silent for a few seconds, the always polite and somewhat shy Frenchman giggled and replied, "Well, when the entire euro economy is on the balance sheet of the ECB, then the asset purchase program will have hit its limits."

I couldn't find words for a response to his remarkable statement and instead mustered an expression that suggested, "Come on, you're joking." Cœuré's response was similarly silent, but his expression indicated, "I'm joking indeed…but not completely."

These encounters with Draghi and Cœuré became ingrained in my memory—particularly Draghi's reminder that he wasn't a magician. To me, they are a perfect reflection of the policies and the intellectual environment shaped by the 2007–2009 global financial crisis and its aftermath. In the Western world, monetary policy became "the only game in town" to fight the financial crisis and subsequent economic instability. There is no question that these actions by central bankers prevented the global financial crisis from evolving into a twenty-first -century Great Depression. Creatively and courageously, they developed a distinctively unconventional monetary policy toolbox.

But as the years passed, after the worst of the financial crisis was over, the major central banks of the world continued their expansionary monetary policies. Then came 2020 and the COVID-19 pandemic. The disease spread quickly from its origin in China to most parts of the world, and many governments responded with aggressive measures, including complete and partial lockdowns. Economies suddenly tanked in ways far worse than they had during the financial crisis; in response, central bankers immediately doubled down on the same unconventional monetary interventions.

Radiating Confidence

Raghuram Rajan was among the first to refer to central bank policy as "the only game in town"—and to add that a heavy burden accompanied that reality. Rajan served as the chief economist at the IMF from 2003 to 2006 and as governor of the Bank of India from September 2013 to September 2016. He is a unique combination of academic excellence and tough, hard-earned, real-life policy experience. During a June 2013 speech at the Bank for International Settlements (BIS), the central bankers' bank in Basel, Switzerland, Rajan noted,

> Central bankers do get aggrieved when questioned about their uncharacteristic role as innovators. "What would you have us do when we are the only game in town," they say. But that may well be the problem. When the central banker offers himself as the only game in town, in an environment where politicians only have the choice between the bad and the worse, he becomes the only game in town. Everyone cedes the stage to the central banker, who cannot admit that his tools are untried and of unknown efficacy. The central banker has to be confident and will constantly refer to the many bullets he still has even if he has very few.[2]

I visited Rajan in his office at the University of Chicago's business school in September 2019, six years after he made that argument. "I see no reason to change these words," he said. "On the contrary. Due to the constant suggestion that, if necessary, central bankers can even do more than what they are already doing, they create for themselves, willingly or not, a sort of otherworldly aureole. Unsurprisingly, these suggestions lead other policymakers, not least of all the political class, to…relax and [assume a] laid-back attitude."

After serving in the Belgian government for more than four years, I find that I must concur. Why bother to make painful and probably unrewarding—electorally speaking—decisions on structural reforms and budget policies if central bankers confidently proclaim that they can do *even more* to keep the machine humming? A belief that central bankers are somehow gifted with magical abilities is widespread among the broader public and also in political circles. They may not be magicians, but they certainly possess a mythic aura more akin to those of supernatural creatures than ordinary mortals.

That said, there's another side to this coin. Central bankers are viewed in some circles, mostly on the extreme left and right of the political spectrum, as dictatorial money kings who impose their financially dominated views on society.[3] In this view, these mystical men and women stalk misty trails guided by a road map drawn for the rich and privileged and never consider the needs of the poor, the unlucky, and the destitute. According to this reasoning, central bankers are masters of an untouchable enclave within the kingdom, accountable only to themselves. At the same time, central bankers are feared most of all for their power to manipulate, secretly or not, the mystical money machine.

During and after the 2007–2009 global financial crisis, central bankers became entangled in a catch-22 that the COVID-19 pandemic only intensified. For their policies to be maximally effective, they must radiate confidence and trust, even in times full of uncertainty and stress. Former World Bank chief economist Kaushik Basu once wrote, "One thing that experts know and that nonexperts do not, is that they know less than nonexperts think they do."[4] Basu's dictum on experts and nonexperts certainly applies to central bankers.

Central bankers' obligation to appear perfectly in control has forced them to promise a lot, leading to their current position as "the only game in town." Consider the confidence exhibited by Ben Bernanke in his presidential address to the annual meeting of the American Economic Association on January 4, 2020, on the eve of the COVID-19 pandemic. He announced that the US Federal Reserve Board (Fed) still possessed ample policy room to attack a slowing of the economy.[5] The confidence central bankers—even *former* central bankers like Bernanke—radiate so easily results in an elevation of their stature and prestige. In the minds of large segments of the public, they are perceived as gifted mystics.

Pivotal Players

By enacting extremely low and even negative policy rates, developing new refinancing mechanisms as the 2007–2009 global financial crisis and COVID-19 pandemic unfolded, and creating massive asset purchasing programs, central banks created an entirely new environment for financial markets. Through these channels, central banks now play an increasingly decisive role in the real economy of investment, spending, saving, and employment. Central bank policies have always had a noticeable impact on the economy and society at large, but during and after the financial crisis and the COVID-19 pandemic, their additional interventions made their impact even more pervasive. Their execution of monetary policy not only affected the general cost and availability of credit but also steered credit toward specific sectors, borrowers, and even regions.[6] That's what happens when the Fed purchases mortgage-backed securities. The Bank of Japan does the same with corporate bonds and even equities, and the ECB buys bonds of specific euro-area member nations. And by taking interest rates into negative territory, central bankers behave as a taxation authority (which, by the way, they also do if they allow inflation to escalate, a possibility that has become uncomfortably real as this book goes to press).

Over the past decade, it has become clear that in order to get high returns on their ventures, investors must closely watch the Fed or the ECB—more so even than they must watch the evolution of economic fundamentals and broader societal evolutions. "Investor dependence on the thoughts and actions of central banks isn't new," as one commentator noted back in 2013, "but it seems to have reached unparalleled and absurd heights…Normal market operations are no longer normal. Investors have had to turn into part-time political scientists in order to anticipate market movements."[7] This unfortunate reality is even more prevalent today than it was in 2013. Investors now talk openly about central banks "having their backs" and that they "feel secure" about the risks they take as a result.

All Those Hands

Sixteenth-century Scottish moral philosopher Adam Smith, the founding father of economics, famously argued that in a well-organized free market economy, an *invisible hand* moved by the combined driving forces of competition and the pursuit of self-interest steers individuals and organizations toward decisions and actions that benefit the public interest.[8] In his magnum opus, *The Wealth of Nations*, Smith argued every individual "intends only his own gain, and he is in this, as in many other cases, led by an invisible hand to promote an end which was no part of his intentions…By pursuing his own interest, he frequently promotes that of society more effectually than when he really intends to promote it. I have never known much good done by those who effected to trade for the public good."[9]

According to Smith, the invisible hand reconciles self-interest and social interest as the market behaves as a constantly "equilibrating mechanism that transforms individual greed via competition into general welfare."[10] Smith's formal recognition of that insight was the origin point of economics' existence as a separate discipline of the humanities.

From Smith's notion arose policies that permitted dramatic improvements in the welfare and well-being of people around the world. These changes began to occur more or less simultaneously with the publication of *The Wealth of Nations;* economic historian Deirdre McCloskey referred to this shift as the "great enrichment."[11]

In their seminal textbook on general equilibrium economics, Nobel Prize in Economics winner Kenneth Arrow and his co-author Frank Hahn wrote, "Adam Smith's 'invisible hand' is a poetic expression of the most fundamental of economic balance relations."[12] For those on the extreme left, however, the invisible hand is symbolic of an economic system that generously rewards the ruthless and powerful at the expense of the poor and powerless. This notion is a great injustice to Smith, a major figure of the Scottish Enlightenment, as he recognized and acknowledged that there is much more to human behavior and motivation than the pursuit of narrow self-interest.[13]

Given the resonance that Smith's invisible-hand theorem has acquired over the centuries, it's surprising that in his entire *oeuvre*, Smith mentions the term *invisible hand* only four times.[14] In each instance, the context is the unintentional beneficial consequences of individual actions. In one, Smith describes a wealthy landowner who does not realize that his pursuit of luxuries provides jobs and income for thousands of poor people. In another, he talks of a capital owner who creates jobs and income for hundreds by deploying his capital in a way that he believes will bring him the greatest profit. It took a genius like Smith to understand the cause and effect at work in the invisible hand, but the field of economics has produced many more hands than the invisible one about which Smith wrote.

The twentieth-century American economic historian and corporate economist Alfred Chandler Jr. wrote that by the mid-1970s, Smith's invisible hand had to a large extent been supplanted by the *visible hand* of corporate management as the most powerful institution in a modern economy. "The theme propounded here," Chandler claimed in the introduction to his masterpiece, *The Visible Hand,* "is that modern business enterprise took the place of market mechanisms in coordinating the activities of the economy and allocating its resources. In many sectors of the economy the visible hand of management replaced what Smith referred to as the invisible hand of market forces."[15]

Chandler described American business in terms of two narratives: one pre-1850 and the other post-1850. The transformative event that split the two was the rise of big railroads around 1850. Small, single-unit firms that produced a single product for consumers in a limited geographic area were dominant in the earlier of the two periods, and these firms' activities "were coordinated and monitored by market and price mechanisms."[16] After 1850, large, multi-unit companies that produced many different products for consumers distributed throughout a wide geographic area became dominant. Their activities were "monitored and coordinated by salaried employees rather than the market mechanisms,"[17] because this visible coordinating hand "permitted greater productivity, lower costs, and higher profit than coordination by market mechanism."[18]

Today, two and a half centuries after Smith's observations and half a century after Chandler's, reflecting on the nature of the relationship between the invisible hand and the visible hand remains an intriguing prospect. For example, to what extent and under which circumstances can the visible hand of the managerial capitalist elite ignore the invisible hand of market forces? Isn't the visible hand of managerial coordination necessarily bound by the actions of product markets controlled by consumer sovereignty and input and capital markets? Perhaps it's more appropriate to say that Chandler's visible hand is a way of dealing with the forces that are unleashed by the invisible hand. Even a casual review of corporate history will quickly show that the invisible hand of the market ultimately determines what type of organization survives. The visible hand of managerial coordination cannot be successful—or even survive—if it neglects the invisible hand of the competitive market.

Regardless of the merits of Chandler's original visible-hand concept, today the term is firmly ensconced in the economic lexicon in the context of actions made by politicians, bureaucrats, and regulators. These actors influence economic, social, and political processes in a much more visible way than Smith's invisible hand, but that's not to say the visible hand of government doesn't influence in hidden and subtle ways as well.

The visible hand of government is able to focus on corrections of market failures and on production of the public goods that private markets don't produce or tend to underproduce. But the visible hand can also *replace* the market, as it does in countries that follow the model of state capitalism.[19] State capitalism models combine traditional state planning with elements of free-market competition and some degree of openness toward free trade and international investment. The most notable example is post-1978 China. China's success has attracted many admirers and followers to the state capitalist model.

Still another way in which to look at the visible hand of government and regulation is to make a distinction between the *helping hand* and the *grabbing hand*.[20] The helping hand is evident when politicians and bureaucrats are intimately involved in the economic and industrial sphere, steering the processes in the interest of the state but also toward their own positions and priorities. Corruption certainly exists in the helping-hand model, but it tends to be rather limited and well organized. When the helping hand dominates, government failures do happen, but they're relatively limited.

But if the grabbing hand becomes the norm, government become destructive and predatory, and corruption prevails alongside arbitrary taxation and regulation. Talent is diverted from productive activities to rent-seeking ones. When the grabbing hand dominates, the visible hand fails to improve general welfare. History teaches us that the helping hand often transforms into the grabbing hand.

The Mystic Hand

Now, in the third decade of the twenty-first century, the hands steering the economy have become even more complicated than they were in the years leading up to the 2007–2009 global financial crisis. The mighty hand of the central bankers has taken its place alongside Smith's invisible hand and the visible hand—either as defined by Chandler or as the government and regulation version that is prevalent today. Whether it is visible or invisible—arguments for either can be made—the central bankers' hand now plays a more direct and intrusive role in many financial and economic decisions throughout society than ever before. While market forces, managerial decisions, and the efforts of politicians and bureaucrats still play a significant role, in the past ten years each has come under the direct influence of central bankers' policies. The central bankers' hand is more complicated than just a visible or invisible one.

Other than during wartimes, central banks' policies on the economy and society at large have never had the impact that they have since the onset of the 2007–2009 global financial crisis. Then, the outbreak of the COVID-19 pandemic intensified the already unconventional monetary policies that have predominated and accentuated the impact these policies have had on society at large. Back in 2013, *New York Times* journalist Neil Irwin argued, "Central bankers determine whether people can get jobs, whether their savings are secure, and, ultimately, whether their nation prospers or fails."[21] Although Irwin's claim is somewhat of an exaggeration, it has never been more true than it is today. Draghi may have told me that central bankers "are no magicians," but now, they're about as close as humanly possible. When your hand is felt everywhere and by everyone, magic is what you get.

Invisible hand, visible hand, helping hand, grabbing hand: all of these elements are somewhat applicable to central bankers, but none quite captures the essence of twenty-first century central banking. British economist and former Deputy Governor of the Bank of England Paul Tucker, who served as chairman of the Systemic Risk Council, characterized these men and women as "the poster boys of the technocratic elite...the new third pillar of the unelected power, alongside the judges and the generals."[22]

Many years ago, the late Paul Volcker, arguably the most impressive central banker in modern history, boiled down what central banking is all about into a single word. British economist Mervyn King had solicited Volcker's advice before joining the Bank of England in 1991, and he provided a one-word response: "Mystique."[23] William Davies, co-director of London's Political Economy Research Club, went a step further, titling his joint review of memoirs by Ben Bernanke and Mervyn King as "The Big Mystique."[24] Indeed, central bankers—certainly those from major central banks—touch the world around them in almost all respects with their *mystic hand*.

According to Dictionary.com, the word *mystique* refers to "a framework of doctrines, ideas, beliefs, or the like, constructed around a person or object, endowing the person or object with enhanced value or profound meaning."[25] That's a spot-on definition of central banking, as far as I'm concerned. Synonyms for the adjective form *mystic* include "arcane, esoteric, hidden, impenetrable, mysterious, occult, otherworldly, supernatural, unaccountable, unknowable, wizardly."[26] These apply well to the activities of central bankers.

Another touch of the supernatural comes from the alchemy at the heart of central banking. *Alchemists,* the forerunners of modern chemistry, were tasked with turning ordinary metals into gold. Like those medieval counterparts, modern central bankers create money, so to speak, out of nothing. King, who served as the Bank of England's governor from 2003 to 2013, characterized central bankers as crucial players in what he termed "the alchemy of modern finance,"[27] and Irwin titled his 2013 book on central banking and the 2007–2009 global financial crisis *The Alchemists.*[28]

The late Karl Brunner, an American economist and a keen observer of central banking, concluded in 1981, "The mystique [around central banking] thrives on a pervasive impression that central banking is an esoteric art. Access to this and its proper execution is confined to the initiated elite. The esoteric nature of the art is moreover revealed by an inherent impossibility to articulate its insights in explicit and intelligible words and sentences. Communication with the uninitiated breaks down. The proper attitude to be cultivated by the latter is trust and confidence in the initiated group's comprehension of the esoteric knowledge."[29]

More than thirty years after Brunner made those succinct observations, Adam Posen, president of the Peterson Institute for International Economics, concluded, "Central bankers have always carried a mystique beyond justification. Even as their policies and procedures have become markedly more transparent, the air of secrecy and power about them persists."[30] William White, a Canadian economist who has held top functions at the Organisation for Economic Co-operation (OECD) and the BIS, argued, "For much of the postwar period, central banks cultivated a mystique of knowledge based essentially on the principle 'never apologize, never explain.'"[31]

The way central bankers juggle billions and even trillions of dollars, yens, or euros is mind-boggling to most ordinary people. It's beyond their comprehension and becomes steeped in an atmosphere of mystique—if not even outright black magic. The same holds true for the money creation and destruction processes that central bankers control. To extend the metaphor created by King and Irwin, central bankers look and feel like alchemists who brew proprietary formulas that fill society with joy and optimism under certain circumstances and depression and mayhem in others. The world of money, credit, and debt creation remains a mystery for most people, and only those who are gifted with a mystic touch can master and control it.

The mystique characterized by Brunner and Posen fits the image of the modern central banker surprisingly well. First, central bankers are generally seen as keeping their heads cool during major crises, when fear and uncertainty reign. In such times, people tend to defer to authority figures, and during the 2007–2009 global financial crisis, central bankers were exactly that. Second, a central banker is often seen in the role of "the heroic fireman containing the blaze."[32] These men and women have battled crises via some highly unusual policy interventions, such as the prolonged period of very low and even negative interest rates that has prevailed since the onset of the financial crisis, and there simply has to be a mystic touch behind such stunts. Central bankers have gained more power and prestige in the wake of the global financial crisis and the COVID-19 pandemic, but this could have a boomerang effect.

The verbal virtuosity of most central bankers is often beyond the comprehension of even informed laymen, which further strengthens their image of being mortals gifted with mystic talents. It's hardly an accident that central bankers tend to express themselves in a way that is "incomprehensible to anyone other than the cognoscenti."[33] Consider this remark, made with utmost seriousness: "I know you believe you understand what you think I said, but I am not sure you realize that what you heard is not what I meant." These were the words of former Fed Chairman Alan Greenspan, who earned his reputation as "the most bedazzling obfuscator of them all."[34] Central bankers and mystique go together well.

Greenspan's levels of opacity and purposeful vagueness are unsurpassed, but he is not particularly exceptional. Sophisticated and mystical-sounding communication remains, despite a recent emphasis on transparency and forward guidance, part and parcel of central bank talk: one of the first books on the modern Fed was titled *Secrets of the*

Temple.[35] Unfortunately, but inevitably, this manner transforms into outright arrogance from time to time. In December 2019, during the hearing in the European Parliament for her confirmation as a new member of the ECB's executive committee, German economist Isabel Schnabel declared, "There are very few people who really understand what is going on" with respect to monetary policy and the economy—an astonishing statement.[36] In my capacity then as chairman of the Committee on Budgets of the European Parliament, I replied that I respectfully but totally disagreed with her thesis about the ignorance of others. Schnabel walked back her statement and promised to be clearer in the future, but she could rightfully have argued that very few people understand *what central bankers are saying most of the time,* rather than implying that knowledgeable people don't understand what monetary policy is all about.

Back and Forth

Central bankers did not always occupy such a central role within societies—in fact, far from it. During the first quarter of the twentieth century they took center stage, but the fallout from the 1929 stock market crash, the unraveling of the gold standard, and the deep shocks of the Great Depression led to the loss of a tremendous amount of prestige, status, and power for central banks.[37] During World War II, central banks' major contribution to the war effort was making sure governments could borrow as cheaply as possible to finance military spending. After the war, the reconstruction of the international economic order left central bankers in a bystander role, or as Paul Tucker put it, "backroom advisers and agents as the West was rebuilt and the Cold War negotiated."[38]

The Bretton Woods regime, a system comparable to the gold standard but with somewhat more room for national policymaking, was dependent on the willingness of governments to subordinate domestic priorities, like growth and employment to the exchange rate. Since the Bretton Woods regime was based on fixed exchange rates and capital mobility, the degree of freedom for domestic monetary policy was very limited.[39] This was simply too much to ask, and Richard Nixon's presidential administration ended the gold convertibility of the dollar in the United States in 1971.

As the Bretton Woods regime unwound during the 1970s, central bankers returned to the forefront. Inflation's stubborn persistence threatened their position and prestige again, but when Volcker, then the Fed chairman, masterminded its conquest in the early 1980s, their star rose once again. It's not an exaggeration to say central bankers "saved" the political elite in those days, since the latter's attempts to gain control over inflation through, among other factors, wage and price controls, had—if anything—only made matters worse. The "Great Moderation" period that ensued, which was characterized by low inflation and reduced variability in growth performance, only enhanced the reputation of central bankers.[40]

As I describe in this book, this reputation was not entirely deserved, as the actions of central bankers contributed significantly to the forces behind the 2007–2009 global financial crisis. Yet remarkably, the crisis did not reduce their prominence—in fact, the reverse is true. Instead, they were catapulted to only-game-in-town status, and also gained regulatory and supervisory responsibilities—mostly because of the abject failures of reigning supervisors and regulators in the years leading up to the crisis.

The rationale behind the central bankers' rise in power and importance was simple: when the financial crisis really got underway, they acted swiftly and courageously, and the COVID-19 pandemic only reinforced their prominence. Central bankers became "Plato's guardians in modern garb...[even]...new, reluctant masters of the universe."[41] Of course, as with Rajan's only-game-in-town remarks, I have some doubt as to whether *reluctant* is appropriate. And aren't "masters of the universe" by definition not supposed to be guided by something like a mystic hand?

The Mystic Hand at Work

This book focuses on the perception of central bankers as being guided by a mystic hand and, as such, that they are worshipped, feared, or detested. It is not an exhaustive history of central banking, since it is largely limited to the role that central banks play during major financial and economic crises.[42] Here, we take a close look at central banks acting as lenders of last resort,[43] which is, of course, not the primary function of central banks. Their main function is to focus on price stability, which requires, as you will read in Chapter 5, continuous attention to financial stability.

A central bank acts as lender of last resort when it moves to resolve financial panics and crises by preventing the collapse of solvent but liquidity-constrained financial institutions, as such a collapse would devastate the stock of money available for the economy. By acting as lender of last resort, a central bank protects sound financial institutions facing liquidity problems from insolvency. Such a dramatic chain of events would inevitably lead to economic depression, mass unemployment, and deep political and societal upheaval—an evolution that would endanger the economic and social fabric of society. In his memoirs, Bernanke referred to the dangers created by "self-feeding liquidity dynamics."[44] Given the hyper-fast speed of the modern financial system, a liquidity-constrained institution's tumble to insolvency can transpire very quickly, so central banks must move boldly and quickly.

According to economic historian and professor Perry Mehrling, "Lender of last resort intervention involves the central bank extending credit when no one else will (or can)…Used wisely, such intervention can control the downturn and prevent it from turning into a rout. Used unwisely, such intervention can foster further continuation of unhealthy bubble conditions."[45] University of Chicago law and economics professor Eric Posner remarked that the lender of last resort "makes loans to banks and other financial institutions until confidence is restored."[46] In his book on the 2007–2009 global financial crisis, Bernanke argued, "We saw our responses to the panic as fulfilling the classic central banking role of lender of last resort."[47] In 1933, UK Treasury economist Ralph

Hawtrey stated unequivocally, "The central bank is the lender of last resort. That is the true source of its responsibility for the currency."[48]

When modern central banks act as lender of last resort, central bank policies are very visible to the public, and they directly affect society. That's why central banks captured the world's attention during the 2007–2009 global financial crisis and its aftermath. Discussing the lender-of-last-resort function of central banks, however, cannot happen in a vacuum, because monetary policy often gives rise to circumstances that oblige a central bank to act as a lender of last resort further down the road. In short, what happens in the realms of monetary and financial stability policy has a direct connection to the development of lender-of-last-resort actions on the part of central banks.

What to Expect in These Pages

Chapter 1 concentrates on the Great Depression, which was once described quite correctly as "an international disaster of perverse economic policies."[49] The chapter specifically explores the monetary explanation of that devastating social, economic, and political event, with detail on the crucial role of blunders made by central bankers during that time. To a large extent, the Great Depression is the sorry tale of a miserable failure of the mystic hand. The central bankers of those days should have paid more attention to the writings of eighteenth-century economist Henry Thornton and his nineteenth-century compatriot Walter Bagehot on episodes of financial crisis and the central bank's role as lender of last resort. Had central bankers followed their analyses and policy advice during the 1920s and 1930s, things would have likely been very different. *By 1930, central banks completely ignored the critical lender-of-last-resort lessons so deeply engrained in Thornton's and Bagehot's writings.*

Chapter 2 focuses on the 2007–2009 global financial crisis and the period leading up to it—ground zero for the unconventional monetary toolbox. Once again, major policy mistakes—not limited to those made by central bankers—threw the world into chaos. The difference this time was that as soon as the crisis began, lessons of the past were taken seriously. Around the world, central bankers followed the advice of Thornton and Bagehot and enacted the policies that were necessary to turn the tide. *As lenders of last resort, central banks relearned what they had unlearned in the years leading up to the Great Depression.* The complicated nature of the modern financial system obliged them to act in ways they never had before in peacetime. When the COVID-19 pandemic hit in early 2020, central bankers doubled down on the intervention playbook they had deployed successfully during the financial crisis.

Chapter 3 explores the timeline of the financial crisis. At several points—notably, during the week of pure horror in September 2008, when Lehman Brothers failed—the world financial system came close to complete meltdown. Had this meltdown occurred, an economic depression of catastrophic proportions would have been unavoidable. In large part because of the bold interventions made by central banks, this did not come to pass. However, over time, the measures taken to arrest that meltdown have created new problems that are now further accentuated by their response to the COVID-19 pandemic. The learning curve for central bankers is now totally in uncharted waters. *Central bankers' successful war on the global financial crisis and the COVID-19 pandemic has created a new phase in their learning process, and they still have a lot to learn.* The distinct possibility of a return of inflation complicates this learning process even further.

Chapter 4 covers the immediate aftermath of the 2007–2009 global financial crisis. During that period, central bankers kept following the same playbook—keeping interest rates very low or even negative and creating massive asset purchase programs. This is better known as the policy of quantitative easing. The Fed was the first, and so far, the only, central bank to change direction—albeit only for a short while—but American monetary policy has remained quite accommodative (though not to the level of policies set in Europe, Japan, and China). Central banks expanded their reach beyond these QE efforts to include the creation of specific new refinancing windows to deal with the realities of the modern financial world. The COVID-19 pandemic only exacerbated existing problems and caused central banks to intensify these policies and even explore ways to further their reach.

Chapter 5 examines the unintended, and mostly negative, consequences of this most unconventional monetary toolbox. In the chapter, I classify these unintended consequences into eight types, or in my parlance, syndromes:

- stealing wealth, income, and jobs from the future and from neighboring nations (Butch Cassidy Syndrome)
- stimulating excessive leverage and debt accumulation (Michael Jackson Syndrome)
- punishing savers (David Copperfield Syndrome)
- facilitating bubbles and expanding the shadow banking system (Semper Augustus Syndrome)
- bullying the traditional financial sector (Savior-Turned-Bully Syndrome)
- contributing to wealth inequality (26 = 3.8 Billion Syndrome)
- weakening productivity performance and real economy growth potential (Zombie Syndrome)
- incentivizing politicians to neglect substantive structural reforms (Sloth Syndrome)

The longer that central banks adhere to unconventional policy stances, the more pronounced these consequences become. The fundamental characteristics of these effects, and the way in which central bankers have to take them into account when formulating their policies, are what the central bankers' latest learning process is all about. These problems are clear indications that the mystic hand doesn't always strike in ways that are benign to society as a whole.

In Chapter 6, the policy framework of central bankers is closely examined. I argue that the most commonly used framework in recent years—targeting an inflation rate of 2 percent—is both too narrow and obsolete. It's too narrow because price stability and financial stability must be considered together, like conjoined twins. It's obsolete because the determinants of inflation mostly fall outside of the control of central bankers. Financial stability must be taken into consideration *ex ante* into the policy framework; cleaning up *ex post*, a strategy most central bankers adhered to in the recent past, is no longer viable.

Chapter 1: An Ode to Henry and Walter

Honoring nineteenth-century wisdom would have prevented the Great Depression

I WOULD LIKE TO SAY TO MILTON AND ANNA: REGARDING THE Great Depression—you're right, we did it. We're very sorry. But thanks to you, we won't do it again." With those words, Ben Bernanke concluded his speech at a November 2002 conference held in commemoration of Milton Friedman's ninetieth birthday at Friedman's alma mater, the University of Chicago.[1] At that moment in time, Bernanke, who had built a solid reputation as an economics professor and researcher at such institutions as MIT, Stanford, and Princeton, was a little more than three months into his first term on the Board of Governors of the Fed.

On February 1, 2006, Bernanke succeeded Greenspan as Fed chairman, a post he held until January 2014. Given the dominance of the US economy and the US dollar, Bernanke was destined to hold a place among the crucial players during the 2007–2009 global financial crisis.[2] Philipp Hildebrand, vice chairman of investment management firm BlackRock and chairman of the Swiss National Bank from 2010 to 2012, once remarked, "Whenever I talk about central banking during the 2008–2009 crisis, I refer to Ben Bernanke as something like the chief architect of policy at the time. We all had to design our own plans to suit our own problems and our own legal, political, and economic circumstances, but there is no doubt that the master plan came from Bernanke and shaped our thinking and our actions."[3]

The Friedman Coup

In the above quote, of course, Bernanke was referring to the Great Depression and to the landmark work *A Monetary History of the United States*[4] by Friedman and his co-author Anna Schwartz. Friedman and Schwartz's *Monetary History* is the definitive work on the origins of that major social and economic disaster, and hardly anyone was in a better place to bestow such praise on the authors than Bernanke, since the Great Depression was the primary focus of Bernanke's academic research.[5] Specifically, Bernanke was an expert on the Depression's *financial accelerator,* the vicious cycle of bank failures and economic weakness as they fed upon one another to produce financial, economic, social, and even political mayhem.

In Bernanke's words, Friedman and Schwartz's monumental *Monetary History* was "nothing less than…what has become the leading and most persuasive explanation of the worst economic disaster in American history, the onset of the Great Depression."[6] Arguments similar to those of Friedman and Schwartz were voiced while the Great Depression was ongoing, namely by Ralph Hawtrey of the UK Treasury and Lauchlin Currie of Harvard University.[7] According to Hawtrey, "The year 1929 saw a disastrous reversal of policy" by the Fed.[8] He added, "The mistake of the Federal Reserve Banks was in their hesitation to lower rates and relax credit after the crisis of October [1929] broke out. That was the moment when prompt action was needed to prevent pessimism getting hold and the vicious circle of deflation getting hold."[9] Currie laid blame on the Fed not only for causing the Great Depression but also for its persistence and depth. He wrote, "The course of events in 1930–'32 is clear evidence that grave mistakes were made by the reserve administration."[10]

Friedman and Schwartz blamed the Fed for not intervening once the banking system collapsed and took first the money supply and then the economy with it. In addition to delivering the most coherent explanation of the forces that unleashed the dramatic Great Depression, they brought about a fundamental rethinking of macroeconomics in general. In those days, John Maynard Keynes' masterful analysis of and policy prescriptions for the Great Depression[11] were still predominant in the study of macroeconomics—money by and large plays a passive role in the economy. Simply put, money doesn't matter. In 1949, Arthur Pigou, a contemporary and intellectual opponent of Keynes at the University of Cambridge, argued in *The Veil of Money* that the real sphere of the economy (growth, employment, investment, *et. al*) can be perfectly analyzed and determined without taking money and the financial sphere into account.[12] The canonical formulation of general equilibrium theory, which was derived in the 1950s and inspired vast amounts of further research in economics, had no space whatsoever for money.[13]

Friedman and Schwartz, armed with innovative empirical and historical research, argued forcibly to the contrary. They convincingly showed that the causal relationship between money on one side and prices and output on the other runs from the first to the latter; thus, money does matter a lot. In the long run, Friedman and Schwartz concluded, changes in the money supply mainly affect prices, but in the short run, they also affect output and employment levels. Despite some methodological criticism ("measurement without theory"), their analysis of the Great Depression has become part of mainstream macroeconomics. As Bernanke pointed out in 2002, it remains the dominant explanation of the Great Depression and the ravages it caused.

The Annihilation

The Great Depression was a truly apocalyptic economic and social event in the United States and many other countries. In the words of banker and author Liaquat Ahamed, the Great Depression "hung over the world, poisoning every aspect of social and material life and crippling the future of a whole generation."[14] This catastrophe directly contributed to the rise of Adolf Hitler and his Nazi party specifically, and to the ascent of fascism, communism, and other political extremism in general. Of course, political extremism set the world on the path to the horrors of World War II. In addition to being deeper and more severe than any other financial crisis to date, the Great Depression also arrived unexpectedly.[15] The world had been blinded by the impressive economic and social progress that was achieved throughout the Roaring Twenties, as they were known. In November 1928, American politician Herbert Hoover boldly claimed in his acceptance speech for the Republican presidential nomination, "We in America today are nearer to the final triumph over poverty than ever before in the history of any land. The poorhouse is vanishing from among us."[16] One is hard pressed to find a prediction proven to be so utterly wrong, so fast.

The data give a clear picture of the enormity and drama of what took place between 1929 and 1933. Between the end of the preceding economic expansion and the deepest point of the Depression, industrial production declined by 47 percent in the United States and Poland, 42 percent in Germany, 33 percent in Italy, 31 percent in France, and 16 percent in the United Kingdom.[17] Given industry's dominance in the economic landscapes of that period, these declines are a very good indication of the contraction of economic activity in general. Unemployment rates skyrocketed, reaching 44 percent of the working population in Germany and 38 percent in the United States (arguably, these were the hardest-hit nations among the larger countries of the world during the Depression). In the United Kingdom, the unemployment rate peaked at 27 percent. The Great Depression was deeply felt beyond North American and European borders as well—between 1929 and 1933, the volume of international trade declined by 25 percent and the price index of internationally traded goods declined by 31 percent.[18]

The massive blows delivered to production, employment, and international trade during the Great Depression were followed by intense deflation. Between the end of 1929 and the end of 1933, the consumer price index declined by 24 percent in the United States, 23 percent in Germany, and 15 percent in the United Kingdom.[19] In the United States, the price of a dozen eggs fell from 50 cents to 13 cents, and the price of gasoline dropped from 10 cents a gallon to less than 5 cents. Deflation proved to be destructive for the economy in many ways, as described elaborately in 1933 by economist and deflation scholar Irving Fisher.[20] Unfortunately, policymakers were insufficiently aware of the destructive forces of deflation, "an annihilating event that...Hoover never understood and Roosevelt understood incompletely."[21] Deflation is undeniably a significant factor in the origin of the Great Depression, but it is not the primary cause.[22]

Despite the resonance of Friedman and Schwartz's analysis, a lively debate on the origin of the Great Depression continues today, almost sixty years later.[23] Some observers point to the great stock market crash of October 24, 1929, known as Black Thursday. The event followed a spectacular bull period on Wall Street powered by an enormous credit boom in the United States, the United Kingdom, and Japan.[24] It destroyed wealth on a huge scale and unleashed uncertainty in the minds of producers, investors, and consumers alike.[25] The Black Thursday crash certainly played a role in the Great Depression's evolution, but research has proven that it was not its point of origin. After all, a downturn of the American economy was already in full swing by the time the crash occurred.

Others argue that the rise of protectionism, which engulfed the world economy during the 1930s, was responsible. The rise began with protectionist actions on the part of countries such as Germany, France, and Italy during the second part of the 1920s, and reached its apex when the US Congress passed the Smoot-Hawley Tariff Act in June 1930. A full-scale trade war involving more than sixty countries ensued.[26] According to historian Harold James, this worldwide protectionism revival was part of a general "backlash against globalization that had been developing progressively since the last third of the nineteenth century."[27] While protectionism likely intensified the Depression, it was not the cause.

On the extreme left of the political spectrum, another faulty explanation of the Depression holds that it was an inevitable consequence of the dominance of monopoly capital and ultimate proof of the historically determined failure of capitalism. Each time a serious economic downturn has occurred during the past two centuries, this mantra has reared its head.

The only explanation of the Great Depression that holds up well over time is the monetary one. It consists of two parts. First, many countries rushed to return to the gold standard after World War I. As predicted by Swedish economist Gustav Cassel,[28] the rush to gold laid the groundwork for a serious economic downturn, and once the downturn arrived, it accelerated quickly from a garden-variety recession to the Great Depression. This overshooting has everything to do with the second part of the monetary explanation of the Great Depression— the failure of the Fed and European monetary authorities to halt the dramatic drop in the money supply caused by massive bank failures.

As the stock of money available to the economy sharply declined, spending on goods and services fell off a cliff. This obliged companies to cut prices, reduce investment, and lay off workers. As borrowers' incomes diminished or disappeared entirely, they could not repay their loans, which led to massive defaults and bankruptcies. These annihilating deflationary forces intensified a vicious spiral of bank failures, further money stock declines, and rapidly accelerating drops in output, employment, and prices. First, we will discuss the gold standard issue in depth, and then we'll dig deeper into the inadequate responses of central banks once the downturn began to wreak havoc in the banking world.

A "Barbarous Relic"

The gold standard was an international monetary system in which the currency of every participating country was expressed in a fixed amount of gold, making each currency perfectly exchangeable in gold.[29] It functioned remarkably well between, say, 1880 and the start of World War I in 1914. The monetary stability that came along with it certainly contributed to the social and economic progress of that period, which in turn contributed significantly to the increased standing and prestige enjoyed by the central bankers who supervised the monetary system.

The start of World War I led to suspension of the gold standard, not least because suspending it allowed governments to turn to the printing press to finance their war efforts. Moreover, no central bank or government wanted to see its gold reserves leave its borders and end up in the hands of enemies. Most believed that the conflict would end relatively quickly, and nations that had previously adhered to the gold standard would be able to return to it soon after hostilities ended.

Yet the war lasted much longer than most anticipated, and it led to important changes in Europe's political map. Three royal houses that had long played crucial roles in Europe's political scene simply disappeared from power: the Habsburgs, who ruled the Austro-Hungarian empire; the Hohenzollern dynasty, which held the levers of power in Prussia; and the house of Romanov, the czars who had ruled Russia since 1613. As these seismic political changes were taking place, Europe was pummeled by the 1918 influenza pandemic. The deadly virus ravaged the continent, taking the lives of between fifty and one hundred million people—several times the military casualty rate of World War I.[30]

Despite these momentous events, a desire to return to the gold standard soon after the end of the war remained widespread; many policymakers believed that returning to it was necessary in order to tame postwar inflation. The United States returned to the gold standard in June 1919, and most other important nations, with the exception of China and the Soviet Union, followed between 1924 and 1926.

Most policymakers vigorously defended their return to the gold standard, but some economists warned that it was a mistake. Keynes famously described the gold standard as a "barbarous relic...[that allows]...the tides of gold to play what tricks they like with the internal price level...[and making impossible]...the attempt to moderate the disastrous influence of the credit cycle on the stability of prices and employment."[31] From the early 1920s on, Swedish economist Gustav Cassel argued that a return to the gold standard by most countries would lead to a shortage of gold and would set into motion the destructive forces of deflation. He wrote, "The prospect of a long period of falling prices would kill all enterprise and impede that reconstruction of the world that is now so very urgent."[32] Cassel's prediction was as right as Hoover's was wrong.

During the postwar period, the gold standard didn't function well, to say the least; two interrelated elements were at fault. First, there was no true world leader—certainly not in terms of monetary matters— that could set and uphold basic rules for the international system. Great Britain and its pound sterling had been the dominating force in monetary affairs prior to World War I, but the war weakened the nation to such a degree that it was unable to maintain a leadership role. The United States was the obvious successor but, as historian Edward Carr put it, "In 1918, leadership was offered, by almost universal consent, to the United States…[and]…was declined."[33]

A refusal to engage in world leadership occurred despite the fact that US presidents like Theodore Roosevelt, who served from 1901 to 1909, and Woodrow Wilson, who served from 1913 to 1921, clearly recognized that doing so was in the country's best interest.[34] Economic historian Charles Kindleberger concluded, "Part of the explanation for the length, and most of the explanation for the depth, of the world depression is the inability of the British to continue their role of underwriter to the system and the reluctance of the United States to take it on until 1936."[35] Later, American politician Harry Truman, who served as president from 1945 to 1953, reflected that the catastrophes of the 1930s and 1940s were caused by America's refusal to step up and accept its "responsibility as a world power."[36]

The second element that contributed strongly to the gold standard's downfall was asymmetry among economies; some countries had external surpluses, and some had external deficits.[37] Those with trade surpluses experienced an inflow of gold, and their gold reserves increased. According to the rules of the gold standard mechanism, an increase in gold reserves should result in an increase in the money supply. Increased money supplies lead to increased internal price levels, reduced international competitiveness, and the disappearance (or at least a significant reduction) of trade surpluses. Countries that bore deficits were subject to the reverse process: their loss of gold reserves led to reductions in their money supplies, subsequent reductions in internal price levels, improvements in international competitiveness, and thus reduction of trade deficits.

Nations with external deficits were strictly obliged to follow these rules, since going against them meant a continuous loss of gold reserves and, inevitably, an inability to participate in the international gold standard. Political elites in those days found this to be quite unacceptable. Countries with surpluses could neutralize the effect of increased gold reserves on their money supply and keep their international competitiveness intact.[38]

Only a strong "underwriter of the system," as economic historian and author Charles Kindleberger aptly put it, could have avoided the asymmetry that inevitably resulted in insufficient worldwide money supplies and strong deflationary forces throughout the international economic system. The most consequential surplus nations that refused to play by the rules of the gold standard were France and the United States; between 1920 and 1930, gold reserves of the United States increased by $450 million, yet no discernable impact to its money supply transpired.[39] In fact, rather than adjusting to this inflow of gold, the Fed *tightened* monetary policy considerably in 1928 and 1929, mostly in an attempt to stop excessive speculation. This tightening followed a period of rapid credit expansion in the United States, mainly due to financial innovations that produced an artificial real estate boom in several states, among other things.[40]

The asymmetric approach was reinforced by the important societal changes occurring in the United States and elsewhere at that time, such as the extension of the right to vote to women and the rise of labor unions. These changes obliged politicians to consider growth and employment much more seriously when formulating policies, and they also reduced the downward flexibility of wages and prices, which was indispensable for smooth operation of the gold standard. Ultimately, these fundamental economic and societal changes substantially undermined the public's acceptance of the gold standard.[41]

The asymmetry in the working of the gold standard greatly contributed to the rise in trade tensions, as every country was desperately fighting for trade surpluses and the ensuing gold inflow. Clearly, the gold standard intimately linked all participating countries, and the destructive deflationary forces it set in motion spread quickly on an international scale. Unsurprisingly, the nations that elected to leave the gold standard first were also the first to recover from the Great Depression.[42] But that's getting too far ahead. The return to the gold standard set the stage for serious economic contraction, but severe mismanagement of the banking crisis was the catalyst for the contraction to become the horrendous Great Depression.

Banks Fall Like Autumn Leaves

The US banking crisis started in the autumn of 1930—specifically in the mostly agrarian states of Missouri, Arkansas, Indiana, Illinois, Iowa, and North Carolina. Pressured by declining prices and falling demand, farmers began to default on their outstanding loans. The highly fragmented nature of the American banking system in those days, with huge amounts of small and very small banks, complicated matters considerably.[43] In November and December 1930 alone, more than 600 banks closed.

On December 11, 1930, New York City's Bank of the United States went bankrupt. The bank was privately owned, but its name suggested involvement of the public sector. Word that US authorities had let one of its own banks go bankrupt spread quickly and caused a panic. In March 1931, September 1931, and March 1933, additional bank crises and financial panics shook the United States; with each, the overall economic and social situation deteriorated further.

Initially, the New York branch of the Federal Reserve System reacted adequately by injecting substantial amounts of liquidity into the system. However, the New York Fed's approach was immediately opposed by most other members of the Fed Board.[44] Among most of the Board members, a fear of inflation, rather than deflation, predominated. Board opposition to moves made by the New York Fed was also inspired by continued adherence by some to the *real bills doctrine*, which held that the creation of money must be strictly linked to short-term commercial paper. The real bills doctrine also implied that Fed interventions to support the banking system were permitted only if the banks could offer first-class commercial paper for the Fed to discount; if no commercial paper could be offered, no liquidity support could be given, as a lack of paper was taken as a clear indication of insolvency.

The real bills doctrine created significant procyclicality in the credit creation process. If the economy performed well, more commercial paper linked to the increasing economic activity would become available. This would allow banks to increase the credit volume on offer, thereby further stimulating the economy. If, however, the economy entered a downward phase, the volume of available commercial paper would decline as well, leading to a contraction in the credit allocation by banks. With that, the initial decline in economic activity would intensify. The real bills doctrine also created another problem—the Fed did not categorize commercial paper based on the activities of small farmers as first class and thus did not permit discounting it. This policy stance accelerated financing problems in the farming sector of the US economy.

Essentially, American authorities stood by and let the banking crises run their ruinous course. Between October 1930 and the end of 1933, more than 9,000 of the 24,700 banks in the United States went bankrupt.[45] Between the end of 1929 and the end of 1933, the money supply in the United States dropped by a third, from $60 billion to $40 billion.[46] As previously explained, the Fed's refusal to let the money supply increase as a consequence of the trade surplus-induced inflow of gold only made matters worse. Deflationary forces strengthened while aggregate demand shriveled, leading to massive unemployment and escalating poverty.

While the US banking crisis was in full swing, a similar crisis developed in Europe. During the winter of 1930–1931, rumors circulated about serious problems in the European banking sector, especially in Germany and Italy,[47] but ultimately, an Austrian bank, the Credit-Anstalt, ignited the crisis.[48]

During the heyday of the Austro-Hungarian Empire, the Austrian capital of Vienna served as the financial center of eastern and middle Europe. After World War I, the empire began to crumble; this, coupled with the ravages of high inflation, obliged the financial sector to restructure. From this process rose the Credit-Anstalt, the dominant financial institution in Austria. Once trouble began at Credit-Anstalt, the Austrian government tried to save it but failed—in part due to opposition to their rescue proposals by the French, which was caused by their frustration over the customs union to which Germany and Austria had agreed.

Credit-Anstalt failed in May 1931 and caused a panic that spread like wildfire to neighboring countries, including Germany,[49] Poland, Hungary, and Romania. The Germans were hard hit by a banking crisis that, in turn, soon spread to the whole of Europe. In July 1931, the failure of the second largest bank in Germany, Danatbank, reinforced the overall loss of confidence and sense of panic.

Central banks in Europe made the same mistakes as the Fed and stood by idly while bank failures significantly reduced the money supply. All across mainland Europe, banks withdrew large amounts of gold from London in a desperate attempt to survive the fast-developing liquidity crunch. These withdrawals placed the pound sterling under heavy and continuous pressure, and finally, on September 21, 1931, the United Kingdom decided to leave the gold standard. The pound devalued by 25 percent almost instantly, and within a few months' time, the recovery of the British economy had begun.

These events in Europe led to increased pressure on the United States and heavy speculation against the dollar. The Fed refused to bow; instead, at the end of 1931 it jacked up interest rates dramatically, making things even worse. In their analysis *The Great Depression: An International Disaster of Perverse Economic Policies,* Thomas Hall and David Ferguson echoed Friedman and Schwartz in their description of the situation: "The US economy was on the brink of disaster, and in several other countries the situation was no better…Due to a combination of economic ignorance, confusion, and incompetence, US policymakers pursued policies that were highly contractionary. They deepened and transformed the recession into a Great Depression."[50]

To be clear, "economic ignorance, confusion, and incompetence" was not solely the domain of the United States; that unholy trinity reigned in Europe as well. Andrew Mellon, the US secretary of the Treasury in those days, famously claimed that in order to deal effectively with the Depression, one had to "…liquidate labor, liquidate stocks, liquidate the farmers, liquidate real estate. It will purge the rottenness out of the system. High costs of living and high living will come down. People will work harder, live a more moral life. Values will be adjusted, and enterprising people will pick up from less competent people."[51] Mellon's substantial lack of insight into what was transpiring in the years leading up to and during the Great Depression was also shared by policymakers in Europe, though they tended to be more subtle about it.

The Great Depression ended when, as previously indicated, countries threw off the yoke of the gold standard and took measures to contain the banking crisis.[52] In the United States, the banking crisis came to an end after President Franklin D. Roosevelt started his first term on March 6, 1933, with a four-day-long national banking holiday.[53] During that short period, important new laws were pushed through introducing government-backed deposit insurance and restructuring of the financial sector. Roosevelt also took control of monetary policy away from the Fed and placed it with the Treasury instead. In June 1933, the United States left the gold standard, which led to the resignation of Fed Chairman Eugene Meyer. Confidence was restored, and from 1933 to 1937, the American economy grew by an average of 8 percent per year.[54] As more countries left the gold standard, recovery also took hold in Europe. In Germany, the Nazi regime's build-up of its military forces contributed strongly to its economic recovery, and the same occurred in Italy. In France and several other European countries, the recovery was much weaker. Then World War II began.

In Venice

Almost a century has gone by since the onset of the Great Depression. It was the most horrific economic event of the twentieth century, and it led directly to political extremism and the disaster of World War II. Evidence that responsibility for the Great Depression lay with the monetary authorities is overwhelming—the mystic hand of central bankers failed to deliver, in a big way. Their neglect of the negative forces unleashed by the return to the gold standard during the 1920s and the destructive consequences that transpired after serial bank failures were allowed to occur were the basic ingredients of a poisonous cocktail. Their failures led to massive economic contraction, sky-high unemployment, a dramatic rise in poverty, and subsequent successes for extremist political parties.

As a member of the guild of central bankers, Bernanke was right to take the blame for the Great Depression, but the political leaders and central bankers of the 1920s and 1930s should not have been blind to the turmoil developing around them. History could have taken a totally different turn if more attention had been paid to the wisdom of economists from earlier generations. Much had already been learned about how adequate monetary policies were capable of preventing and addressing the developments that made the Great Depression so disastrous. *The central bankers of the 1930s effectively unlearned the lessons they should have been thoroughly aware of, given the stock of knowledge that was available to them.*

If Smith's *The Wealth of Nations* (1776) is the canonical text that created economics as a modern science, then it can also be argued that Henry Thornton performed the same *tour de force* in monetary economics (more specifically, regarding the crucial task of the central bank as lender of last resort) in his 1802 book, *An Enquiry into the Nature and Effects of the Paper Credit of Great Britain*. Even now, in the twenty-first century, every economist still owes a debt to Smith, and every temporary monetary economist owes Thornton as well. Thornton's writings are "the peak achievement of classical monetary theory,"[55] and they provide us with "lessons that continue to inform policymakers to this day."[56] Central bank specialist Charles Goodhart referred to *Paper Credit* as "the greatest treatise on the conduct of monetary policy ever written."[57] Thornton was well known as a "seminal monetary theorist and father of the modern central bank."[58]

In all fairness, the honorary title of "father of the modern central bank" could also be claimed by Alexander Hamilton, the first Secretary of the Treasury of the United States. Throughout his too-short life, the poorly educated Hamilton proved to be a brilliant politician with a powerful mind, a strong will, and abundant common sense.[59] During the very first financial crisis faced by the newly formed United States of America, the panic of 1792, the prices of securities dropped by 25 percent in two weeks' time. Faced with such a calamity, Hamilton forcefully intervened as the lender of last resort to the imploding financial system; his act minimized the effect of the financial turbulence on the real economy.[60] In effect, Hamilton "formulated and implemented 'Bagehot's rules' for central-bank management eight decades before Walter Bagehot wrote about them in *Lombard Street.*"[61]

With common sense and intuition as his only tools, Hamilton applied most of the rules and policy prescriptions that Thornton and later Bagehot would document during the nineteenth century. The same can be argued for certain moments in the history of the city-states in Europe that thrived economically during the Middle Ages.[62] Foremost among these medieval city-states was Venice, which, through its monopolization of the spice trade, reached the peak of its economic power during the fifteenth century. By that time, the Venetians had developed a sophisticated system of bank transfers for settling payments. Despite the fact that this system was advanced and even revolutionary for the time, the Venetians eventually faced what we now define as liquidity crises and deposit runs, which jeopardized the financial infrastructure and threatened the broader economic and trade environment. The Venetian elite soon realized that such crises limited the government's ability to borrow.

As these banking crises began to occur regularly in the fourteenth and fifteenth centuries, Venetians were obliged to think seriously about what we now know as central bank policies—without creating a central bank as a specific institution. Over the decades, the Venetians "developed a wide range of regulatory tools that were not unlike those in force nowadays. These included *ex ante* interventions like the establishment of legal restrictions to operations, of specific supervisory bodies, and of disclosure requirements, but also *ex post* interventions like lending of last resort."[63] The perils of crisis prevention and resolution led to the 1587 creation of the Banco della Piazza di Rialto, a privately owned bank that received a concession, making it a *de facto* central bank of sorts, including lender-of-last-resort responsibilities. The Banco della Piazza di Rialto was replaced in 1619 by the Banco del Giro, which operated quite successfully until it was liquidated by the Napoleonic administration that took over Venice in the early nineteenth century.

Early in the seventeenth century, the city-state of Amsterdam created its own public bank, the Wisselbank, with a mission to clean up the hodgepodge of debased currencies that circulated in those days; the bank largely succeeded in its mission. By the end of the seventeenth century, the Wisselbank had been given several other functions, and its success "allowed the government and government-sponsored entities (especially the Dutch East India Company) to monetize nonnegligible amounts of debt through the bank. Moreover, the bank started to indirectly behave as a lender of last resort, as it provided a liquidity backstop to the fund of mutual assistance that had been created in order to extend loans to cash-strapped merchant banks."[64] Over time, the Wisselbank was transformed into the Nederlandsche Bank, which is still today the central bank of the Netherlands.

In the German city-state of Hamburg, the Hamburger Bank, which was modeled on the Wisselbank, intervened as lender of last resort on occasion—especially during the 1763 crisis. The Hamburger Bank was merged into the Reichsbank in 1875. The Reichsbank in turn was the forerunner of the notorious Bundesbank, which in the post-World War II era became the symbol *par excellence* of rigorous and orthodox central banking.

Despite these many historical precedents, the institutional forerunner of the present-day version of a central bank didn't come about until the end of seventeenth century. First was the Sveriges Riksbank, a central bank established in Sweden in 1668. After several crises transpired, the Sveriges Riksbank was finally allowed to take up the main functions of modern central banking.[65] The Bank of England, founded as a private bank in 1694, delivered the template for the modern central bank,[66] and more than a century later, in 1800, the next central bank, the Banque de France, arrived on the scene.[67] The Bank of England's creation was the result of a deal between a group of British bankers and William of Orange, who became king of Britain and the Netherlands in the Glorious Revolution of 1689. The bankers agreed to lend William £1.2 million, quite a sum in those days, to rebuild his naval fleet so it would rival that of the French. In return for this loan, the bankers got the privilege of setting up the Bank of England and the ability to issue banknotes. Quickly, the Bank of England evolved into the banker of the British government.

Banker and Evangelist

Explicit references in the economic literature to a central bank and its role as lender of last resort were scarce prior to Thornton's treatise, despite the practices applied in several of medieval city-states and Alexander Hamilton's uncodified crisis approach. When Smith discussed the role of the state in society and in the economy, he mentioned the obligation of the state to create "certain public institutions," but the installation of a central bank was not among them.[68] Smith's comments on monetary and banking issues were heavily influenced by the Scottish banking crisis of 1772.[69] As a result of the crisis, Smith realized that safeguarding financial stability was important for social and economic development overall—that it was crucial for, to use his own parlance, "the wealth of nations." Smith indicated that the Bank of England should act "not only as ordinary bank, but as a great engine of state;" arguably, he was suggesting that it function in some way like a lender of last resort, but he did not develop that theme as such.[70]

Smith may have given a very indirect indication of the need for a lender of last resort, but not even the vaguest hint is present in the work of David Ricardo (1772–1823), another shining light of classical economics. Ricardo's pamphlet entitled *Plan for the Establishment of a National Bank*, which was published posthumously, stressed the necessity of such a bank to control the money supply in accordance with the needs of the economy.[71] Ricardo also warned of the potential for misuse of the printing press by the political elite, but at no point did he suggest that central banks should take up a lender-of-last-resort function when financial crises occurred. Like most classical economists, Ricardo trusted market forces to be largely self-regulating—certainly in the context of gold convertibility of currency.

Sir Francis Baring (1740–1810) was a lot more specific about lender of last resort than Smith or Ricardo. Baring founded, with his brother John, a London merchant house that evolved into the bank known as Baring Brothers & Co. (Its modern incarnation, Barings Bank, went under in 1995 due to losses caused by rogue trader Nick Leeson.)[72] During the nineteenth century, the Barings and the Rothschilds were the leading bankers in London. In 1797, Baring published a remarkable treatise on the Bank of England that described the bank as follows: "[It] must be considered solely as the center or pivot, for the purpose of enabling every part of the machine to move in perfect order."[73] He went on to specifically refer to the Bank of England as "the *dernier* resort...[because]...there is no resource on their refusal" to stand by the banking system. (*Dernier* is French for "last.")[74] Despite his reference to a central bank's function as lender of last resort, Baring's treatise fell short in adequately developing the economic and monetary framework necessary to position this lender-of-last-resort function. It was up to Henry Thornton to perform that *tour de force.*

Thornton was born into the business world.[75] In the late seventeenth century, his grandfather Robert started a trading house dealing mostly with Russia and the Baltics. Thornton's father, John, continued in the trading business and was a member of the Evangelicals, a puritanical sect within the Church of England. John Thornton was known as "the Great and Good," due to the fact that he donated large amounts of his fortune on charity.

Henry Thornton inherited his father's deep senses of piety and generosity. He was the youngest of three brothers; the eldest, Samuel, was also a figure of considerable importance in London who served as both director and governor of the Bank of England.

Against the advice of his father, Thornton joined the banking house of Down and Free in 1784, and it soon became Down, Thornton & Free. He began serving in the House of Commons at the young age of twenty-two. As part of Thornton's engagement with the Evangelical sect, he led the campaign for the abolition of slavery. His successful banking activities made him a wealthy man, and he continued his father's tradition of charity. Up until his marriage in 1796—he and his wife Marianne raised nine children who all survived their parents, remarkable in those days—Thornton gave away as much as six-sevenths of his income to charity. By the time of his marriage, he was closely engaged in discussions on credit and monetary issues related to various financial crises that occurred during the 1790s.

In 1793, a war began between Great Britain and revolutionary, Napoleonic France. Fought in varying degrees of intensity, it lasted almost twenty-five years. The start of the war set off a financial crisis during which several banking houses in London and the countryside failed. In 1797, another major crisis erupted following rumors that French soldiers had landed on British soil. This time around, the Bank of England was obliged to suspend the gold convertibility of its notes. The suspension was meant to be temporary, but it persisted until 1821. Thornton played a central role in parliamentary discussions about the financial situation as it evolved.[76] Most prominent was the constant demand that the British government, under pressure from war expenditures, must be able to borrow directly from the Bank of England.

During this turbulent period, Thornton's thinking on monetary affairs crystallized into what he recorded in his magnum opus, *Paper*

Credit. In it, he defended the feasibility of a monetary system without gold as an anchor. After the publication of his book, Thornton was regarded by his generation as *the* authority in England on credit and banking policies. As the attention for his book faded, so did his reputation, but he remained active as a banker and continued to devote much time, energy, and money to his religious beliefs for the rest of his life. Although he delivered several brilliant speeches during his tenure in Parliament, Thornton gradually lost interest in parliamentary work, not least because his defense of the Bank of England was heavily criticized as a result of a case of mistaken identity—it was his brother Samuel who had been director and governor of the Bank of England, not Henry. Thornton died after a prolonged illness on January 6, 1815, at the age of fifty-four.

Way Ahead

A careful analysis of the problems of the day, Thornton's *Paper Credit* stands the test of time as a brilliant exposition on the fundamentals of not only monetary and banking policies but also of the economic system in general. The breadth and depth of Thornton's approach was succinctly described by Anna Schwartz, Milton Friedman's co-author of *A Monetary History*, in her 1981 Henry Thornton Lecture:

> [Thornton] understood: the fallacy of the real bills doctrine; the distinction between the first-round and ultimate effects of monetary change; the problem market participants faced in distinguishing relative from general price changes; the distinction between internal and external gold drains; the factors influencing the foreign exchanges including the role of purchasing power parity; how to bring inflation under control; the relation of the Bank of England to other English banks; types of effects of monetary disturbances on interest rates; the distinction between the market rate and the natural rate of interest and between nominal and real rates of interest.[77]

Schwartz's list proves that Thornton was far beyond his contemporaries in terms of monetary discussions—he also laid out a basic set of topics that kept monetary economists busy for the two centuries that followed. Yet Schwartz's list is incomplete. Thornton didn't just stress the importance of confidence and trust for the smooth functioning of the economy and its monetary system; he also clearly acknowledged the existence and relevance of what we now call *moral hazard*—i.e., the fact that people change their behavior when government interventions change the environment in which people live and interact. Thornton's insights into the workings of credit markets; the way in which credit can stimulate economic activity (with the caveat that too much credit can become highly destructive); and the inflationary and deflationary processes and their consequences for the economy were way ahead of his time. According to Thornton, the difference between the loan rate in the economy and the profit rate to be earned by using borrowed money was crucial. A loan rate below the profit rate produces inflation, and one higher than the profit rate leads to deflation.

Thornton keenly comprehended the determinants of economic fluctuations—specifically with respect to the role played by inventory investment and by wage rigidity in particular. With this last observation, Thornton was squarely counter to the classical dogma of perfectly flexible markets, which dominated economic debate in those days. In the *Handbook of Monetary Economics,* Lucas Papademos and Franco Modigliani stated, "According to classical theory all markets for goods, including the market for labour services, clear continuously, with relative prices adjusting flexibly to ensure the attainment of equilibrium. Resources are fully utilized, and thus aggregate employment and output are always at the 'full-employment' or 'natural' level...In such an economy, money...does not influence the determination of relative prices, real interest rates, the equilibrium quantities of commodities, and thus aggregate real income."[78] Thornton realized that this classical picture of the economy was incomplete and that major rigidities in the system—most of all wage rigidity—make money not neutral. Changes in monetary policies bring about, at least in the short run, changes in the real economy.

Throughout *Paper Credit*, Thornton made clear his awareness of the ways in which the financial and banking systems have an impact on the overall state of the economy or, in modern parlance, on the overall macroeconomic stability. Business failures can produce banking failures and financial upheaval, but the opposite can also be true. Coherent and prompt central bank policies are necessary to turn vicious circles into virtuous ones. These may sound like truisms, but they're not. As will be described more in detail in the portion of this book dealing with the 2007–2009 global financial crisis, the awareness of the close link between financial upheaval and macroeconomic stability had largely disappeared from the mindset of most central bankers in the years leading up to that crisis. It certainly had disappeared from the econometric models on which they relied to formulate their policies.[79] *Having relearned the lesson that inadequate central bank interventions contributed significantly to the Great Depression, most twenty-first-century central bankers and their economic advisors had unlearned the reality of important interactions between the real and financial sectors of the economy.*

A substantial part of *Paper Credit* deals with the central bank's function as lender of last resort. "If any single theme stands out as the dominant message of *Paper Credit*," historian of economic thought Neil Skaggs pointed out, "it is the importance of the Bank of England as the guarantor of liquidity of the British financial system."[80] Throughout the book, Thornton focused on the public responsibility of the Bank of England to preserve the quantity of money (the money supply) available in the economy at an adequate level through adjustments in the emission of its notes, which by virtue of their soundness and general acceptability formed the non-gold component of the money supply. This duty meant that the Bank of England had to behave completely differently than commercial bankers. This is especially true in times of distress or crisis, when commercial bankers contract their loan engagements. In those circumstances, the central bank must expand its note issue and its loans.

Thornton strenuously argued that it was imperative for the Bank of England to uphold and restore confidence in the credit system and use all possible means at its disposal to achieve that goal. These policy prescriptions did not fall on deaf ears at the Bank of England. The policies pursued by the Bank of England during the crises of 1825, 1836, 1847, and 1866 clearly had the imprint of Thornton's analysis. Jeremiah Harman, governor of the Bank of England during the crisis of 1825, declared that panic was stemmed through lending "by every possible means and in modes that we had never adopted before; we took in stock on security, we purchased Exchequer bills, we made advances on Exchequer bills, we not only discounted outright, but we made advances on the deposits of bills of exchange to an immense amount, in short by every possible means consistent with the safety of the Bank, and we were not on some occasions over nice."[81]

Thornton pointed to several policy issues or problems that might arise in the context of fulfilling this lender-of-last-resort task. First, there's the issue of possible contradictions between the central bank's duty to control the growth of the money supply and its obligation to step forward as lender of last resort. The following quote from *Paper Credit*, described by Joseph Schumpeter as the "Magna Carta of central banking,"[82] expresses Thornton's resolution of this seeming contradiction:

> To limit the total amount of paper issued, and to resort
> for this purpose, whenever the temptation to borrow
> is strong, to some effectual principle of restriction; in
> no case, however, materially to diminish the sum in
> circulation, but to let it vibrate only within certain
> limits; to afford a slow and cautious extension of it, as the
> general trade of the kingdom enlarges itself; to allow of
> some special, though temporary, increase in the event of
> any extraordinary alarm or difficulty, as the best means
> of preventing a great demand at home for guineas; and
> to lean on the side of diminution, in the case of gold
> going abroad, and of the general exchanges continuing
> long unfavourable; this seems to be the true policy of

the directors of an institution circumstanced like that of
the Bank of England. To suffer either the solicitations of
merchants, or the wishes of government, to determine
the measure of the bank issues, is unquestionably to
adopt very false principle of conduct.[83]

Thornton advised that in order to avoid inflation, as well as deflation,
money growth should be roughly consistent with the growth rate of
real output within the economy, but central bankers must stand ready
for *ad hoc* interventions when extraordinary circumstances develop.
In Thornton's day, money supply under control of the central bank
consisted of gold reserves. Thornton regarded the Bank of England
as the custodian of the gold reserve and notes issued by the Bank of
England. What he labeled as "external drains" and "internal drains"—
what we today describe as external or internal crises or shocks—might
permit deviation from this rule. If the external drain (for example, trade
deficits) is thought to be temporary, the stock of gold reserves available
for the country should be used to meet the drain. If that external drain
is persistent, then restrictive monetary policies to bring internal prices
back in line with foreign ones are necessary in order to bring the loss of
gold reserves to a halt. In case of an internal drain due to a panic, the
central bank would have to increase its note issuance and its loans to
keep the money supply from contracting. Thornton emphasized that the
Bank of England's interventions would be more efficient if it was explicit
about its intentions and strategy.

The second policy issue Thornton addressed was the distinction
between the central bank's responsibility for the money supply and the
banking system as a whole and its responsibility for individual banks
and institutions. He was very clear on this issue, arguing that only the
general responsibility must be fulfilled. Bank runs and the accompanying
panics that ensue must be countered quickly and firmly in order to avoid
deflation and contraction of economic activity and to restore confidence
as quickly as possible.

Yet Thornton strongly argued against rescuing banks that misbehaved or were poorly managed:

> It is by no means intended to imply, that it would become the Bank of England to relieve every distress which the rashness of country banks may bring upon them... The relief should neither be so prompt and liberal as to exempt those who misconduct their business from all the natural consequences of their fault, nor so scanty and slow as deeply to involve the general interests. These interests, nevertheless, are sure to be pleaded by every distressed person whose affairs are large, however indifferent or even ruinous may be their state.[84]

Clearly, Thornton is speaking of the too-big-to-fail issue. A central bank should only give support on unfavorable terms, not least because of the problem of moral hazard. Insolvent banks should be allowed to fail.

A Man on a Mission

Thornton's treatment contained all the basic ingredients of the lender-of-last-resort function of a central bank embedded in a sophisticated (for the time, certainly) broader monetary and economic framework. Yet Walter Bagehot (1828-1871) is better known than Thornton for his clarity on the lender-of-last-resort doctrine. Mervyn King called Bagehot's *Lombard Street* (1873) "a book that was to become the bible for those interested in how to handle financial crises."[85] There are numerous parallels between Bagehot's analysis and policy recommendations in *Lombard Street* and Thornton's in *Paper Credit*. It's remarkable that, as far as I could verify, Bagehot makes no reference whatsoever to Thornton's seminal work on monetary economics in general and the lender-of-last-resort topic specifically. Although Thornton should unquestionably be regarded as the pioneer of the idea, Bagehot's contribution to the doctrine of lender of last resort also remains highly relevant in our modern world.

Despite living a short life, Bagehot left behind an impressive legacy—and not only in terms of monetary matters. It's quite impossible to put

Bagehot in a category as an intellectual. Bagehot was characterized by Norman St. John-Stevas, a British politician, author, lawyer, and editor of Bagehot's works, as "Victorian England's most versatile genius."[86] Historian George M. Young described Bagehot as "the greatest Victorian."[87] A contemporary said of Bagehot, "[He is] the human element in all the affairs of life, whether it relates to literature, history, politics, economics, sociology, religion, or science."[88] Woodrow Wilson, the US president from 1913 to 1921, claimed, "Occasionally, a man is born into the world whose mission it evidently is to clarify the thought of his generation, and to vivify it; to give it speed where it is slow, vision where it is blind, balance where it is out of poise, saving humor where it is dry—and such a man was Walter Bagehot."[89] Bagehot's collected works consist of fifteen volumes.

Born on February 3, 1826, in Langport, Somerset, a county in southwestern England, Bagehot was the second child of his mother Edith's second marriage (the first child died in childhood). Edith Stuckey was ten years older than Bagehot's father, Thomas. Edith lost two of the three children from her first marriage in childhood as well, and the third was severely mentally disabled. The trauma of these events led Edith to suffer from periodic bouts of insanity. Bagehot became his mother's chief support, and her death in 1870 devastated him. It's likely that his closeness to his long-suffering mother led Bagehot to write that "every trouble in life is a joke compared to madness."[90]

Bagehot's parents sent him to Bristol for grammar school and then to University College of London, where he studied mathematics, classics, and philosophy. He was a brilliant student with his share of troubles, including prolonged periods of mental exhaustion (partly explained by his mother's issues). After Bagehot left the university in 1848, his father pressured him into the study of law. He was called to the bar in 1852, but by that time, Bagehot had decided against a legal career.

Following his short foray into the law, Bagehot traveled to Paris to report on Napoléon's *coup d'état* for the *Inquirer*. As was typical of his eclectic style and way of looking at things, his articles defended Napoléon's use of force and curtailment of the French press—and he received plenty of criticism for this position. After Paris, Bagehot returned to Somerset and joined the Stuckey Bank, where his father was a partner (the bank had been founded by his mother's uncle). He kept his position at the bank, but by that point, writing had become essential to him. He first focused on historical and literary essays, but everything changed for Bagehot after a fateful meeting in 1857 with James Wilson, a member of the British Parliament, financial secretary to the treasury in London, and the founder and owner of the weekly magazine *The Economist*.

At Wilson's invitation, Bagehot began a series of articles on banking for *The Economist*. Over time, Bagehot became involved with Wilson's eldest daughter, Eliza, and they married in 1858. Wilson was called to India on a Treasury mission, and he appointed Bagehot and Richard Holt, a friend of Bagehot's from college who had been serving as editor of the magazine, to serve as joint directors of *The Economist* in his absence. The move became permanent in 1860, after Wilson died in India, and a year later, Holt left to become editor of *The Spectator*. Bagehot became the sole editor of *The Economist*, a position he held until his untimely death in 1877.

Given his responsibilities at the magazine, Bagehot moved to London and supervised the local branch of the Stuckey Bank there. During the 1860s, he ran for Parliament four times but failed each time. His health was delicate throughout his life; in March 1877, a cold quickly worsened and ultimately proved fatal.

In addition to his enormous catalog of contributions to *The Economist,* primarily to the topics of politics and economics, Bagehot authored three books. In 1867, he published *The English Constitution*, a practical, down-to-earth analysis of the British form of government— including great emphasis on the importance of the mystery of the monarchy to British society. "The use of the Queen, in a dignified position, is incalculable," Bagehot argued. He continued to explain that in the constitution there are "two parts…first, those which excite and preserve the reverence of the population…and next, the efficient parts, those by which it, in fact, works and rules."[91] Five years later, Bagehot published *Physics and Politics,* the objective of which was clearly put forth by the book's subtitle, "Thoughts on the Application of the Principles of 'Natural Selection' and 'Inheritance' to Political Science." Both books are remarkable intellectual achievements, but his third book, *Lombard Street,* is of relevance to the subject at hand—the central bank and its role of lender of last resort. Bagehot began the book by noting, "Money will not manage itself."[92]

"Permanent Chancellor of the Exchequer"

Twentieth-century economist and historian Richard Sayers succinctly assessed Bagehot's reputation as an economist: "When the two outstanding central bankers in the 1920s, Strong and Norman, correspond across the Atlantic on current policy, Bagehot was the authority they quoted to each other. This is a formidable record."[93] In the 1920s, Benjamin Strong served as director of the New York branch of the Federal Reserve. As previously discussed, Strong's untimely death was, according to Friedman and Schwartz, an important factor in the policy mistakes the Fed made in the years leading up to and during the Great Depression. Montagu Norman was the eccentric but powerful governor of the Bank of England from 1920 to 1944. During Bagehot's lifetime, politicians of all parties sought his advice on monetary and banking issues; he was once described as the "permanent Chancellor of the Exchequer."[94]

Comparing Bagehot's contributions to those of Thornton can be tricky. Thornton's insights on economic and financial life in general were superior to those of Bagehot. When discussing prevailing myths about the lender of last resort, British economist Charles Goodhart argued, "The very first myth is that the fount of all wisdom, the *fons et origo,* on the subject is to be found in Bagehot's great book *Lombard Street.*"[95] Goodhart believed that honor belonged to Thornton's *Paper Credit.* But Thornton's dominance extends beyond the terrain of lender of last resort—for example, Thornton's penetrating remarks on the business cycle and the impact of market rigidities.

The monetary situation of Bagehot's time was totally different than that of Thornton. By the time Bagehot was writing *Lombard Street* and reflecting on monetary issues, Great Britain had restored the gold convertibility of the pound sterling. *Paper Credit* was published while gold convertibility was suspended. The existence of gold convertibility made Bagehot less attentive to the need to stabilize the money supply, a central tenet of Thornton's argument. Fixed gold convertibility provided a high degree of automaticity with respect to the evolution of the money supply.

In his analysis and policy prescriptions, Bagehot echoed Thornton's writings on the distinction between internal and external drains on reserves, moral hazard, and the need for clear communication on the central bank's objectives. Bagehot stressed the need for a firm commitment on the part of the central bank to pursue these objectives stringently and without compromise. The Bank of England, Bagehot wrote, must make clear beyond the shadow of a doubt that it will stand ready to lend as much as is necessary to stem panics. There must be "a clear understanding between the Bank and the public that, since the Bank holds our ultimate banking reserve, they will recognize and act on the obligations which this implies."[96]

Bagehot also agreed with Thornton on the issue of moral hazard. He was adamant that the Bank of England should not bail out or support unsound institutions, no matter how big or how well connected they might be. As for external drains, Bagehot stressed the need to increase interest rates in order to protect the country's reserves, a divergence from Thornton that can logically be attributed to Bagehot's need to consider gold convertibility.

Yet Bagehot was just as insistent as Thornton on the crucial issue of trust: "The peculiar essence of our banking system is an unprecedent trust between man and man. And when that trust is much weakened by hidden causes, a small accident may greatly hurt it, and a great accident for a moment may almost destroy it."[97] This is reminiscent of the teachings of the Chinese philosopher Confucius, who claimed in the fifth century BC, "Three things are necessary for government: weapons, food, and trust. If a ruler cannot hold on to all three, he should give up weapons first and food next. Trust should be guarded to the end: without trust we cannot stand."[98]

Bagehot and Thornton agreed on rules the central bank must obey in acting as lender of last resort during times when financial turmoil threatens the economic system. Bagehot wrote that advances or loans made by the Bank of England under such circumstances should

> ...Stay the panic. And for this purpose, there are two rules. First. That these loans should only be made at very high rate of interest. This will operate as a heavy fine on unreasonable timidity and will prevent the greatest number of applications by persons who do not require it...Secondly. That at this rate these advances should be made on all good banking securities, and as largely as the public ask for them...The way to cause alarm is to refuse someone who has good security to offer...If it is known that the Bank of England is freely advancing on what in ordinary times is reckoned a good security... the alarm of the solvent merchants and bankers will be stayed.[99]

In other words, during panics, central banks must lend freely and boldly at high interest rates and against good collateral, whatever the collateral's origin might be. This became known as "Bagehot's dictum," but it could just as well be called "Thornton's dictum."[100]

To Bagehot, it was key that the Bank of England focused on preventing the failures of unsound institutions from starting a wave of failures among the sound institutions of the system. To achieve that objective, Bagehot believed, in a panic during which the Bank of England inevitably becomes "the sole lender," the bank must lend to all solvent borrowers—not just banks.[101] In order to avoid moral hazard, this crisis lending must involve an interest rate high enough to ensure that those seeking loans from the central bank first exhausted all other possibilities for financing. Moreover, high interest rates ensure a quick ending to emergency lending once a panic is over, and they also help protect the nation's gold reserves. Given the growing internationalization of economic activities, this last aspect became more relevant during Bagehot's time than it had been during Thornton's life.

Continuing Relevance

Clearly and systematically, Thornton and Bagehot outlined what it meant for the central bank to fulfill its role as lender of last resort to the financial and economic system. Over time, Bagehot received most of the credit for this intellectual achievement—a peculiar twist in the history of economic thought, as Thornton provided a more profound analysis three quarters of a century earlier than Bagehot.[102] Economist and historian Peter Bernstein claimed in his foreword to Bagehot's *Lombard Street*, "Bagehot invented crisis management; after 150 years his wise words are still the prescription of choice for containing financial crises, as well as a handbook for avoiding them." The same argument stands for Thornton's *Paper Credit*.

Together, the writings of Thornton and Bagehot developed a coherent picture of the basic mission of a central bank. Without making explicit reference to those nineteenth century giants, former Bank of England governor Mervyn King summarized that picture as such: "[The central bank is] responsible for two key aspects of the management of money in a capitalist economy. The first is to ensure that in good times the amount of money grows at a rate sufficient to maintain broad stability of the value of money, and the second is to ensure that in bad times the amount of money grows at a rate sufficient to provide the liquidity...required to meet unpredictable swings in the demand for it by the private sector."[103] Appropriate execution of the lender-of-last-resort function of central banks is crucial in this context.

Historian of monetary thought Thomas Humphrey summarized Thornton and Bagehot's take in six succinct points: "(1) protecting the aggregate money stock, not individual institutions; (2) letting insolvent institutions fail; (3) accommodating sound institutions only; (4) charging penalty rates; (5) requiring good collateral; and (6) preannouncing these conditions well in advance of any crisis so that the market would know exactly what to expect."[104] These policy prescriptions that a central bank must follow in order to maintain crucial trust and confidence in the system remain as valid today as they were in the nineteenth century, when Thornton and Bagehot formulated them. Moreover, both Thornton and Bagehot warned about the problem of moral hazard. The known availability of emergency lending by the lender of last resort may inspire investors to double down on risky ventures, which could potentially lead to crises of greater magnitude. Obviously, political, economic, and financial circumstances have changed enormously—in Thornton's and Bagehot's time, for example, the world was dominated by Great Britain and its pound sterling. But that makes the continuing relevance of their contribution all the more remarkable.

Clearly, if these prescriptions had been respected by monetary authorities during the years leading up to and during the Great Depression, the result would have been substantially different. *Unfortunately, the lessons taught by Thornton and Bagehot were unlearned by the central bankers of the 1920s and 1930s.* The economic and social collapse suffered worldwide would certainly have been much more limited, and there would have been fewer opportunities for political extremists to rise to power as a result of economic and social ruin. This is, of course, a matter of historical speculation, but if the world—and the United States specifically—had followed the lender-of-last-resort doctrine laid out by Thornton and Bagehot, quite a different history could have been possible.

As Bernanke pre-announced in his November 2002 speech at the celebration of Milton Friedman's ninetieth birthday, central bankers didn't forget this lesson when the 2007–2009 global financial crisis transpired. Thanks to the research of Friedman and Schwartz, *central bankers had relearned the lessons taught by Thornton and Bagehot.* When the financial crisis started to hit hard, in the summer of 2007, they acted quickly and resolutely to prevent the collapse of the financial system. With that, a twenty-first-century variant of the Great Depression was averted. We were saved from destructive deflation and economic and social collapse, as well as the dire political consequences of such a chain of events. Interest rates were cut deeply, and imaginative new programs and intervention schemes were developed to save the financial system from implosion. And central bankers, with some help from fiscal efforts by governments, succeeded in turning the tide.

And Then There Was COVID-19

Yet once the acute phase of the 2007–2009 global financial crisis was over, a new situation for central bankers emerged. Suddenly, they found themselves in circumstances never before experienced in peacetime. The lessons of the Great Depression had been applied—great, so now what? No textbook or scenario was close at hand for central bankers to apply in the real world. The financial markets were still very fragile, and the risk of a newly escalating recession was very real. How long would the system require very accommodating monetary policies? What risks were involved in turning policies around, and should that happen quickly or slowly? What would the unintended consequences of these policies be over time? Did those risks and consequences outweigh the positive impact on inflation (deflation) and growth? There were many more questions than reliable answers. *Central bankers soon discovered that, on top of what they had relearned from the nineteenth-century masters, many things remained to be learned about their role in the reality of the post-crisis world.* This was strongly reinforced when, in early 2020, the COVID-19 pandemic fell upon an unprepared world.

In December 2019, news outlets began to report on an outbreak of an unknown type of viral infection in the Chinese city of Wuhan, capital of the province of Hubei. As the news began to seep out, most of the world expressed various shades of indifference. The Chinese authorities began intense efforts to conceal the truth about the situation in and around Wuhan, and as a result, on January 23, 2020, the World Health Organization (WHO) saw no reason to declare an international emergency situation.[105] Exactly one week later, however, the WHO indicated that an emergency was underway; by March 11, the organization declared the COVID-19 outbreak to be a pandemic. By then, the number of people infected and dying was rising exponentially around the world. Cancellations of mass events, partial and total lockdowns and shutdowns, and measures to ensure social distancing were imposed all over the world. Normal life as we had known it came to an abrupt stop.

The COVID-19 pandemic led central bankers to double down on their use of unconventional monetary policy tools to prevent the pandemic from setting off a deep depression. New sanitation and social distancing rules were organized in many countries, and the effects they had on people and the economy made such a scenario frighteningly possible. Kristalina Georgieva, managing director of the IMF, declared, "This is a crisis like no other…It is way worse than the global financial crisis."[106] In April 2020, Martin Wolf, the well-respected economics commentator of the *Financial Times,* concluded, "The world economy is now collapsing…[This]…is the biggest crisis the world [has] confronted since World War II and the biggest economic disaster since the Depression of the 1930s."[107] French President Emmanuel Macron stated, "We have stopped half the planet to save lives; there are no precedents for that."[108] Former US Secretary of the Treasury and Harvard president Larry Summers claimed, "No event since the Civil War has so dramatically changed the lives of so many families."[109]

By early May 2020, the Bank of England warned the UK was "On the brink of the worst recession in 300 years."[110] The World Bank predicted that the economies of emerging and developing countries as a whole would shrink for the first time in at least six decades; the Group's chief economist, Carmen Reinhart, noted, "Even by the standard of systemic crises, this is a once-in-a-century, global—truly global—crisis."[111] The International Labor Organization warned that at least 195 million jobs worldwide would be wiped out.[112] Laurence Boon, chief economist of the OECD, said, "The loss of income exceeds that of any previous recession over the last one hundred years outside wartime, with dire and long-lasting consequences for people, firms, and governments."[113] The

International Labor Organization estimated that during the first nine months of 2020, income earned by workers dropped worldwide by more than 10 percent ($3.5 trillion).[114]

Given the grave social and economic consequences of the COVID-19 pandemic, central bankers felt obliged to postpone policy actions aimed at normalizing monetary policy and instead intensified and broadened the use of the unconventional monetary toolbox. In March 2020, former ECB president Mario Draghi set the tone by declaring, "We must mobilize as if for war."[115] The Fed put out a statement early on in the crisis stipulating, "The Federal Reserve is committed to using its full range of tools to support households, businesses, and the US economy overall in these challenging times."[116] On the same day, Christine Lagarde uttered her own version of the "whatever it takes" argument made by Draghi, her predecessor at the ECB, by arguing, "There are no limits to our commitments to the euro." Claudio Borio, the head of the BIS Monetary and Economic Department, concluded, "[During the first weeks of the pandemic] monetary policy has broken new ground. Central banks have gone one step further than in the past, seeking to cover 'the last mile' to reach businesses directly…They have done this through backstops for bank funding…In the process, central banks have gone down the credit scale more than ever before."[117]

To best understand the issues faced by central bankers, we must first closely examine the 2007–2009 global financial crisis and its broader context. The COVID-19 pandemic accelerated and deepened current economic troubles, but the unconventional monetary tools that central bankers originated during the global financial crisis remain in use today. Chapter 2 documents the drivers of the financial crisis: an extreme real estate bubble; a financial technique (securitization) gone wild, transgressing into fraud as rating agencies reneged on their role; leverage and debt accelerating through the roof; over-expansionary monetary policies; and, last but not least, psychological factors, including herd behavior (madness of the crowds) and risk myopia. Chapter 3 focuses on the timeline of the global financial crisis's evolution.

Chapter 4 documents in detail the policies pursued by central banks during and after the global financial crisis: very low and even negative policy interest rates; the creation of new refinancing mechanisms appropriate for the extraordinary circumstances of the crisis; large-scale asset-buying programs (quantitative easing); and forward guidance. These are the tools in the unconventional monetary policy toolbox used by most central banks to fight the financial crisis, and their use was accelerated in response to the pandemic. During the pandemic, central banks pushed the limits of their lender-of-last-resort operations even further. By largely ignoring collateral value, central bankers became buyers of last resort for almost any asset class on a worldwide scale.

Chapter 5 provides an overview of the unintended consequences of these unconventional monetary policies. Over time, these unintended consequences grew in importance and increasingly overshadowed the positive impacts they originally offered. Chapter 6 assesses the shortcomings of the inflation-targeting framework used explicitly or implicitly by most central banks in recent decades. The analysis reveals a need for a new framework for central bank policy that focuses on conjoined twins: price stability and financial stability.

Chapter 2: The Leverage Poison

The five drivers of the greatest financial crisis in history

FED CHAIRMAN BEN BERNANKE, US TREASURY SECRETARY Hank Paulson, and New York Fed President Timothy Geithner, American policymakers who were intimately involved in the fight to control the 2007–2009 global financial crisis, described it as "The worst financial crisis in generations…a conflagration that chocked off global credit, ravaged public finance, and plunged the American economy into the most damaging recession since the breadlines and shantytowns of the 1930s." They claimed that "the financial shocks of 2008 were by many measures greater than the shocks before the Great Depression," and that it was "hard to overstate just how chaotic and frightening it was."[1]

Bernanke's individual recollections were even more direct: "In public I described what was happening as the 'worst financial crisis since the Great Depression,' but privately I thought that—given the number of major financial institutions that had failed or come close to failure, its broad-based effect in financial and credit markets, and its global scope— it was almost certainly the worst in human history."[2] Mervyn King, who was governor of the Bank of England at the time, argued, "Within the space of little more than a year, between September 2007 and October 2008, what had been viewed as the age of wisdom was now seen as the age of foolishness, and belief turned into incredulity."[3]

Just like the Great Depression, the 2007–2009 global financial crisis took the world by surprise, as illustrated by the following quotes from IMF publications. In its Global Financial Stability Report, published in April 2006, a little more than a year before the crisis began, the IMF noted, "There is growing recognition that the dispersal of credit risk by banks to a broader and more diverse group of investors...has helped to make the banking and overall financial system more resilient... The improved resilience may be seen in fewer bank failures and more consistent credit provision. Consequently, the commercial banks, a core segment of the financial system, may be less vulnerable today to credit and economic shocks."[4] A year later, the IMF's World Economic Outlook was similarly optimistic: "Notwithstanding the recent bout of financial volatility, the world economy still looks well set for continued robust growth in 2007 and 2008...Overall risks to the outlook seem less threatening than six months ago."[5]

Queen Elizabeth II visited the London School of Economics toward the end of 2008 and asked, "Why did no one see it coming?" A deafening silence filled the room. British businessman and academic Adair Turner remarked, "On Saturday, September 20, 2008, I became chairman of the UK Financial Services Authority. Lehman Brothers had failed the previous Monday...We faced the biggest financial crisis in eighty years. Seven days before I started, I had no idea we were on the verge of disaster. Nor did almost everyone in the central banks, regulators, or finance ministries, nor in the financial markets or major economics departments."[6]

Turner's assessment is somewhat unfair, as some economists did indeed see "it" coming. But only a rare breed had the foresight to realize what was happening *and* gathered the courage necessary to go against the all-is-well consensus that prevailed as the dangerous situation unfolded. Those doomsayers included the University of Chicago's Raghuram Rajan,[7] Harvard's Kenneth Rogoff, Yale's Robert Shiller, New York University's Nouriel Roubini,[8] and William White and Claudio Borio of BIS—all Cassandras who predicted the coming financial storm.[9]

Not everyone appreciated their pessimistic straightforwardness on the developing financial situation.[10] When I spoke to Rajan, Roubini, and Borio years later, all three admitted that although they had acknowledged that serious trouble was on the horizon, they were surprised by the intensity of the crisis and the speed at which it spread throughout the financial system. Everyone who lived through the horrible days, weeks, and months when the crisis raged through the economy and our lives will never forget the experience.

During the heyday of the crisis, I was the director of a think tank in Belgium. The developments of the fall of 2008 frightened me so much that at one point, I told my wife to discreetly withdraw a substantial amount of cash from our bank account. I feared that we were descending into chaos, with bank closures and failures that would inevitably lead to mass panic. Years later, during my tenure as Belgium's minister of finance, I brought up this episode in a discussion with a government official and a top banker who had been closely involved at the highest level in the discussions and deliberations during those days. Both confessed they'd done the same. We had truly feared the sky was falling in on us.

Five Drivers

August 9, 2007 was a windy and exceptionally cool day in Paris. On that day, BNP Paribas, France's largest bank, announced that it would shut down three of its in-house hedge funds. The rationale: They were facing problems with their portfolios, which were largely based on American mortgage paper—specifically the subprime segment of that market's collateralized debt obligations (CDOs).[11] In terms of quality, subprime loans are the lowest segment of the mortgage loan market.

To many, the BNP Paribas announcement is the starting point of what would bloom into the 2007–2009 global financial crisis.[12] Paribas's acknowledgment that it could not value the assets of its hemorrhaging funds was a profoundly alarming signal—and one the markets did not miss. If a top-notch institution like a French megabank couldn't figure out the worth of its assets, "How could any other bank know its real exposure to mortgage-backed securities?"[13] Paribas was in fact the third warning of danger in the summer of 2007, and even those who had failed to take notice of the first two could no longer deny the clouds on the horizon.

In June of that year, Bear Stearns, the smallest of the five big American investment banks,[14] confronted the first clear signal of major trouble in the financial markets. The bank was obliged to pump $3 billion into two of its funds, which were drowning in subprime CDOs. (There will be more on the Bear Stearns saga in Chapter 3.) A few weeks after the Bear Stearns alert, another warning shot came from Germany. The German government was forced to step in and save IKB Deutsche Industriebank and two regional Landesbanken, Sachsen and Nord Rhein-Westfalen, as all three were loaded with American subprime paper. At the time, they claimed the subprime problems were a purely American problem—later proven to be incorrect.

In July, Chuck Prince, chairman of Citigroup, launched a veiled warning: "When the music stops, in terms of liquidity, things will be complicated. But as long as the music is playing, you've got to get up and dance. We're still dancing."[15] By August, several institutions in the United States, France, and Germany were in serious trouble. The cause was the same—collateralized American real estate paper that the whole world had been eagerly buying. Prince's remarkable and unusual warning made clear that this *crisette* wouldn't be limited to a few countries or a few markets. Things were about to get ugly, and not just here and there—on a global scale.

The drivers of the worst financial crisis since the Great Depression of the 1930s were already clearly visible when the troubles faced by Bear Stearns, BNP Paribas, and the three German institutions surfaced during the summer of 2007. The first was the enormous bubble that had developed in the American real estate market—specifically, the huge expansion of the subprime segment of that market. The second was the securitization process, which gradually suffered destructive excesses and abuses. The third was the massively increasing degrees of leverage that had begun to dominate Western economies—primarily the United

States, the United Kingdom, and some of the euro-area economies. The fourth was the monetary policy that had been pursued in the United States and elsewhere in the years leading up to the crisis, which was consistently accommodative and asymmetric. Last but not least, the fifth driver was myopic herd behavior that amplified the shocks the financial and economic system was undergoing. Intimate links among each of these drivers made the mixture even more explosive, as the remainder of this chapter will document extensively.

Real Estate Freebies

In mid-2005, *The Economist* warned that the levels of US house prices were so high that they threatened the health of the entire world economy[16]—prophetic words, to be sure. On average, housing prices in the United States rose by 125 percent between 1997 and 2006 in real terms, i.e., after correcting for inflation. Prices peaked in 2006; by the end of 2007, they averaged 10 percent below peak. In the end, they plunged by 30 percent or more. The evolution of the subprime segment was particularly disruptive; the percentage of seriously delinquent or foreclosed subprime mortgages soared from just under 6 percent in the fall of 2005 to more than 30 percent by the end of 2009.[17]

Three elements contributed to this massive real estate bubble. The first was the deeply ingrained belief among Americans (and quite a few foreigners, too) that US real estate prices only went in one direction— up—with no real limits. The second was the set of policies pursued in the United States by Fannie Mae and Freddie Mac, the government-sponsored enterprises (GSEs) focused on refinancing the mortgage market. The third element behind the bubble was the insatiable appetite foreign investors had for yields offered by American real estate securities.

The mistaken belief that housing prices in the United States only went up began as pure speculation but came to be viewed as a sound investment. That's a recipe, history has taught us, for disaster.[18] Homebuyers whose yearly incomes were insufficient to cover a mortgage eagerly took them on anyway because they believed they could sell later for an even higher price—getting them off the hook, plus a tidy profit. Policies pursued by the Clinton and Bush administrations to stimulate home ownership throughout the entire income distribution, especially the lower parts of it, also bolstered the subprime segment of the mortgage market.[19] Subprime mortgages are extended to those who, on the basis of standard requirements for mortgage loans (income and credit history), should not be entitled to them.

This discussion of the subprime mortgage market segues well into the second element that fueled unhealthy developments in the US real estate market—the policies pursued by Fannie Mae and Freddie Mac. These policies took shape in the wake of housing policies of different presidential administrations.[20] Bernanke, Geithner, and Paulson considered Fannie and Freddie to be "basically the corporate embodiment of moral hazard"—quite a categorical statement for top-notch policymakers.[21] At the start of the crisis, the two institutions were responsible for refinancing more than half of the $12 trillion outstanding mortgage loans in the country, and Fannie and Freddie were frequently pushed by legislators to increase the subprime component of their overall refinancing activity. In 1996, the Clinton administration ordered Fannie and Freddie to have at least 42 percent of its refinancing activities in mortgages for people with incomes below the regional median, and the Bush administration increased it twice more, to 50 percent in 2000 and 52 percent in 2005.

For a fee, Fannie and Freddie would guarantee their mortgage-backed securities against borrower defaults, which meant that purchasers of these securities faced no credit risk at all. The guarantees were thought to be as good as those made by the US Treasury, an assumption that proved to be correct (see infra). Naturally, the market cooperated and produced mortgage loans that fit the requirements of these policies. Horrific irresponsibility and outright fraudulent practices played a part, as well, but misguided government regulation decisively pumped up the subprime mortgage bubble.

Charles Calomiris, finance professor at the business school of Columbia University, summarized the role of Fannie and Freddie as such:

The politicization of Fannie Mae and Freddie Mac and
the actions of members of Congress to encourage reckless
lending by GSEs in the name of affordable housing
were arguably the most damaging policy actions leading
up to the crisis...Fannie and Freddie ended up holding
$1.5 trillion in exposure to toxic mortgages...It is likely
that absent the involvement of Fannie and Freddie in
aggressive subprime buying beginning in 2004, the
total magnitude of toxic mortgages originated would
have been less than half its actual amount.[22]

Calomiris' conclusion was confirmed by four New York University
economists, who argued, "It is certainly true that the vast expansion of
mortgage finance could not have taken place without the involvement of
the GSEs...The tale of the financial crisis is that homeowners, mortgage
lenders, securitizers, and investors in mortgage-backed securities all took
advantage of the freebies thrown at them either directly or indirectly by
the GSEs."[23]

The third factor behind the real estate bubble was foreigners' huge
appetite for paper from the US real estate securitization machine.
Following the economic liberalization in China and India and the
implosion of the Soviet empire, emerging markets experienced a huge
increase in income growth. Moreover, after the Asian and Russian financial
crises of 1997 and 1998, governments reduced their budget deficits
substantially, which contributed to an increase in national savings rates
in many emerging countries. These actions, which resulted in impressive
surpluses on the current account of the balance of payments, built up
substantial international reserves that shielded their economies from
the consequences of sudden massive capital movements. This evolution
produced what Bernanke described in 2005 as a "global savings glut."[24]
The savings rate in emerging markets rose from 24 percent of GDP
in 1999 to 34 percent of GDP by 2007. As investors looked for yield
in a broadly low interest rate environment, these savings increasingly
flowed to the United States. Foreign savings were attracted by the higher

yields—particularly in the bubble of the American real estate market—
and also by the deep liquidity of American financial markets and the
strong rule of law in those markets.

At the peak, foreign investors held close to $1.5 trillion in securities
directly related to the American real estate sector, and China was a major
source of these capital inflows. By 2008, China held more than $700
billion in mortgage-backed securities, mainly from Fannie and Freddie,
an amount slightly higher than the Chinese holdings of US Treasuries
at that time. This massive Chinese investment in US paper was the
inevitable consequence of the country's stubborn policy to keep its
currency undervalued *vis à vis* the US dollar and other major currencies.
China wanted to keep its export machine in overdrive, so its currency
had to remain undervalued. Massive purchases of dollar-denominated
assets were unavoidable.

Clearly, years of reckless behavior in and around the American real
estate sector (especially the subprime market) played a crucial role in
the development of the 2007–2009 global financial crisis. But to keep
things in perspective, consider that there was much more going on as
well. In the words of Bernanke, Geithner, and Paulson, "The spark for
the financial fire of 2008 came from irresponsible lending in America's
subprime mortgage sector. But the turmoil in that chaotic but relatively
small corner of the credit markets could not have created a global
inferno if dry tinder hadn't accumulated throughout the entire financial
system."[25]

Agent of Contagion

The second driver of the global financial crisis was *securitization*—
specifically, the unhappy course the securitization process had followed
in the years leading up to the crisis. This financial technique consists of
packaging future revenue-producing assets into securities that can be
offered to investors in the present. Loans of all types qualify as assets
suitable for securitization, but other assets can be considered as well.
For example, in 1997, the late British pop star David Bowie securitized

the future expected revenues from the royalties of his catalog. Investors paid $55 million for the securities Bowie's management brought into the market. (Bowie was an innovator in more than music alone.)

During the 1990s, securitization of mortgage loans really took off, especially in the United States. The process generated a huge stream of collateralized debt obligations, *asset-backed securities,* and *mortgage-backed securities.* Financial institutions competed ferociously to develop new and increasingly sophisticated CDO variants. Despite the fact that they weren't invented until the latter half of the 1990s, close to $600 billion in new CDOs were issued in 2006 alone.[26] At the same time, enormous amounts of credit insurance related to these products was developed. Known as *credit default swaps* (CDS), these brought down insurance giant AIG in September 2008. By the end of 2007, the nominal amount of outstanding CDSs was almost $60 trillion.[27]

This securitization process was supposed to make the financial system more resilient and safer by spreading risk more efficiently throughout the markets and by allowing more sophisticated risk management. For example, securitization allowed banks to take loan risks off their balance sheet and bring them to the market, where the risks could be absorbed by those best placed to manage such risks and/or those with the appropriate risk appetite. Many economists, including Fed Chairman Alan Greenspan, firmly believed at the onset of the twenty-first century that securitization had made the financial system much safer and less prone to devastating banking crises.[28] Unfortunately, things worked out, say, a little differently in the real world. In the words of Bernanke, "Securitization was supposed to disperse risk by packaging thousands of loans into securities...[but instead it became]...an agent of global contagion."[29]

The derailment of securitization and, specifically, securitized mortgage paper was best described by Bernanke: "In the years just before the crisis, neither banks nor their regulators adequately understood the full extent of banks' exposures to dicey mortgages and other risky credit."[30] In mortgage securities, the excesses were most striking, but the securitization of other types of loans caused severe difficulties as well.

First, securitization led underwriters to pay much less attention to the credit quality of those who applied for mortgage loans.[31] Why invest in exhaustive screening of homebuyers if mortgage loans could be securitized, brought to the market, and taken off the balance sheet of the loan's originator in a matter of weeks? Demand for securitized mortgage paper was overwhelming, so no matter what the securitization machine churned out, interested buyers were ready to scoop it up. Everyone seemed to forget that distributing the risk through trade in securitized paper didn't make the risk disappear. On the contrary, as securitization allowed banks to take loans of their balance sheets, they increasingly pursued new loans that could be dumped in the same way. As more and more loans were created and securitized, their quality deteriorated, as banks catered first to the least risky borrowers.

Intense usage of securitization techniques shuffles risk around, and as it does, it also builds more risk into the financial system. Yet the securitization process creates, in the words of Janet Yellen, Bernanke's successor as Fed chairman, "an illusion of low risk."[32] This situation led to almost instant panic once people finally began to wonder where the risks were, which securities were toxic, and who was stuck with that garbage in their portfolio. As Bernanke wrote, during the financial crisis, securitization became "an agent of global contagion" moving at lightning speed. It was COVID-19 *avant la lettre* (before the concept existed), so to speak.

The second derailing force at work was the continuous slicing and dicing inherent in the securitization process—the repackaging of securitized paper. The slicing and dicing of packages of mortgage loans was originally intended to fine-tune the packages to meet the different tastes of investors. Investors willing to accept higher risks could earn higher returns than those who were more risk averse. But increasingly, the repackaging of securitized mortgages began to conceal where the real risks were hidden. The IMF estimated that 90 percent of subprime mortgages originated in the US eventually found their way into the highest-rated (AAA) securitized paper. The rating agencies, egged on by competition and eager to collect fees, turned their rating responsibilities into a joke—and they knew it.[33] Jean Tirole, laureate of the 2014 Nobel Prize in economics, elegantly put it in tongue-in-cheek language, "The agencies' incentives were not fully aligned with the regulators' objectives."[34] Once it became clear that the agencies' (Moody's, Standard & Poor's, and Fitch were three most important ones) ratings for the ocean of mortgage-related securities floating all around the world were utterly unreliable, even more contagion and panic infused the developing storm in the financial markets.

The third factor that turned securitization into a doomsday vector was the perverse manner in which the process interacted with bonus payouts in the financial sector.[35] Most bonus systems were oriented toward the short term—i.e., a bonus calculated on profits produced during the fiscal year or an even shorter time period. This bonus system created strong incentives to package and repackage mortgage loans as much as possible to maximize the AAA ratings, realize handsome profits on these transactions, and pocket fee-related bonuses, no matter what problems those securitized time bombs might create down the road.[36] In short, the situation became a prime example of *après moi, le déluge* (a selfish disregard for problems that may occur in the future).

Securitization wasn't the only new financial technology that went off the rails—the blind mathematization of risk management also played a role. Some believe it all began in 1989, when Dennis Weatherstone, then the CEO of JP Morgan, demanded that his employees present him with a quantitative risk evaluation of the company's balance sheet by 4:15 each afternoon. Soon, the variance-at-risk (VaR) method became the ubiquitous quantification effort for the risks faced by financial institutions, and the era of the quants (people specialized in mathematical and statistical methods) was underway.[37] There's no need to go deep on the VaR method and other sophisticated measurement exercises, as the takeaway is that these analyses—and especially, the way in which they are used by the leadership of financial institutions—often flagrantly ignore tail risk.[38] The American-Lebanese author Nassim Nicholas Taleb referred to tail risks as black swans, or events that have a very low probability of occurring.[39] Unfortunately, when black swans occur in financial markets, as several did during the financial crisis, the consequences are dramatic. Blind faith in a mathematical approach to risk management had left many institutions unprepared for the devastation of black swans.

The clear failure of these quantitative models to prevent major management mistakes recalls a claim by Albert Einstein, "Not everything that counts can be measured, and not everything that can be counted counts." Andrew Haldane, director of the Bank of England, insightfully noted, "All models are wrong. The only model that is not wrong is reality, and reality is not, by definition, a model. But risk management models have during this crisis proved themselves wrong in a more fundamental sense. They failed Keynes' test—that it is better to be roughly right than to be precisely wrong. With hindsight, these models were both very precise and very wrong."[40]

Leveraged to the Hilt

The third driver behind the 2007–2009 global financial crisis was the substantial amount of leverage that riddled the financial system and the rest of the economy. Leverage is a fancy word to describe the degree of indebtedness faced by an economy, a financial institution, a company, a household, or an individual. Throughout economic and financial history, a healthy dose of leverage has been shown to be a good thing, as it can facilitate economic growth and social progress. But too much of a good thing can quickly become a very bad thing. As Mervyn King noted, "For all the clever innovations in the world of finance, its vulnerability was, and remains, the extraordinary levels of leverage."[41] Excessive leverage was probably the dominating destructive force behind the financial crisis.

In order to come to meaningful conclusions on leverage, indebtedness must be measured against the repayment capacity of the debtor, which is mainly determined by available income. In the case of an individual or family, an equal amount of debt means something substantially different if your annual net income is $50,000 instead of $250,000. Across an entire economy, gross domestic product (GDP) provides a fairly good estimate of the income streams a government can generate to honor its debt obligations. Thus, public debt as a percent of GDP is the most relevant parameter to judge national leverage. Profitability and cash flows provide basic metrics for the debt service capabilities of companies and financial institutions, and households and individuals depend on disposable income to honor the debt burden they take on.

Of course, the net asset position (assets minus debt) of debtors is also an important element in judging debt burdens and degrees of leverage, since sovereigns, companies, financial institutions, households, and individuals can sell assets to honor debt obligations. For the purposes of this book, we will focus on debt as measured against some income metric, because measuring leverage in terms of net asset position can lead to misguided conclusions. If expanding credit causes asset prices to rise (for example, real estate or equities), then looking only at the relation of outstanding credit to asset values may give the impression that leverage hasn't changed much or has even diminished, in the case of rapidly rising asset prices. When asset prices drop, however, leverage can explode in the blink of an eye, leaving many investors, to paraphrase the words of Warren Buffett, swimming in the sea without a bathing suit.

In the period preceding the 2007–2009 global financial crisis, leverage measured as debt against income metrics exploded. *Debt rose faster—much faster—than the economy grew.* Large parts of the world went on one of the wildest leverage binges ever seen. By the end of 2007, the total debt outstanding reached $142 trillion, or 269 percent of world GDP, up by $57 trillion, or 23 percentage points of GDP against the number from the end of 2000.[42] This massive increase in leverage worldwide was visible in every sector of the economy. Leverage would really go through the roof in the period after the acute phase of the financial crisis and certainly with the arrival of the COVID-19 pandemic.[43] In developed countries, credit grew between 10 percent and 15 percent per year in the two decades before 2008, while annual nominal income grew by around 5 percent during the same period.[44]

Throughout the developed world, especially in the United States and the euro area, debt increase over the period leading up to the financial crisis was significant. Total debt in the US economy soared from around 250 percent of GDP in 2000 to more than 350 percent of GDP by the start of the financial crisis. In contrast, it previously took almost 50 years, rather than 8, for overall debt in the US to increase by 100 percentage points of GDP. The euro area saw a similar result, with total debt evolving between 2000 to 2007 from 280 percent of GDP to 350 percent of GDP.[45] In both the US and the euro area, private leverage (companies, households, and, most of all, financial institutions) saw the fastest increases. In China, too, leverage increased considerably between the end of 2000 and the end of 2007—debt rose from $2.1 trillion to $7.4 trillion, or from 121 percent of GDP to 158 percent of GDP.[46] The leverage increase in China mainly occurred in local layers of the government sector and the financial sector, as the corporate sector substantially deleveraged.[47]

A distinction must be made here between the public and the private sectors. In democracies, governments generally have continuous problems with controlling their budget deficits—call it the wrong side of the Keynesian legacy.[48] When the economy sags, automatic stabilizers like spending on unemployment and other welfare benefits rise, and tax revenues go down. This results in budget deficits, and that is as it should be. But in good times, the deficits should disappear as the automatic stabilizers work in reverse. As a result, the government's leverage (debt as a percentage of GDP) shouldn't change that much. This approach also leaves room for necessary public investments and interventions that are critical when unexpected emergencies like the financial crisis and the COVID-19 pandemic occur. Governments must have room to maneuver in order to do what is needed for the benefit of their citizens.

Unfortunately, history tells a different story. In the hands of politicians, the Keynesian legacy is used to justify deficits across the board far too often. In an economic downturn, the argument is made that everything needs to be done to fight the downturn—to spend, cut taxes, reap the electoral benefits of throwing money around, and not worry too much about the deficit and debt. When the economy improves, so the argument goes, we can't do anything that would disturb the upswing, so worries about the deficit should be kept quiet. In a democratic society, the reality is that deficits appear easily and consistently, but they don't disappear in the same way. Simply put, economics get derailed by politics. As they keep their eyes focused on the next election, politicians prefer expanding spending to cutting it. The ideological objective among leftist parties to increase government expenditures adds to the problem.

In the United States, despite frequent rhetoric on budget deficits that sometimes gets heated, a kind of structural neglect of budget deficits prevails. This attitude has a lot to do with the fact that these deficits, given the still dominant role of the dollar in world economic and financial affairs, can be financed relatively easily. Charles De Gaulle, the legendary French president who served during the middle of the twentieth century, first termed this advantage *exorbitant privilege*.[49] In 1971, John Connally, who served as Richard Nixon's secretary of the Treasury, remarked to a group of astonished European ministers of finance, "The dollar is our currency, but it's your problem."[50] Of course, that exorbitant privilege will become less relevant as the dominance of the US economy and its currency slips.

In Europe, the tendency to accumulate budget deficits, and thus to increase government leverage over time, has more to do with the past promises made in the sphere of social security benefits. That's not to say that the United States isn't confronted with the delicate issue of promises launched in the past, but Europe has gone further down this road. Former German chancellor Angela Merkel famously commented that Europe accounts for 7 percent of the world's population, 25 percent of the world's economy, and half of the world's social spending.[51] Programs that are easy to pay for in times of persistently high growth rates and positive demographics become much more difficult to deliver when growth declines and an aging population turns the demographic tables. Politically speaking, reneging on promises of social expenditures (especially pensions) is extremely difficult, especially when tax rates are so high that they become a drag on the economy. Kicking the can down the road by letting outstanding debt rise is practically the only political option that remains—especially when the mystic hand of central bankers *seems* capable of containing any crisis that comes along.

A Long Tail

In the period leading up to the financial crisis, the private sector was leveraged to the hilt. In the private sector, leverage can substantially increase return on capital. Suppose you invest $10 million of your own capital in an investment and the investment brings you a $1 million profit, which is a return of 10 percent. Now suppose you use only $2 million of your own capital and $8 million in borrowed funds to make the same investment. If you assume a 3 percent cost of interest for the borrowed funds, you walk away with $760,000 as a net profit ($1 million minus 3 percent on $8 million). Now the return on your invested capital is 38 percent—almost four times the initial return.[52] In the same example, if you invest only $500,000 of your own capital and borrow the remaining $9.5 million, the return on invested capital shoots way above 100 percent.

The lower the cost to borrow sinks, the more attractive increased leverage becomes. Of course, it's also true that if the layer of capital invested in a venture is very thin, a loss on the investment will wipe out the whole venture very quickly. That's why highly leveraged financial institutions can slide into turbulent waters very quickly once markets turn, just as the financial crisis showed.[53] That most banks had become leveraged to the hilt had a lot to do with the international rules for bank capitalization, which are known as Basel rules.[54] Without getting too technical about the rules, the basic point is that they allowed banks to work with a minimum amount of capital and that the real content of the capital buffer of banks was smaller than most thought.[55] Moreover, practically all banks had created numerous off-balance special purpose vehicles that were very thinly capitalized—just like those of BNP Paribas and Bear Stearns. When all hell broke loose, the banks put these vehicles back on to their balance sheets, which crippled them.

Increased leverage throughout the financial and banking system fueled the growth of the financial sector. In 1950, the financial sector contributed 2.8 percent to the US GDP. This increased to 4.9 percent in 1980 and to 8.3 percent in 2006,[56] so between 1950 and 2006, the US financial sector grew three times faster than the rest of the economy. Similar developments occurred in Europe and Japan. It's undeniable that financial development can positively affect economic and social advancement, but there's also clearly a point at which the contribution of finance turns negative—or at least its benefits diminish significantly.[57] Luigi Zingales, a professor at the University of Chicago Booth School of Business, has argued convincingly that finance specialists have misled society by overstating the benefits of finance, concluding, "Without proper rules, finance can easily degenerate into a rent-seeking activity."[58]

One element that contributes to the less-than-beneficial effect of modern finance is that its ever-increasing relative share of the economy, combined with the industry's ability to pay high wages, sucks human capital away from sectors in which their contributions could be much more beneficial to society.[59] Development of the sophisticated derivative products needed to feed the securitization machine requires armies of PhDs in mathematics, statistics, physics, and computer technology. "Dealing rooms of the world," Turner remarked, "are filled with numerous top math and physics graduates, devoting their skills to trading strategies and financial innovation, rather than to scientific research or industrial innovation."[60]

Leverage is often absolutely necessary to launch ground-breaking innovation. Almost a century ago, legendary economist Joseph Schumpeter concluded, "Capitalism is that form of private property economy in which innovations are carried out by means of borrowed money, which in general, though not by logical necessity, implies credit creation."[61] Most often, people who engage in revolutionary innovative processes lack the resources to make the necessary investments. Rich people are rarely revolutionary innovators who wildly think outside the box. Instead, they tend to be more interested in the status quo. Grassroots innovation often comes from the odd man or woman out.

Attractive as leverage can be, high levels of it pose acute and chronic risks alike. As Carmen Reinhart and Kenneth Rogoff concluded in their book *This Time Is Different: Eight Centuries of Financial Folly*, "Highly leveraged economies, particularly those in which continual rollover of short-term debt is sustained only by confidence in relatively illiquid underlying assets, seldom survive forever, particularly if leverage continues to grow unchecked."[62] Concerns about a debtor's willingness or ability to service debts may lead to a funding crisis in which creditors are unwilling to extend new loans or roll over existing commitments—thus bringing down the house of cards built on a foundation of leverage. If panic sets in, a self-fulfilling loop of doom is set in motion. Risk premiums escalate and fire sales of assets worsen debtors' situations across the board. Funding crises like these played a pivotal role in the development of the financial crisis.

The edifice of modern finance is built on the assumption that liquidity will be sufficiently available at all times. While that's a reasonable assumption in normal times, it quickly becomes a myth when trouble starts. As economics professor Perry Mehrling remarked,

> You don't know what you've got 'til it's gone. Liquidity is like that. One day you've got a nice portfolio of high-yielding fixed income securities, which you can easily finance by using the securities themselves as collateral to borrow in a deep and liquid wholesale money market. The next day, you can no longer borrow at any reasonable rate, and you can't sell your nice portfolio either at any reasonable price. Liquidity is gone, and it is about to take you away with it.[63]

An ironclad law of finance is, "In a crisis, liquidity is king."[64] Leverage increases the risk of financial crises in three forms: banking crises, sovereign debt crises, and external financing crises that can occur when the leverage is substantially financed abroad. Of course, in the real world, financial crises can contain elements of each form simultaneously. Leverage-induced crises tend to have a long tail; they result in slower

GDP growth for a prolonged period and are notoriously costly to resolve.[65] Bubbles that pop up without dramatic rises in leverage tend to have relatively limited effects on the economy as a whole. Examples of rather benign de-bubbling episodes include the periods following the stock market crash of October 1987 and the implosion of the dot-com craze of the early 2000s. In both instances, leverage didn't substantially increase during the growth of the bubbles, and when the bubbles popped, the economy slowed but did not slide into serious recessions. Yet leverage went through the roof in the years before 2007, and in that case, the bubbles led to the greatest financial crisis and the deepest recession since World War II.

Living by the Rule

So excessive leverage, the derailment of securitization and other fancy financial techniques, and enormous real estate bubbles in the United States and some European countries were recognized almost immediately as the main drivers behind the difficulties faced by financial companies like Bear Stearns, BNP Paribas, and other institutions in the summer of 2007. Not surprisingly, suspicion grew that many more financial institutions were in similar or even worse positions. But it's also true that there's more to the story behind the 2007–2009 global financial crisis than those factors. A fourth driver of the crisis was the monetary policies pursued by central banks, especially, but not only, the Fed in the United States, in prior years. Once the crisis got underway, a fifth driver became evident—myopic herd behavior among humans, which was described by a keen nineteenth-century observer as the "extraordinary popular delusions and the madness of crowds."[66]

Let's first take a closer look at monetary policies. Central banks have an important role to play in economic and social progress, and the specific goals of their policies can vary. For example, the US Congress gave the Fed a dual mandate with three explicit goals: "maximum employment, stable prices, and moderate long-term interest rates."[67] The European Central Bank faces what seems to be a simpler and more straightforward task, maintaining price stability within the eurozone.[68] The ECB has defined price stability as an annual inflation rate "below, but close to 2 percent" over the medium term.

Prior to the 2007–2009 global financial crisis, most central banks of the world kept their focus on price stability and betterment of the general economic situation (mainly characterized by economic growth and employment). Essentially, they practiced inflation targeting and always kept at least one eye on the overall state of the economy. Leading up to the financial crisis, the central banks' short-term policy rates were their main tool for steering the economic and financial system and fulfilling their statutory task(s). (The general framework of central bank policymaking is covered in Chapter 6.)

The question of how to judge the quality of central bank policies has long been high on the agenda of researchers, politicians, journalists, and, obviously, central bankers. More specifically, the crucial question in this discussion became whether central bankers should follow specific rules or whether they should act with discretion, in the sense that their actions should be determined by the specific circumstances of the moment. During the 1950s, Milton Friedman argued forcefully for the central bank to follow a strict monetary growth rule in which the annual growth rate of money should equal the real growth rate of the economy.[69] Rules versus discretion became a hot topic during the 1970s and 1980s.[70] During the last two decades of the twentieth century, a relative consensus came about that was in line with the arguments of Thornton and Bagehot—central banks should follow certain rules, but with just enough *souplesse* (flexibility). In specific circumstances, policy interventions could be made that would deviate substantially from what the rules prescribed the actual policy interest rate to be.

John Taylor of Stanford University is an American economist who advised several American presidents, including Gerald Ford, Jimmy Carter, and both George Bushes. In 1993, Taylor launched the idea of a monetary policy rule that soon bore his name; over time, it became the subject of a whole research industry.[71] Gradually, the Taylor rule became recognized as one of the best ways to guide and judge the policies pursued by central banks. It's fair to say "the Taylor rule has revolutionized the way many policymakers at central banks think about monetary policy."[72] Many different specifications of the Taylor rule have been suggested, and some are quite sophisticated. Ultimately, three elements together determine what should be, subject to further analysis and interpretation, the policy interest rate of the central bank. If the actual policy rate comes out above the Taylor rate, then monetary policy is restrictive; if the actual policy rate is below the Taylor-calculated rate, monetary policy is expansionary.

The first of the three variables in a Taylor equation is the natural interest rate. As discussed in Chapter 1, Thornton considered the difference between what he called the loan rate in the economy and the profit rate to be earned in the economy to be of crucial importance. In today's parlance, the first of Thornton's rates would be the central bank's policy rate, and the second would be very similar to the natural interest rate.

The concept of the natural interest rate was fully developed by the great late nineteenth-century Swedish economist Knut Wicksell. The natural rate of interest surfaces if, in an environment of stable inflation, all the factors of production available in the economy are employed—i.e., when the economy is running at its potential output capacity. Estimates of the natural rate of interest run around 2 percent, but in recent times, these estimates have been more toward 1 percent or even lower, certainly in the United States and Europe.[73] Halfway through 2019, the Board of Governors of the Fed placed the natural rate of interest at only 0.5 percent.[74] These estimates are almost unavoidably surrounded by substantial uncertainty.[75]

The second variable in the Taylor equation concerns the inflation rate. A comparison is made between a combination of the inflation rate and inflationary expectations and the inflation rate the central bank aims to set. In the case of the ECB, for example, the latter would be "below but close to 2 percent." If inflation runs higher than the rate targeted by the central bank, the central bank should increase the policy rate to reduce inflationary pressure.

A similar reasoning goes for the rate of growth in the economy, the third variable in the Taylor equation. If the current or expected rate of growth is below the annual rate of growth of potential output (estimated at, say, 2 percent), then the economy requires some stimulus, and the central bank should lower the policy rate of interest. The difference between actual and potential output is most often referred to as the *output gap*, a very attractive concept, theoretically speaking, that is extremely difficult to estimate reliably. Central banks differ in the weights they place on the inflation variable and on the growth variable. More conservative central banks are inclined to put more weight on the inflation variable than central banks that consider the general state of the economy to be the more important variable for their policy decisions.

Let's illustrate the Taylor rate with a simple example. Suppose the natural rate of interest is estimated at 1 percent. The actual and expected rate of inflation hovers around 3.5 percent, with 2 percent being the inflation target of the central bank. Next, suppose that annual growth runs at 3 percent, with potential output growth estimated at 2 percent. For the final piece of the hypothesis, the central bank attaches somewhat more importance to price stability than to growth considerations. That choice implies, for example, a 60 percent weight for the inflation variable and a 40 percent weight for the growth variable. Applying the Taylor rule gives an interest rate of 2.3 percent = [1 + 0.6 (3.5—2) + 0.4 (3—2)]. If the policy rate stands at, for example, 2 percent, the central bank should raise the rate to 2.3 percent or perhaps even higher, given the high inflation rate and the fact that output is increasing faster than potential output is growing. The actual number isn't important in this Taylor-rule exercise; in the example given, it's obvious that the central bank should raise its policy interest rate.

Of course, this example is extremely simple, with a straightforward decision for the central bankers. In reality, the circumstances confronted by central bankers are usually more complex. For example, when the inflation variable indicates a need to restrict monetary policy (to raise the policy rate) at the same time that the growth variable suggests there is room for a policy rate reduction (with actual growth below potential growth), careful judgment and caution is needed on the part of central bankers. But the guidance provided by the Taylor rule is important, as it allows central bankers to have a structured policy discussion that also remains consistent over time. Time consistency is imperative, in order for policy options chosen by the central bank to have maximal resonance in the financial markets and the economy.

Although they lacked the technical expertise and instruments to perform a Taylor-rule-like exercise, one can easily imagine that Thornton and Bagehot would have been rather sympathetic to this kind of approach, as it stresses the importance of rules-based transparency. Both argued in favor of monetary policy taking what is happening in the economy into consideration. Thornton and Bagehot believed that the main tasks of central bankers were to avoid inflation as well as deflation, while also carefully accounting for how the economy evolved. An intelligently used Taylor rule—meaning, among others, consciousness about the difficulties and uncertainties surrounding the calculation of every Taylor rule—is an excellent instrument to help judge whether a central bank has kept its policy on track with regard to inflation and deflation and also to the benefit of the overall economic situation, while taking into consideration concerns about financial stability.

Too Low for Too Long

What does a Taylor-rule analysis of the monetary policies pursued by central banks over the last two decades look like? For the world economy as a whole, calculations by economists at the BIS reveal the effective policy rate and what that policy rate would have been if a Taylor rule had been strictly followed by the central banks.[76] During the 1990s and at the beginning of the twenty-first century, the Taylor and effective policy rates were consistently close. From 2002 until the start of the global financial crisis, the policy rate was way below the Taylor rate, and by 2007, the policy rate was literally half the Taylor rate. During the acute phase of the financial crisis, both rates coincided again. However, from 2009 on, divergence began anew—again, clearly with policy rates substantially below Taylor rates.[77]

Within the developed world, the divergence between rates was greatest in the United States, but elsewhere, the tendency of monetary policies went in the same expansionary direction.[78] It's fairly well established that there was an international transmission element to the monetary policy pursued in the United States that worked through different mechanisms, not least of which was the exchange rate.[79] Many emerging countries joined the very accommodative policies of advanced countries out of fears that not following the easing bias in the US and other developed countries would push up their exchange rates, mortgaging their competitiveness and also their development perspectives. In the words of Claudio Borio, "Easing begets easing across the world."[80] Whether they liked it or not, emerging countries had no real option other than following American monetary policies, given the dominance of the dollar in international finance and trade.[81]

In the period before the financial crisis, two elements explain the consistent divergence between actual monetary policy rates and Taylor-rule rates. First is the Japan Syndrome, the fear that the persistent deflation that Japan had suffered following the early 1990s bursting of its enormous real estate and stock market bubbles would also hit the United States and Europe as a consequence of the twin shocks of the implosion of the dot-com bubble in 2000 and the terrorist attacks of September 11, 2001. Many economists believe that deflation was the main reason Japan suffered through a "lost decade."[82] In November 2002, in one of his first speeches as director of the Fed, Bernanke explicitly stated that everything possible must be done to prevent deflation from gaining traction in the United States.[83] Bernanke's speech contained the major ingredients of what would become Fed policies as the global financial crisis raged five years later.

The second element explaining policy rates systematically coming out below Taylor-rule rates was the risk management approach to monetary policy that came to be identified with Alan Greenspan, Bernanke's forerunner as Fed chairman.[84] This approach was based on the belief that monetary policy has enough powerful tools to react quickly and efficiently after bubbles burst. Greenspan and other adherents to the risk management approach argued first, it is very difficult to detect bubbles in time to address them, and second, proactive prevention of bubbles was too expensive in terms of jobs lost and output forgone. The "clean up afterward" strategy championed by Greenspan gradually gained more credibility as aggressive injections of liquidity seemed to offer solutions to the problems posed by successive crisis situations. Examples include the policies pursued to counter the effects of the savings and loans crisis of the 1980s, the stock market crash of October 1987, the Gulf War, the Asian and Russian financial crisis, the LTCM crisis of the 1990s, and, as previously noted, the dot-com de-bubbling, and the wave of terrorist attacks at the beginning of the 2000s.[85]

In his memoirs, Greenspan summarized the risk management approach to monetary policy as follows:

> After thinking a great deal about this, I decided the best the Fed could do would be to stay with our central goal of stabilizing product and services prices. By doing this job well, we would gain the power and flexibility needed to limit economic damage if there was a crash. That became the consensus within the FOMC (Federal Open Market Committee, the Fed's central policy making body). In the event of a major market decline, our policy would be to move aggressively, lowering rates and flooding the system with liquidity to mitigate the economic fallout.[86]

Mervyn King, Greenspan's counterpart at the helm of the Bank of England, concluded in his memoirs, "As time passed, it became easier to flood the system with liquidity when problems arose than to design a framework that would counter moral hazard."[87] The discussion on whether central banks should "lean" against the wind or "clean up" after the storm has hit, as the risk management approach to monetary policy dictated, became lively during and after the global financial crisis.[88]

No matter why monetary policies were too accommodative or expansionary in the years leading up to the global financial crisis, the way in which central bankers (primarily the Fed) orchestrated policy changes led to systematic expectations on the part of private market participants. Monetary policy became asymmetric: there was quick and aggressive action when markets were down, but far more reluctance to adjust policy stances when markets rose. When the dot-com bubble burst in late 2000, Ed Yardeni, at that time head of Deutsche Bank Securities, declared he "was not too concerned, since I know the Fed is our friend."[89] This situation came to be known as the "Greenspan put," and later the "Bernanke put." This will be covered in Chapter 6.[90]

The Greenspan or Bernanke put gave rise to behavior that can be described as strongly influenced by *moral hazard*. People adjust their behavior when the environment in which they live, work, and invest changes. (For example, if there are changes in regulation or government policies.) The result of the Greenspan or Bernanke put was that investors minimized their concerns about potential losses of their strategies since the Fed, and most other central banks, stood ready to intervene quickly and powerfully when markets turned negative. Slowly but surely, a risk bias entered into the behavior and strategies of many investors.[91] Central bankers like Greenspan and Bernanke seemed to have been well aware of this bias, but their belief in the risk management approach toward monetary policy led them to minimize the risks associated with their monetary policy strategy as well.[92]

The economic and econometric models the central bankers' staffs worked with took on an important role in all these considerations and positions. These models, whether they were of the new classical type or new Keynesian, relied heavily on the rational expectations hypothesis, with the economy reverting rather smoothly to equilibrium as a consequence of that built-in hypothesis. Moreover, these models largely ignored financial developments.[93] Money was supposed to be neutral, in the long as well as the short run. After the worst of the global financial crisis was over, Bank of England governor Mervyn King acknowledged in the dominant econometric model of monetary economics, "money, credit, and banking play no meaningful role."[94] Thornton and Bagehot would have turned over in their graves upon "hearing" this message. *Central bankers unlearned a crucial lesson that Thornton and many others after him thought should be a focal point of central bank policies—that the real and the financial sector of the economy influence each other tremendously.*

Although important authors like Bernanke and Alan Blinder, both distinguished academics and former Fed officials, and Robert Shiller, recipient of the Nobel Prize in Economics in 2013, minimize the role of monetary policy in the period preceding the global financial crisis, arguments and evidence to the contrary are quite persuasive.[95] Highly accommodative monetary policies and asymmetry in policy reactions fueled investors' expectations of ever-increasing asset prices and thus contributed to development of a mania, which is "a general atmosphere of euphoria, simultaneously boosting asset prices, consumption, and investment spending, and the broad participation of all social layers in the speculative wave."[96] As twentieth-century economist Hyman Minsky pointed out in the formulation of his "financial instability hypothesis" in the 1980s, an abundant supply of credit, at least partially inspired by accommodative monetary policies, plays a crucial role in an evolution toward financial instability.[97] The 2007–2009 global financial crisis became an extreme illustration of this chain of events, and it had disastrous social and economic consequences.

Cold Turkey

So overly accommodative monetary policies leading to abundant supply of credit fueled increasing degrees of leverage, and the additions of the real estate craze and the securitization follies helped create an environment in which the human psyche was much more vulnerable to euphoric, if not downright manic, behavior. In line with Minsky's analysis that financial stability invariably sows the seeds of instability, Rajan noted, "cyclical euphoria…the euphoria generated by the boom" regularly gets the upper hand.[98] In their seminal *This Time Is Different: Eight Centuries of Financial Folly*, Reinhart and Rogoff concluded, "Technology has changed, the height of humans has changed, and fashions have changed. Yet the ability of governments and investors to delude themselves, giving rise to periodic bouts of euphoria that usually end in tears, seems to have remained a constant."[99] When euphoria settles in, people forget basic truths, like the old finance adage that there is no return without risk. In general, the higher the return on an investment, the higher the risks. It's often forgotten that concealed risks are still risks, and often, they're the most dangerous of all.

The phenomenon of financial euphoria, with all the excesses that go along with it, has been the subject of several remarkable books.[100] One of the first extensively documented bubbles was the tulip mania that hit the Netherlands in the 1630s.[101] Mathematician, astrologist, philosopher, and central banker *avant la lettre* (before the concept existed) Isaac Newton knew the dangers of a bubble as well. Sensing that the South Sea bubble was about to implode and that he himself would lose a lot of money as a result, Newton muttered in 1720 that he "could calculate the motions of the heavenly bodies, but not the madness of the crowds."[102]

Different psychological factors conjure up financial euphoria at regular intervals. The *turkey illusion*, a concept first advanced by the great British historian, philosopher, and mathematician Bertrand Russell, describes the dilemma of a turkey who believes that his cosseted lifestyle, in which he is fed each day at more or less the same hour, will continue forever.[103] The turkey is completely surprised when at a certain moment—perhaps a few days before Thanksgiving—the farmer stops feeding the turkey and kills the animal. Plenty of people get caught up in the turkey illusion. When euphoria ends in tears (and hopefully not in blood), those who are crying are the most surprised as events unfold.

Russell's turkey illusion is clearly linked to the phenomena of *disaster myopia* and *groupthink*. Disaster myopia is the observation that people assume as more time passes since a certain type of disaster—a financial crisis, for example—has happened, it's less likely that such a disaster will occur again.[104] As Bernanke, Geithner, and Paulson concluded, "Financial crises recur in part because memories fade."[105] In fact, 2005 was the first year since the Great Depression during which no bank failed in the United States, which fed the belief that major bank crises had become a thing of the past. Disaster myopia is reinforced by group pressure to confirm a prevailing sentiment; no one wants to be the party pooper. Referring to the euphoria of the late 1920s that preceded the Great Depression, John Kenneth Galbraith remarked, "By the summer of 1929, the [stock] market not only dominated the news. It also dominated the culture."[106] Robert Shiller referred to the "social contagion of boom-think."[107] History shows that contagion also strongly influences the behavior of regulators and legislators.

It's no coincidence that the concept of the Great Moderation gained traction in the years leading up to the 2007–2009 global financial crisis.[108] The idea was the evolution of the economy had gradually become more stable with respect to growth and inflation because of the successful monetary policies followed by the leading central banks, among other factors. Some suggested society at large was close to knowing all that was to be known about macroeconomics.[109] The fact that several major crises had been successfully managed in the decades prior to the global financial crisis reinforced the idea that markets and policymakers (most of all, central bankers) had become more efficient in dealing with adverse developments.[110] But, as former Fed chairwoman Janet Yellen emphasized, the Great Moderation concept also fed "incaution."[111]

It's important to note that, during the 2005 session of the Jackson Hole Symposium, extreme praise was showered on Alan Greenspan, who was then regarded as the "maestro" who navigated the American and world economies through several major crises.[112] In 2007, the late US senator John McCain famously said of Greenspan, "If he's alive or dead, it doesn't matter. If he's dead, just prop him up and put some dark glasses on him like *Weekend at Bernie's*."[113] Soon afterward, Greenspan would become a more controversial figure. The global financial crisis destroyed economies, companies, lives, and reputations. And the Great Moderation proved to be, at least in part, a "Great Illusion."[114]

Chapter 3: A Deadly Inferno

A timeline of the world's descent into fear and uncertainty

THE GIGANTIC STORM THAT BROUGHT THE WORLDWIDE financial and economic system to the precipice of the abyss during the 2007–2009 global financial crisis can be summarized as follows: the consistent easing bias in monetary policies, primarily in the United States, created a benign environment that allowed credit to boom and fueled debt buildup and leverage across the system, mostly but not exclusively in the financial sector. Unstable short-term financing went through the roof based on the assumption that sufficient liquidity would always be available in the markets. Lackluster and counterproductive regulation helped drive leverage to levels never seen before. A continuously accommodative monetary environment contributed to a real estate bubble that was further exacerbated by unwise government regulation, blatant misuse of the securitization technique, and an abdication of responsibility among the rating agencies.

Gradually, euphoria prevailed, making market participants, governments, central bank officials, and the public at large less aware of risk and the consequences of possible adverse developments. Moral hazard, disaster myopia, and groupthink were all at play. The 2007–2009 global financial crisis was brought about by a collective of wrong and even perverse incentives and shortsighted, naïve, or flat-out wrong policies.[1] British businessman and academic Adair Turner described the crisis as "entirely self-inflicted and avoidable."[2] It seemed that no one was concerned that a black swan, an event that's highly unlikely to occur but that creates massive damage when it does, could bring the whole system down. Former Fed chair and current US Secretary of the Treasury Janet Yellen concluded,

> We experienced a *perfect storm* in financial markets: runs on highly vulnerable and systemically important financial institutions, dysfunction in most securitized credit markets, a reduction in interbank lending, higher interest rates for all but the safest borrowers, matched by near-zero yields on Treasury bills, lower equity values, and a restricted supply of credit from financial institutions. Once this massive credit crunch hit, it didn't take long before we were in a recession. This recession, in turn, deepened the credit crunch as demand and employment fell, and credit losses of financial institutions surged.[3]

First Dominoes

How did the crisis develop? As previously discussed, the news in summer 2007 that Bear Stearns, three German financial institutions, and BNP Paribas were facing massive losses related to real estate set the crisis events in motion. On learning of the problems at BNP Paribas, Jean-Claude Trichet, then president of the ECB, immediately sensed that he must act. Within hours, the ECB announced it would provide "unlimited" liquidity to the markets. *This was the first clear indication that the lessons of the Great Depression had been learned, and that the advice of Thornton and Bagehot would to be taken seriously this time around.*

The ECB promptly made available €95 billion in emergency lending, and the Fed stepped in with $64 billion. Immediately, a problem arose for central bankers, especially in the US—how could they get funds to the shadow banking system (investment banks, hedge funds, money market mutual funds, and so on), which had no direct access to central bank financing? Levels of nervousness, discomfort, and outright suspicion shot through the roof. The growing uneasiness and uncertainty in the markets was clearly illustrated by a pronounced hike in the LIBOR, the rate at which international banks make loans to each other.[4] Distrust and uncertainty predominated throughout the financial system.

The next domino to fall was the British bank Northern Rock, which was highly leveraged and up to its ears in mortgage financing. Moreover, most of Northern Rock's financing was very short term. For the first time in 150 years, a British bank run made news in September 2007; people stood in line for hours at Northern Rock branches to get their money out. Some observers regard the bank run on Northern Rock as the event "that heralded the global financial crisis."[5] In February 2008, the British government nationalized Northern Rock.

In the meantime, unease and outright worries about the evolving situation escalated around the world. A precipitous drop in real estate prices in many parts of the United States accelerated the concerns. Central banks drastically lowered their policy rates and provided ample liquidity where it was needed. They also showed a clear awareness of the international nature of the troubles and provided each other with substantial credit lines. The Fed recognized the worldwide need for dollar financing and acted accordingly through extensive swap agreements with other central banks, a step that proved to be crucial in fighting the crisis. All these actions were clearly twenty-first-century updates to the Thornton and Bagehot playbook.

A hastily agreed-upon $150 billion fiscal stimulus package in the US was not enough to prevent intensification of the crisis in the first months of 2008. Stock markets tanked and banks announced huge losses. At the end of January 2008, news broke that rogue trader Jérôme Kerviel had caused $7 billion losses at Société Générale, one of France's major banks, through a cascade of disastrous transactions. This further fueled uncertainty, fear, and suspicion, as everyone wondered if rogue traders were wreaking havoc in other banks as well.

March 10 was the beginning of what historian Harold James described as "the slow-motion collapse of Bear Stearns."[6] After the bankruptcy of the Carlyle Capital Corporation, of which Bear was an important financier, it became impossible for Bear, a highly leveraged investment bank with no direct access to Fed lending facilities, to find sufficient market financing.[7] In four days' time, $18 billion of cash reserves that Bear Stearns had on hand disappeared. Over the weekend of March 14–16, authorities feverishly sought to prevent Bear's outright collapse. Bear Stearns, the reasoning went, wasn't *too big to fail*; rather, it was *too interconnected* to the rest of the financial sector to be allowed to fail. After a generous intervention by the Fed, JP Morgan Chase stepped forward to take over Bear Stearns.[8] Bernanke, Geithner, and Paulson concluded, "The Fed crossed a Rubicon by intervening to prevent the implosion of a nonbank."[9]

The resolution of the Bear Stearns saga calmed the markets to some extent, but by July 2008, the crisis was back with a vengeance. Several US officials openly questioned whether the government-sponsored mortgage refinancers Fannie Mae and Freddie Mac could survive the crisis. When IndyMac, a major California bank that was heavily loaded with mortgage loans and related derivatives, went bankrupt on July 11, the pressure on Fannie and Freddie increased dramatically. Fear and uncertainty intensified and increasingly crippled financial markets. Traditional funding markets began to freeze up, necessitating the fire sale of assets, mostly mortgage-related, by those who were unable to refinance. These fire sales led to a plunge in asset prices that worsened the situation and the outlook.

On August 20, Kenneth Rogoff, an economics professor at Harvard who served as the IMF's chief economist from 2001 to 2004, dared to say what many had feared: "The worst is to come…We're not just going to see mid-sized banks go under in the next few months, we're going to see a whopper, we're going to see a big one, one of the big investment banks or big banks."[10] Less than one month later, his dire prediction came true.

Global Inferno

During the month of August, pressure on the mortgage refinancers Fannie Mae and Freddie Mac increased even further. Considering their combined losses of $15 billion, there was no way that enough private sector capital could be found to reinforce their balance sheets. The fact that foreign investors held securities from Fannie and Freddie—to the tune of at least $1.5 trillion—substantially influenced what transpired in Washington. The US government felt compelled to save Fannie and Freddie from bankruptcy, so on September 6, both government-sponsored entities were put into a conservatorship run by the Federal Housing Finance Agency. They were effectively nationalized when Treasury Secretary Hank Paulson committed $200 billion in taxpayer money to recapitalize them. Disapproval of this intervention was rampant, especially among the rank and file of then-President Bush's Republican Party.

The Fannie and Freddie saga was only the beginning. Lehman Brothers, the fourth largest of the five big American investment banks, was believed to be next in line to fail after Bear, the smallest of the five, was taken over. Also leveraged to the hilt and deeply engaged in mortgage-backed securities and derivatives, Lehman had to raise $100 billion in the markets *on a monthly basis* to keep its investment portfolio financed.[11] Once the markets started to freeze, Lehman was confronted with a massive financing shortage. Negotiations with the Korean Development Bank, the Chinese investment fund Citic Services, at least two sovereign wealth funds from the Middle East, the MetLife insurance company, and even Warren Buffett to find fresh capital for Lehman all failed, at least to some degree because of the brutality, arrogance, and stubbornness of Richard Fuld, Lehman's CEO, better known on Wall Street as "The Gorilla."

With losses at Lehman running into the billions, the American government desperately sought to avoid its bankruptcy over the weekend of September 12–14. ECB President Jean-Claude Trichet warned during that weekend that a failure of Lehman would lead to a "total meltdown."[12] Bank of America was already focused on a hasty takeover of the collapsing investment bank Merrill Lynch, which was generally expected to be next in line for the guillotine after Lehman and Bear. A last-minute attempt to get Britain's Barclays Bank involved failed, and with it, attempts to get to a Bear Stearns scenario for Lehman Brothers came to naught. Lehman urgently needed $100 billion in additional liquidity, and it was impossible to raise such an amount.

On Monday, September 15, 2008, at 1:45 a.m., Lehman Brothers filed for bankruptcy. With more than $600 billion in outstanding debt, Lehman was by far the biggest corporate failure in American history;[13] its derivatives holdings were twice those of Bear Stearns. The world held its breath as surprise, bewilderment, desperation, and outright panic dominated. Fed chairman Ben Bernanke summarized those hours in his memoirs: "It was a terrible, almost surreal moment. We were staring into the abyss...Lehman's failure fanned the flames of the financial panic...Two iconic Wall Street firms that had survived world wars and depressions, Lehman and Merrill, had disappeared in a weekend...I knew that the risks the two firms had taken had endangered not only the companies but the global economy, with unknowable consequences."[14]

Yet a major puzzle persists. In his memoirs, Bernanke went on,

> We had little doubt a Lehman failure would massively disrupt financial markets and impose heavy costs on many parties other than Lehman's shareholders, managers, and creditors, including millions of people around the world who would be hurt by its economic shockwaves...I never heard anyone from the Fed or the Treasury suggest that letting Lehman fail would be anything other than a disaster, or that we should contemplate allowing the firm to fail. We needed to put the fire out.[15]

This statement completely contradicts what Bernanke said before a committee of the US Senate one week after the Lehman collapse: "The troubles at Lehman had been well known for some time, and investors clearly recognized...that the failure of the firm was a significant possibility.

Thus, we judged that investors and counterparties had had time to take precautionary actions."[16] Even a Fed chairman can't simultaneously argue that a failure of Lehman would be a massive disaster *and* that he and other policymakers in Washington thought the markets would be well prepared for the shock.

So the question remains: what really happened in those dramatic hours before the morning of September 15, 2008? Why was Lehman allowed to fail? Why did the Fed "cross the Rubicon" for Bear Stearns and not for Lehman? Bernanke and other officials involved argued that there was no legal basis for the saving of Lehman Brothers. It's true that the Fed is empowered by law to lend only to banks and savings institutions. As Lehman was an investment bank, these rules didn't apply. But section 13(3) of the Federal Reserve Act gives the Fed the authority in "unusual and exigent circumstances" to lend to any individual, partnership, or corporation. It's hard to argue that those days in mid-September 2008 didn't constitute "unusual and exigent circumstances." Bernanke's description of what a failure of Lehman would ignite clearly falls under that heading. Why wasn't section 13(3) invoked for the rescue of Lehman Brothers? The argument of legal obstacles to save Lehman does not fly.[17]

Although no private takeover candidates stepped up for Lehman like JP Morgan had for Bear Stearns, there's a case to be made that Lehman's failure was permitted for political reasons. First, pressure was on due to the upcoming presidential election in November of that year. The Bush administration feared that after the poorly received and costly rescues of Bear Stearns, Fannie, and Freddie, a government-sponsored rescue of another financial institution of which the greedy executives had clearly misbehaved—or perhaps even committed outright fraud—would have been political suicide, particularly since more rescue operations were potentially on the horizon.[18]

Second, among the leaders of the fight against the crisis—Paulson, Bernanke, and Geithner—desperation had seeped in; they could see that members of Congress did not realize the gravity and urgency of the situation. The three make a veiled reference to this situation in their collective memoir of the crisis, remarking that Washington politicians are capable of doing courageous things in a crisis, "though perhaps no earlier than that."[19] Furthermore, Bernanke, Geithner, and Paulson argued, "without a spectacular failure like Lehman" they never would have gotten Congressional approval to inject capital into banks (see infra).[20]

If letting Lehman fall into the abyss was meant to awaken a sleeping Congress, the strategy succeeded brilliantly. However, the global inferno that developed in the wake of Lehman's bankruptcy brought the world's financial and economic system to the brink of a catastrophe, one that threatened to be even worse than the Great Depression. Further complicating matters was the fact that Fed and the Treasury were seen as flip-floppers in the markets. Saving Bear Stearns and not Lehman was inconsistent behavior, and Thornton and Bagehot both believed that inconsistency was detrimental in a crisis. So, everyone wondered, what would they do next: intervene or let go?

Hardcore Horror

Two days after the Lehman debacle, a new shock hit. The American International Group (AIG), the world's largest insurance company, came under scrutiny as the activities of a division of the company, AIG Financial Products (AIG FP), brought the entire organization to its knees. The nucleus of AIG FP came to AIG after the failure of the investment bank Drexel Burnham Lambert at the end of 1980s. AIG FP jumped into the real estate craze with both feet, including developing credit default swaps to insure securitized paper based on subprime mortgages. By the middle of 2008, AIG FP had issued CDSs covering more than $500 billion of securitized paper. These insurance products made the situation even more dangerous, since the AIG coverage was assumed to be enough protection to reduce the need for capital. Huge fees were collected by AIG, but once the real estate bubble burst, holders of CDSs issued by AIG FP came forward to collect.

By September 16, AIG's back was against the wall, overwhelmed by AIG FP's huge losses. Bernanke noted in his memoirs that although financial conditions were very chaotic at that moment, "they could become unimaginably worse if AIG defaulted—with unknowable but assuredly catastrophic consequences for the US and global economies."[21] AIG was completely entangled with the international financial system. With more than $1 trillion of assets, AIG's balance sheet was twice that of Lehman Brothers. The insurance conglomerate was active in 130 countries and had 74 million individual and corporate clients, including government entities, major corporations, and numerous pension funds. Estimates of immediate market losses following an AIG failure came to $180 billion or higher.[22]

After feverish discussions, the authorities acted on September 16. The Fed stepped in with a massive $85 billion loan and became an 80 percent owner of the company; the injection was increased by $37.8 billion three weeks later. The loan agreements carried high interest rates and obliged AIG to sell off assets to repay the loans. AIG's CEO, Robert Willumstad, was ousted. When you total up the money pledged to rescue Bear Stearns, Fannie Mae, Freddie Mac, AIG, and various smaller rescue deals and loans, the American taxpayer was on the hook for close to $1 trillion. In his memoirs, Bernanke made no secret of his feelings about the AIG drama, writing that it made him "angry...I understand why the American people are angry. It is absolutely unfair that taxpayer dollars are going to prop up a company that made these terrible bets."[23] Yet AIG, Fannie Mae, Freddie Mac, and Bear Stearns were saved, and Lehman wasn't.

As if the AIG debacle wasn't enough that week, the meltdown of credit markets was in full progress. On the day of AIG's rescue, another bomb went off in the financial markets, this time in *money market mutual funds* (MMMFs). MMMFs are investment funds that typically invest in debt securities characterized by short maturities and low risk profiles. They were first launched in the 1970s to allow investors to buy into a pool of securities that offered a better return than a standard banking account without losing easy access to the money. When MMMFs can't immediately provide their investors with every dollar invested in the fund, they're said to have "broken the buck"—a situation that MMMFs try to avoid at all times.

The worldwide investment community suffered a shock on September 16, when the Reserve Primary Fund effectively broke the buck and declared its net asset value as ninety-seven cents on the dollar. The fund, created in 1970 by Bruce Bent, who went on to be known as the father of the money-fund industry, was among the industry's flagships. At that moment in time, 56 percent of its $65 billion portfolio consisted of mortgage-backed and financial-sector related securitized paper. Only 1.2 percent of Reserve Primary Fund's holdings were directly related to Lehman, but that was enough to cause a stampede among its clients. Within twenty-four hours of Lehman's bankruptcy, demands to withdraw from the fund amounted to more than 50 percent of its assets. Like wildfire, withdrawals from other MMMFs spread exponentially.

Given the immense importance of MMMFs, in which something like $3 trillion was invested, the Treasury had to intervene. Withdrawal orders from the MMMFs were blocked, and the Treasury put out a guarantee for MMMF portfolios called the Temporary Guarantee Program for Money Market Funds. In response to the troubles in MMMFs, the Fed created yet another facility to allow provision of liquidity to this market segment.[24] Again, central bankers took a page from the Thornton and Bagehot playbook.

The week that began with the horrors of Lehman's bankruptcy ended with important changes for the two remaining large investment banks on Wall Street, Goldman Sachs and Morgan Stanley. The Fed agreed to transform each into bank holding companies, which allowed them direct access to financing facilities at the Fed. On top of that, both attracted substantial fresh capital: Warren Buffett injected $5 billion into Goldman Sachs, and the Japanese group Mitsubishi UFJ added $9 billion to Morgan Stanley's capital pool. These actions reduced uncertainty in the markets to some degree, but more was needed to quell the crisis.

The Big European Freeze

In the wake of the Lehman Brothers collapse, a devastating wildfire raged through the financial system around the world. In the United States, Washington Mutual, one of the largest savings banks in the country, saw a massive outflow of deposits as clients were spooked by the bank's huge exposure in the real estate sector. At Wachovia, the sixth largest bank in the country, the situation quickly became untenable. Washington Mutual was taken over by JP Morgan Chase, and Wachovia acquired Wells Fargo after a bitter struggle with Citigroup. The financial storm wasn't limited to financial institutions; at one point, even the formidable industrial giant General Electric had a hard time rolling over its commercial paper.

In Europe, things went from bad to worse at breathtaking speed. If policymakers in the United States were somewhat late to realize the urgency of the developing crisis, the surprise and lethargy among European policymakers was even worse. In late September, several declarations made by crucial players indicated their total unawareness of the gravity of what was happening right under their noses. Christian Noyer, governor of the Banque de France and director of the ECB, said that he saw "no drama" developing in Europe.[25] German minister of finance Peer Steinbrück could hardly disguise his *Schadenfreude* when he declared, "The days of the United States as superpower of the financial world are numbered."[26] Europe, many believed, was an island of stability in a world destabilized by American mistakes and misconduct.

Tiny Iceland, one of the most developed countries in the world,[27] became headline news around the world when it underwent a spectacular collapse of its financial system and the largest banking crisis in economic history.[28] The nation is small, with a surface area close to that of the US state of Kentucky, and in 2008, it had a population of only 320,000 souls. In the preceding decade, Iceland, a nation traditionally focused on fishery and related industries, had turned itself into a huge banking center. But in reality, the Iceland of 2008 was a gigantically leveraged hedge fund. The numbers were mind-boggling: the total assets of its three leading banks—Kaupthing, Landsbanki, and Glitnir—stood at eleven times the Icelandic GDP when the crisis began. These banks had financed massive involvement in long-term securitized paper with short-term deposits mostly attracted from abroad. In the middle of 2008, foreign debt stood at no less than seven times the country's GDP.

Uncertainty and fear paralyzed financial markets following the Lehman bombshell, and as a result, the Icelandic banking sector was blown away like a house of cards. The country's banks went bankrupt. The huge financial collapse led the nation into a depression. As GDP dropped by more than 10 percent, thousands of jobs were lost, and citizens saw serious declines in their living standards. Without a $5 billion aid package provided by the IMF and other Nordic countries, the Icelandic depression would have been much worse.

An international incident developed when the Icelandic authorities refused to honor the government's deposit guarantee for foreign depositors. Eager to cash in on the high interest rates offered by Icelandic banks during the go-go years, Dutch and British citizens in particular had made significant deposits in Iceland or in European branches of Icelandic banks. After a massive devaluation of the krona, the Icelandic economy began to recover more quickly and more vigorously than expected.

Back on the mainland, Belgium became the epicenter of yet another banking crisis. Fortis bank, formerly known as the Générale de Banque de la Belgique, had spent most of the 2000s engaged in expansion and takeovers throughout Europe, the United States, and Turkey. The partial acquisition of the ABN AMRO group, Europe's eighth-largest bank, in 2007, was the crowning achievement of Fortis' aggressive takeover strategy. As the bank was leveraged to the extreme and heavily engaged in real estate paper and credit in southern Europe, shrapnel from the Lehman bomb hit Fortis in a deadly way. As Fortis was no longer able to mobilize the necessary funds to keep its balance sheet financed, the governments of the three Benelux nations had to step in with a capital injection of €11 billion during the last weekend of September 2008.[29] A month later, Fortis bank became part of the French banking behemoth BNP Paribas.

Didier Reynders, who was in the Belgian government as minister of foreign affairs during my tenure as minister of finance, served as minister of finance during that frightful autumn of 2008. Of the time, Reynders told me, "We really had the feeling that the sky was falling in. Enormous decisions that in normal times should have taken weeks, if not months of careful preparations, had to be made within a few hours' time. The lack of information and the amount of uncertainty was staggering. It was an experience that you take with you for the rest of your life. Still today I'm sometimes wondering what really happened during that dark period."

It wasn't just Fortis that kept Reynders and many others awake at night. On the day Fortis was rescued, it was Dexia's turn to go belly up. Dexia was a French-Belgian banking conglomerate that was created in 1996 out of a merger of the Belgian Gemeentekrediet and the French Crédit Locale de France. Originally focused on the financing of local communities in both countries, Dexia began a rash of international expansion that was archetypal of growth in the banking sector in the decade prior to the eruption of the financial crisis. Its balance sheet swelled to more than forty times its capital base—an even worse ratio than Lehman's. To finance its assets, Dexia had less than 20 percent in stable deposits, and the rest came mostly from short-term wholesale funding. It built up a derivative portfolio that was not only mind-bogglingly complex but also very risky. Through its American subsidiary, Dexia also took substantial positions in American securities and real estate-related paper. When all hell broke loose in the markets, it became clear that Dexia would go under, too. On September 30, the French and Belgian government stepped in with €6.4 billion in capital to prevent a bankruptcy. Dexia became a bad bank whose rundown required another €85 billion in guarantees underwritten by the French and Belgian states.

Belgium wasn't the only hotbed for the financial crisis in Europe.[30] During the last days of September, the German government had to inject €35 billion into Hypo Real Estate, the second-largest mortgage company in the country. In the Netherlands, several banks had to be bailed out by the authorities. In the United Kingdom, the government was forced to nationalize three of the biggest banking institutions of the country, Royal Bank of Scotland, Lloyds Bank, HBOS, and Bradford and Bigley, an important real estate financier, had to be saved by the government as well. In Switzerland, that most orthodox of all financial centers, the world's largest asset manager at that time, UBS, lost more than $40 billion on American real estate-related assets and had to be bailed out by the Swiss authorities. Across Europe, stock markets tanked all over the place—the FTSE 100 index declined by 15 percent on September 29—and recessionary winds began to blow with gusto.

A situation almost as horrific as the Icelandic drama unfolded in Ireland. Between 1988 and 2007, the country experienced an average of 6 percent annual growth, catapulting Ireland from one of the poorest to one of the richest member states of the European Union. In the process, it earned the nickname "Celtic Tiger,"[31] and in 1999, it became one of the first countries to adopt the euro.

The creation of the euro monetary union led to a substantial decline in interest rates across the euro area. All members of the union inherited the credibility of the German Bundesbank, which was respected worldwide for its unshakable adherence to monetary orthodoxy. The resulting spectacular decline in interest rates, in combination with lax regulatory oversight, produced a massive real estate and banking boom in Ireland. Just like their Icelandic colleagues, Irish banks financed their skyrocketing real estate loans mostly with short-term funding, largely from abroad. Between 1994 and 2006, real housing prices in Ireland tripled. Needless to say, the Lehman bomb also torpedoed the extremely fragile Irish banks. On September 30, the Irish government issued a state guarantee for *all* liabilities of Irish banks, which amounted to €440 billion, 60 percent *more* than the country's GDP. A few years later, the Irish crisis would become an integral part of the general euro-area crisis.

TARPing the Crisis

While the crisis ran its disastrous course in Europe, consensus grew among policymakers in the United States that drastic measures were required to stop it. The Fed could not continue to shoulder the burden alone. Treasury secretary Hank Paulson came up with an initiative called the Troubled Asset Relief Program (TARP). TARP's mission was to buy up $700 billion in troubled or toxic assets from banks, effectively cleaning up and strengthening their balance sheets. Paulson hoped that TARP would restore confidence in financial markets. But TARP faced fierce opposition in Congress, which rejected the proposal on September 29. Bernanke remarked that the decision made him feel "like [he] had been hit by a truck."[32]

Under pressure from continued upheaval in the markets, Congress approved TARP in a second vote on October 3—but for half the amount Paulson had requested. The idea to buy toxic assets was dropped for practical, financial, and political reasons; instead, the funds would be used to strengthen the banks' capital. The Fed could provide unlimited liquidity, but banks urgently needed capital to strengthen their balance sheets. On October 13, Paulson muscled all US banks into agreeing to the TARP proposal, which resulted in a *de facto* partial nationalization of the American banking industry. The nine largest banks received $125 billion, and a comparable amount was channeled to the rest of the banking sector;[33] the direct capital injections came in the form of *non-voting preferred stock*—preferred to ensure the government would be first in line to receive dividends, and non-voting to avoid making it a true nationalization of the industry. If the banks' stock prices rose, taxpayers would share the gains. In the UK, comparable actions were made to strengthen the capital base of banks.

Although many observers consider the capital injections in the American and British banking sector to be a turning point in the 2007–2009 global financial crisis, a positive effect wasn't immediately reflected in the markets. At the end of 2008, Bernie Madoff, the former chairman of technology stock exchange Nasdaq, was arrested for a massive fraud scheme that had been exposed by the crisis.[34] At Citigroup, a bank historically in need of government assistance,[35] things went from bad to worse. An initial TARP injection of $25 billion wasn't enough to restore confidence in the banking behemoth, so on November 23, it required a second injection of $20 billion from TARP, accompanied by additional government guarantees totaling almost $300 billion. Public outcry against the use of taxpayer money to save the banking giant once again was deafening.[36] But Citigroup wasn't the only bank in need. Larger-than-expected losses at Merrill Lynch meant trouble for Bank of America, which took over Merrill at the height of the crisis, so Bank of America's capital was strengthened with $20 billion of TARP money. In the meantime, Congress had agreed to release a second tranche of funds to TARP—$350 billion. In the years since the crisis, every dollar of TARP money flowed back to the Treasury, with a profit on top.

Of course, the implosion of the financial markets heavily affected the real economy. The American economy officially went into recession in December 2007 and didn't begin to recover until the third quarter of 2009. Unemployment soared, and consumption expenditures tanked. Many other countries experienced a similar evolution. In 2009, advanced countries as a whole saw their economies shrink by 3.4 percent, and emerging countries grew by 2.8 percent, less than half their pre-crisis growth rate.[37] The world economy suffered a fall in production during the first quarter of 2009 of 6.5 percent, a frightening level. World trade decreased in volume by 12 percent in 2009, a post-World War II record.

Over the course of 2009, things finally started to calm down in the markets. The successful capital injections of the TARP program were instrumental in this recovery, as was the stress test that the US government imposed on the banking sector. The test showed that the ten largest US banks required $75 billion in additional capital, a sum they were able to raise in the market before the end of 2009. Once the markets recognized that the tests were meaningful, confidence and trust were restored. On the value of the stress test, Bernanke is unequivocal: "[It] was a decisive turning point."[38] Private and public forecasters revised their dire growth projections upward. Yet despite the fact that growth came back with a vengeance toward the end of 2009 and in 2010,[39] the Fed felt it was necessary to keep the monetary engine roaring. They fed the engine with zero interest rates and the launch of the first quantitative easing program at the end of 2008. While the skies were beginning to clear in the United States, dark clouds continued to gather over Europe.

Saving the Euro in London

The euro crisis that began in October 2009, following the most acute phase of the financial crisis, kept the ECB and other major central banks on high alert. The triumphant atmosphere that surrounded festivities held at the end of 2008 in honor of the tenth anniversary of the launch of the monetary union and the euro melted like snow in the sun once the euro crisis was underway. In early 2009, hardly anyone had recognized the demand for urgent financial assistance by Latvia, the small Baltic country that joined the European Union in 2004, for what it really was: a harbinger of the euro crisis.[40] The trouble intensified in October 2009 with an announcement by the newly elected Greek government that its budget deficit for 2009 would be at least twice the 6 percent of GDP that had been forecasted. The still-fragile financial markets, which had not yet recovered from the financial crisis, reacted immediately. The spread between interest on Greek securities and the one on German securities shot up. Ireland, Portugal, and Spain followed suit, and Italy and Belgium came under pressure as well.

The reaction among European and national authorities was confused and incoherent. The Eurogroup of ministers of finance and the European Council of heads of state held endless meetings that ran deep into the night, if not the morning, to discuss rescue programs and reforms of the euro area. Hundreds of billions of euros were mobilized to save the countries in crisis and to keep the monetary union from falling apart.

At heart, the problem of the European monetary union was that it lacked a political union. It seems obvious that this was a big mistake made when the monetary union was created, but it's explained by the fact that those who pushed for the monetary union saw it as a means to an end, the end being a political union.[41] Crises, the founding fathers of the European Union firmly believed, would push the member states over time to accept the necessity of "completing the union." That was a lousy bet, since history has shown that a monetary union with no political union can't survive. In the words of Mervyn King, "No monetary union has survived unless it has also developed into a political union, and the latter usually came before the former, as when a single currency followed the unification of Germany under Bismarck."[42]

At the launch of the European monetary union in 1999, there was no majority support for a political union, and now, more than twenty years later, the situation is not different. Thus, there was a need for a number of rules and criteria, encapsulated in the Stability and Growth Pact (SGP), that formed a second-best option for amassing a minimum degree of coherence and responsibility among the member states' economic and social policies. The 3 percent budget deficit limit and the maximum debt ceiling are the best known of these rules and criteria. Yet these rules and criteria are second-best options, and the enforcement of them has been a continuous problem in the euro area. The no bailout clause, which was absolutely essential to maintain discipline in the monetary union, became politically untenable once the euro crisis began. The institutional incompleteness of the euro area openly invited nations to pursue irresponsible policies and led to fundamental disequilibria and structural problems for many member countries. When the COVID-19 pandemic arrived in early 2020, one of the first decisions of the European authorities was to shelve the SGP rules, since massive fiscal interventions were needed to limit social and economic damage caused by the pandemic.

There's much more to say about the euro crisis that unfolded between 2009 and 2012—in Greece, the crisis lasted until 2016—but for the purposes of the subject at hand, the most important aspect came about in the summer of 2012.[43] On the eve of the 2012 Olympic Games in London, Mario Draghi, who was then the president of the ECB, addressed a select group of investors in the British capital. Convinced that a shock was needed to avoid further intensification of the euro crisis and dissolution of the monetary union, Draghi explained, "There is more progress [in fighting the euro crisis] than it has been acknowledged" and that most people tend to "underestimate the amount of political capital invested in the euro." Then he dropped the bomb, with perfect timing and supreme self-confidence: "Within our mandate, the ECB is ready to do whatever it takes to preserve the euro. And believe me, it will be enough."[44]

Draghi's performance in London electrified not only his audience but the financial markets in general. Several elements contributed to the magic of the moment. First, Draghi suggested that he would do what Thornton and Bagehot considered to be a crucial task for the central bank—that is, to take its task as lender of last resort seriously. Given the limiting statutes of the ECB, the markets had harbored doubt as to what extent the ECB could act as a true lender of last resort to stem the tide of a crisis. Second, shortly after Draghi's declaration, the ECB announced its Outright Monetary Transactions (OMT) program, putting the ECB's money where his mouth was, so to speak. The OMT program placed no limit on the amounts that could be refinanced and gave no end dates. Third, German chancellor Angela Merkel and French president François Hollande immediately endorsed Draghi's moves.

It's somewhat ironic that Draghi chose London, the capital of the country that later decided to leave the EU, as the place to launch his successful endeavor to save the euro. Given the continuing incompleteness of the European monetary union, Draghi's rescue of the euro was only a temporary victory. I once asked Draghi whether he thought that the euro had been definitively saved. He replied, "Nothing in life is definitive except birth, death, and taxes." Trouble will return, as long as the monetary union is not embedded in a political union.

The next chapter elaborates on the many programs and policy initiatives taken by central bankers during the financial crisis and its aftermath. These were extended and expanded once the COVID-19 pandemic began early in 2020. Both crises made the mystic hand of central bankers swing into action in a big way.

Chapter 4: Going Unconventional

The twenty-first century's steroidal version of a nineteenth-century playbook

T
HE CRUCIAL ROLE OF CENTRAL BANKERS IN FIGHTING financial crises was recognized and well defined long ago by nineteenth-century economists Henry Thornton and Walter Bagehot, who offered original and lasting insights and created a conceptual framework for the operations of central banks. The basic Thornton-Bagehot playbook gained in importance as economies and their financial systems grew and became more sophisticated. Both Thornton and Bagehot placed great emphasis on the central bank's crucial task of acting as the lender of last resort. In times of crisis, this task is crucial in order to avoid an implosion of the financial system and the resulting dire consequences for the real economy of production, investments, incomes, and jobs—not to mention the impact of a severe economic and social depression on political democracies.

As they carry out this lender-of-last-resort task, central bankers are often perceived as being guided by a mystic hand. It's seen as mystical because while most people realize that central bankers play a crucial role in times of crisis, the how, why, and when of the process remains fuzzy—if not downright mysterious—to them. As Thornton and Bagehot emphasized, central banks should act quickly and decisively, and they should communicate transparently and consistently. And they should lend without limit during times of crisis, but that lending should be at a high interest rate against good collateral, whatever the source. These rules are generally known as Bagehot's dictum, but they could be called Thornton's dictum as well.

According to Thornton and Bagehot, the source of the collateral offered could be traditional banks, other financial institutions, or even some non-financial ones. Under the influence of Thornton's writings, the Bank of England lent aggressively during the crisis of 1825 in the United Kingdom. Jeremiah Harman, who was then the governor of the Bank of England, was quoted saying the bank lent "by every possible means, and in modes that we had never adopted before...seeing the dreadful state in which the public were, we rendered every assistance in our power."[1] The situation faced by the British economy during that crisis was described by William Huskisson, then the chairman of the Board of Trade, as being "within twenty-four hours of a state of barter."[2]

Bagehot was at least as direct as Thornton when he argued central bankers must lend to merchants, to minor banks, to "this man and that man"—whenever the security is good. Central bankers should lend "to all that bring good securities, quickly, freely, and readily" and should not lose sight of the fact they should accept "everything which in *common times* [italics mine] is good banking security."[3] Bagehot's explicit reference to "in common times" means that he, as Thornton before him, expected central bankers to see through the uncommon impact of a major crisis on asset values.

No Atheists, No Ideologues

They did not mention Thornton and Bagehot by name, but the three leading figures in the US's fight against the 2007–2009 global financial crisis—Bernanke, Geithner, and Paulson—unconditionally followed their analysis and crisis prescriptions:

> When panic strikes, policymakers need to do everything in their power to quell it, regardless of the political ramifications, regardless of their ideological

convictions, regardless of what they've said or promised in the past. The politics of financial rescues are terrible, but economic depressions are worse...Once it's clear that a crisis is truly systematic, underreacting is much more dangerous than overreacting, too-late creates more problems than too-early, and half measures can just pour gasoline on the flames.[4]

This statement, which could have been made by any central banker during those dark days, is totally consistent with Bagehot's argument that "bank governors are generally cautious men...in consequence they are very apt to temporize and delay. But inevitably the delay in creating a stringency only makes a greater stringency inevitable."[5]

While the advice of Thornton and Bagehot was largely ignored during the Great Depression, it was broadly followed during the 2007–2009 financial crisis, despite the fact that totally different circumstances and economic, financial, and institutional environments prevailed. Some basic principles and related policy advice are still valid centuries later. What constitutes good collateral is to a large extent a question of appreciation, and what a sufficiently high interest rate would be is also up to interpretation. The central bankers "adapted the time-honored lender of last resort function to the new economic realities—acting, in effect, as dealers (market-makers) of last resort."[6] During the financial crisis, central bankers went to the limits—and even beyond, some would argue—of what Thornton and Bagehot saw as permissible and advisable for the lender-of-last-resort role. Given the spirit of their works and acute awareness of the need to do whatever is possible to avoid a major financial implosion, it is hard to imagine that Thornton and Bagehot wouldn't have *broadly* agreed with the central bankers' actions during the acute portion of the crisis. What they may have thought of the policies central bankers followed after the acute portion was over, however, is less clear.

The broad and intensive lending, or refinancing, that central banks performed during the crisis inspired Mervyn King to describe them as "the pawnbroker for all seasons…a pawnbroker is someone who is prepared to lend to almost everyone who pledges collateral sufficient to cover the value of a loan." Central bankers did indeed pull out all the stops to avoid a devastating depression following both the financial crisis and the COVID-19 pandemic. In both cases, nothing was taboo, or as Bernanke eloquently put it, "There are no atheists in fox holes nor ideologues in a financial crisis."[7] Given his intimate knowledge of what led to the economic disaster of the 1930s, Bernanke was in the opinion of many the right man in the right place at the right time. Among the policymakers acting at that time, no one was more keenly aware of the mechanisms behind the Great Depression than Bernanke.

The actions taken by central bankers to fight the financial crisis and its impact on the real economy evolved into a package of *unconventional monetary policies*. As the COVID-19 pandemic exploded in early 2020, central banks intensified and even broadened their usage of the unconventional monetary toolbox. Instead of just focusing on variations in the policy interest rate, as was typically done prior to the global financial crisis, central banks used all four basic ingredients of that unconventional package: pushing policy interest rates to zero or close to zero (and in some cases, even into negative territory); installing new refinancing facilities as required by specific circumstances; pursuing quantitative easing or massive asset purchase programs; and offering explicit forward guidance on policy rates.

Nothing but Zero

The first action made by most central banks during the financial crisis was to drop their policy interest rates in the hope of easing financial stress in the markets, keeping deflationary forces at bay, and limiting the damage to the real economy. Among advanced countries as a whole, nominal policy rates stood on a weighted basis close to 5 percent at the onset of the crisis.[8] As the severity of the crisis became obvious, central banks slashed their policy interest rates quickly and decisively, bringing them to zero or close to zero in the short term. Eventually, some central banks (for example, the ECB and the Swiss and Swedish central banks) resorted to negative policy rates. These interest policy choices involved many intense and even heated discussions among decision makers at the central banks, as such drastic actions could ignite inflationary wildfires or lead to financial instability.

In real, inflation-adjusted terms, policy interest rates in advanced countries remained negative during and after the crisis. In emerging markets, nominal interest rates were cut substantially, but remained above the zero boundary. Real policy rates ended up close to zero. In the years prior to the crisis, real policy rates in advanced and emerging markets had averaged close to 2 percent. These worldwide actions on policy interest rates were quite unconventional not because they were brought down to more or less zero. Most policymakers realized that the severity of the crisis warranted such a move. Instead, what made them unconventional was the length of time that they stayed at or around zero, and certainly those instances where policy rates went negative were very unconventional.

Taylor-rule calculations showed that policy rates at zero or close to zero were more or less optimal during the peak of the crisis. But after the worst was over, policy rates should have been gradually raised above zero to remain consistent with Taylor-rule logic. Instead, central bankers kept policy interest rates so low for such a prolonged period after that acute phase for four reasons:

- They feared that deflation would gain a foothold in the expectations of investors, producers, and consumers.
- The disappointing performance of the economy fueled fears that the financial system was still very fragile, so they focused on avoiding a double-dip recession that would have pummeled the financial system and the public finances of many countries.
- The euro crisis raged on after the worst of the financial crisis was over. Many policymakers and certainly central bankers feared that the euro crisis might reignite the financial crisis, and thus would intensify the substantial drag the euro crisis represented on the worldwide economy.

- Central bankers found themselves in a catch-22 situation: they were paralyzed by the fear of what might happen if and when rates were to rise.

The Fed attempted to break this negative spiral when it became the first of the major central banks to begin inching up its interest rates after the crisis. After nearly a decade of keeping its policy rates at or close to zero, the Fed increased its policy rates at the end of 2015. The move was made because of the economic recovery that had already taken place, which then received a substantial short-term boost from the tax cut enacted by the Trump administration in 2017 and the receding prospect of deflation. The target range for the federal funds rate, which had been pinned in the 0 to 0.25 percent range since December 2008, was raised by 25 basis points (bp) at the end of 2015. In December 2016, the Fed raised the target range by another 25 bp, followed by three hikes in 2017, and four more in 2018. Each increase was for 25 bp, pushing the target range by the end of 2018 to 2.25 to 2.50 percent.

With volatility rising substantially in financial and equity markets and with the overall economic perspectives becoming gloomier, particularly as a result of the all-out trade war developing between the United States and China, the Fed decided to reverse its policy during the summer of 2019. The American central bank lowered the federal funds rate by 25 bp in early August 2019. Fed chairman Jerome Powell referred to this move as "a mid-cycle adjustment" that he claimed would not fundamentally alter the Fed's basic policy stance.[9] Despite the objections of several members of the Fed board, two further reductions of the federal funds rate's target range, each by 25 bp, followed before the end of 2019. In autumn 2019, no one expected the massive shock that the economic and financial system would face within a few months.

During the first three months of 2020, the COVID-19 pandemic began to spread from China to practically every corner of the world. The measures needed to contain the pandemic, including lockdowns, shutdowns, and strict social distancing policies, would bring the world economy to a virtual standstill. The first action by the Fed came on March 3, when it lowered the federal funds rate by 50 bp, dropping it into the

0.50 to 0.75 percent range. The extent of the crisis developing at light-ning speed inspired the Fed to again cut the benchmark interest rate by 50 bp only twelve days later, which brought it down to essentially zero.

The Fed's decision was driven by turbulence that erupted in the first half of March in the US treasuries market, the $20 trillion bedrock of the global financial system.[10] First, there was a worldwide dash for cash as the COVID-19 pandemic spread, and fear and uncertainty crippled the world's economic and financial system. Second, electronic trading amplified the initial shock—particularly a tactic deployed by hedge funds trying to profit from very small price differences. This sudden and intense turbulence inspired the Fed to make drastic interest rate moves and several other actions.

Stubbornly Negative

While the Fed at least *tried* to move away from the zero-lower bound of its policy rates, the same cannot be said of the ECB and the Bank of Japan. Facing a rapidly deteriorating economic situation, with inflation falling well below the target rate of 2 percent, the ECB lowered its benchmark policy rate for refinancing operations from 4.25 percent in July 2008 to 1 percent by May 2009.[11] The euro crisis and the accompanying economic malaise inspired the ECB to bring this benchmark rate to 0 percent in March 2015.

The ECB went even further with its deposit facility rate. Still at 3.25 percent in October 2008, this policy rate was quickly reduced to zero by July 2012. In June 2014, the ECB remarkably decided to bring the deposit facility rate in negative territory. Initially placed at -0.10 percent, the policy rate subsequently fell to -0.50 percent in September 2019. With a negative deposit rate, the ECB was effectively punishing banks that deposited excess reserves at the ECB so the banks would seek different ways to use these reserves. The hope was that their deployment of the reserves would help the economy and push up inflation. Negative interest rates also tend to weigh down the exchange rate of the euro, providing the euro economy with extra stimulus. However, negative interest rates have important unintended consequences, which are covered in the next chapter.

Although many speculated that the COVID-19 pandemic would inspire the ECB to drop its policy rates further, that did not happen. The ECB left its policy rates unchanged but took other important measures to mitigate the consequences of the COVID-19 shock that will be covered later in this chapter. As far as interest rates were concerned, the ECB's governing council resisted moving more into negative territory than they had done during the last weeks of Draghi's tenure as president of the ECB, in the fall of 2019. When I interviewed Draghi in the European Parliament about this episode and disagreements within the ECB's governing council, he became evasive and was clearly irritated.

Despite, or maybe because of, the tense internal discussions going on within the ECB, the executive board came up with an important innovation, a dual interest rate structure described by some as "monetary rocket fuel."[12] A dual interest rate structure meant that the ECB was separately targeting the interest rate on loans and the interest rate on deposits, allowing it to push down the interest rate on loans without a commensurate decline in interest rates on deposits. The degree to which the rate on ECB-provided loans could drop was based on how much lending the banks extended to the economy. By enacting a dual interest rate structure, central banks (in this case, the ECB) could escape the trap of increasingly negative policy rates. Of course, such operations create negative net interest income for a central bank. This exposure to loss is a serious risk for central banks in general, and it was certainly the case for the ECB, as eventual erosion of the capital base due to losses would immediately become a hot political issue within the euro area.

At the Bank of Japan (BoJ), the reaction to the financial crisis was more or less business as usual—or to be more specific, business as it had *become* usual. After a decade of sky-high real estate prices, off-the-charts equity notations, and absurd levels of leverage, in the early 1990s, Japan's bubble economy exploded. The term "lost decade" was invented for the particular Japanese experience.[13] Over the decade that followed, the Japanese economy sank into a coma of sorts, with low growth levels under the best of circumstances, and persistent deflation, despite the countless aggressive monetary and budgetary policies that were enacted. Since the beginning of the 1990s, Japan's budget deficit stood at more than 3 percent of GDP every year, with the deficits rising above 10 percent in some years. These continuous budget deficits made Japan the most indebted nation in the world, with public debt reaching 266 percent of GDP by the end of 2020 and no end to the rise in sight. During this same period, the BoJ also pioneered quantitative easing. While many assumed that these problems were exclusive to Japan, that belief became less credible after the global financial crisis tipped many other developed countries into similar situations.[14]

The BoJ reduced its main policy rate, the discount rate, from 5 to 2.5 percent between 1985 and 1987, in direct violation of every kind of Taylor-rule guidance. Like the Fed and the ECB in the years leading up to the global financial crisis, the policies pursued by the BoJ fueled different asset booms. In 1988, the central bank started to push up interest rates—raising the discount rate from 2.5 percent in 1988 to 6 percent in 1990—in an attempt to deflate the bubbles without causing too much damage to the real economy, but it was too late. The bubbles burst, as they always do, and the damage was catastrophic, given the enormous leverage that had been built up. The discount rate was cut to 0.5 percent by 1995. In the early years of the twenty-first century, after he had already brought interest rates to zero, BoJ Governor Masaru Hayami was pressured by members of the Japanese Diet (the parliament) to do more. Hayami replied, "We're doing everything we can, but trust me, it will do no good."[15] Policy rates have been close to zero ever since.

Early in 2016, the BoJ placed the interest rate on the excess reserves financial institutions park with the central bank at -0.1 percent. Since then, spokesmen for the BoJ have regularly suggested that this deposit rate go even lower if the economy deteriorates. The COVID-19 pandemic did not inspire the BoJ to push policy interest rates further down, but direct interventions in different markets were substantially stepped up. We'll elaborate on these interventions shortly.

Out of and Into the Shadows

The second broad action central banks took during the financial crisis was the creation of new lending and refinancing facilities tailored for specific situations, and the third was a series of QE programs. Since the division between these two kinds of actions is not always clear cut, they will be covered together. First, the focus will be on the Fed, which was clearly in the driver's seat since the US was the epicenter of the global financial crisis and the dollar was and still is by far the most important international currency. Next, we will examine the actions of the ECB and BoJ, which are the other two most important central banks of the advanced world economy. Other central banks in the developed world and in emerging countries adopted policies similar to those of the Fed, the ECB, and the BoJ following the COVID-19 pandemic.

The Fed needed to create new financing facilities because the financial sector had become a very diverse place, with new players all around. Access to refinancing facilities at the Fed had previously been limited to the traditional banks, but another area had become increasingly important in the financial business—the shadow banking system. The shadow banking system is the group of financial intermediaries facilitating and actively participating in the creation of credit across the global financial system. Organizations in the shadow banking system, which has grown enormously in the past twenty years worldwide, including China and India, carry out other traditional banking functions as well, but they are subject to very little regulatory oversight—or none at all.[16]

Investment banks, money market funds, hedge funds, and even large internet companies are counted as major elements of the shadow banking system. Many feared significant failures in the shadow banking system, which is much less regulated and supervised—if at all—than the traditional banking sector, would drag down the regular banking system and contribute in substantial and perhaps not immediately visible ways to a slide into economic depression.[17] That being said, it has to be recognized that the first two actions undertaken by the Fed with respect to new financing facilities were not directly related to the existence of the shadow banking system.

Bernanke and his board, as well as most other central bankers, realized early that the crisis had international ramifications, with financial institutions involved worldwide. After all, Bear Stearns was considered not too *big* to fail, but too *interconnected* to fail.[18] Since a huge demand for dollars would inevitably develop in foreign markets, the Fed created swap lines with the other major central banks of the world—the ECB and the Swiss National Bank were the first—to be able to absorb the new demand for dollars. Later in the crisis, these swap lines were expanded, and they proved to be an essential part of the toolkit required to contain the crisis. When the COVID-19 pandemic overwhelmed the world, these swap lines were reopened and reinforced.

At the end of 2007, the Fed created the Term Auction Facility (TAF) to allow banks to rely on Fed liquidity support without the stigma of formally addressing the discount window of the central bank. Some feared that the stigma might set in motion a kind of self-fulfilling prophecy in which a specific financial institution's precautions to broaden its liquidity base might be interpreted by the markets as an indication that it was in trouble. Through TAF, the Fed regularly auctioned off set amounts of collateral-backed loans to institutions with access to the Fed, allowing them to support their liquidity position without the stigma of using the discount window. In an "ordinary" crisis, liquidity is king. In an event as severe as the global financial crisis, liquidity is *everything*.

Crossing the Rubicon

In March 2008, Bernanke convinced his colleagues on the Fed Board, as well as the Federal Open Market Committee (FOMC), to launch the Term Securities Lending Facility (TSLF). The TSLF was designed to fight the liquidity crunch that was threatening to shatter major parts of the shadow banking system, including the big investment banks. Around this time, unsustainable pressure was crushing Bear Stearns, and mortgage-related problems were escalating throughout the international financial system. "[The TSLF] is unusual, but so are market conditions," Bernanke wrote in an email to colleagues at the Fed.[19] The TSLF allowed nonbanks, such as the five largest investment banks, to offer less-liquid or even illiquid assets, such as mortgage-related securities, for refinancing. "We're crossing certain lines," Bernanke acknowledged. "We're doing things we haven't done before...I think we have to be flexible and creative in the face of what really are extraordinary times."[20]

Yet the TSLF proved to be insufficient to keep the five big investment banks and other elements of the shadow banking system afloat, so another acronym joined the alphabet soup of intervention mechanisms, the Primary Dealer Credit Facility (PDCF). The PDCF was intended to stem negative market sentiments that quickly escalated following the Bear Stearns rescue by allowing the Fed to accept a broader range of securities as collateral, including riskier assets. Despite the haircuts applied to many of the securities offered at the PDCF window, the Fed was playing a borderline game with the PDCF, according to the Thornton and Bagehot playbook. Just how solid was the collateral that the Fed would accept at the PDCF window? The distinction between illiquidity and insolvency became blurred, and the tremendous amount of uncertainty made judging just how much of a haircut was appropriate very complicated.[21] The Fed opted to err on the safer side in terms of interpreting where the border between illiquidity and insolvency lay, with "safer" meaning avoiding a system-wide financial implosion at all costs. It was ready and willing to accept "less safe" collateral.

Next up was the Commercial Paper Funding Facility (CPFF), a means to block a destructive transmission mechanism from the financial crisis to the real economy. As the financial markets began to freeze up, non-financial companies increasingly encountered difficulty in getting their commercial paper refinanced or placed. European companies generally rely on credit facilities at banks for their financing needs, but American companies rely much more heavily on commercial paper placed in the market. The CPFF allowed the Fed to step in and try to secure sufficient financing for the real economy, despite the turmoil in the financial markets. Once more, the Fed found itself teetering on the limits of the Thornton and Bagehot playbook, since the risks involved in commercial paper were harder to determine.[22] Nevertheless, the need for the CPFF was immediately evident—two days after its launch, on October 27, 2008, $145 billion in three-month commercial paper had already passed through the new facility. A week later, the total rose to $242 billion, and it reached $350 billion at its peak in January 2009.[23]

With the financial system still reeling from the Lehman shock, another new facility was necessary in order to get the situation under control and prevent further deterioration in the real economy. The Term Asset-Backed Securities Loan Facility (TALF) was created to allow the refinancing of securities backed by credit card, student, car, and small business loans. Once again, the Fed decided to push the limits of what could be expected from its task as lender of last resort by permitting these securities to serve as collateral—of course, with haircuts applied. TALF was instrumental in avoiding a further implosion of the consumer credit market, which would have made the recession much worse than it already was. Initially designed with a limit of $200 billion, the TALF facility was expanded to $1 trillion in early 2009 on the insistence of Timothy Geithner, but in the end, it never came close to reaching the ceiling.[24] The amount outstanding in the TALF facility peaked at $71 billion.[25]

Two other initiatives of the Treasury are worthy of mention: the Temporary Guarantee Program for Money Market Funds (TGM) and the aforementioned Troubled Assets Relief Program (TARP). The Treasury created the TGM to protect money market-fund investors from losses in funds that broke the buck, preventing a full-blown stampede out of funds that would have caused havoc in the markets and the real economy.[26] TARP was instrumental in recapitalizing American banks, and most now agree that the TARP-funded bank recapitalizations were a turning point in the crisis.

Reopening the Spigots

By February 2009, most of the *sui generis* facilities created by the Fed during the crisis had ended and the swap lines with foreign central banks were closed; the only facility that stayed in operation was TALF, which was terminated at the end of June 2010. The Treasury guarantee for money market funds and TARP came to an end as well. None sustained losses, in the end—in fact, the fees money market funds had to pay to obtain a Treasury guarantee brought in $1.2 billion.[27] It's hard to deny that the extraordinary facilities created by the Fed and the Treasury played an important, if not decisive, role in the fight against the global financial crisis.[28]

When the COVID-19 pandemic set in early in 2020, the Fed acted almost immediately, slashing policy interest rates to near zero and creating several new refinancing facilities. The new facilities focused on the huge liquidity problems faced by many businesses, households, and government entities, such as municipalities, when the economy nosedived and the financial markets experienced upheaval. No longer just the lender of last resort, the Fed reinforced its status as "buyer of last resort."

Between March and April 2020, the Fed created eleven emergency facilities that promised to make a total of $2.6 trillion available. Among others, these included the Primary Market Corporate Credit Facility (PMCCF), Secondary Market Corporate Credit Facility (SMCCF), Main Street New Loan Facility (MSNLF), Main Street Primary Loan Facility (MSPLF), Municipal Liquidity Facility (MLF), and Paycheck Protection Program Liquidity Facility (PPPLF). During the first phase of the pandemic, the Fed was primarily focused on liquidity in the business sector. The sudden stop in economic activity caused by lockdowns, shutdowns, and social distancing measures placed countless small and large business in peril from life-threatening solvency issues. The potential for a tsunami of bankruptcies became frighteningly real overnight. To fight this, the Fed started buying up existing and newly issued corporate bonds and expanded its interventions in the commercial paper market. By mid-July 2020, the Fed extended access to its billion-dollar lending schemes to nonprofit organizations, including hospitals and universities.

These actions were well received in the markets. "The innovation, the creativity and the size of…[the Fed's actions]…was so large that their credibility is higher than it's ever been…You couldn't have designed it better," remarked Rick Rieder, chief investment officer of BlackRock, an investment management firm.[29] Such reactions are understandable from the short-term market perspective, but from a longer-term and more broadly societal perspective, this praise sounds rather overbaked. Gillian Tett of the *Financial Times* wrote that the pandemic-inspired interventions by Fed chairman Jerome Powell were "not just crossing traditional red lines, but deliberately sprinting over them...The sheer scale...[of the new programs]...will reduce the Fed's future firepower in the face of any fresh financial and economic shocks that might by unleashed by the pandemic. These wild experiments are also creating unprecedented moral hazard; or more accurately, amplifying the hazard that has haunted the financial system since 2008."[30] Chapter 5 will return to these themes in discussing the unintended consequences of unconventional monetary interventions.

Thornton and Bagehot may have had reservations regarding many of the central bankers' actions. Were the Fed and other central banks really accepting only "good collateral" when they launched these targeted refinancing programs? Were the interest rates applied by refinancing facilities sufficiently high? Were the central banks too lenient in terms of the haircuts extended, given the risk-taking extremes of some financial institutions? Yet it's hard to imagine that both Thornton and Bagehot would have disagreed with the broader overall approach. The special facilities created by the Fed and other central banks to deal with the acute phases of the financial crisis and the pandemic certainly helped avert another Great Depression. But under the impetus of Bernanke, the Fed found it necessary to take further steps to recover from the financial crisis and its aftermath, and those steps were dramatic.

Not New but Radical
The Fed's moves on policy interest rates and new financing facilities were quite spectacular, but its policy of quantitative easing got most of the attention. Although important differences exist between the various QE programs launched by central bankers worldwide, they all aim to

reduce long-term interest rates through large-scale purchases of long-term bonds initially issued by public and private entities.[31] While it's tempting to attribute the persistent decline in long-term interest rates to QE policies, to do so would be wrong. The decline began during the 1980s, a clear indication that there's more to this phenomenon than QE interventions. Slower productivity growth, global saving surpluses, and demographic shifts have also played roles in the remarkable structural decline in long-term interest rates.[32]

Buying bonds and other securities on a large scale causes their prices to increase and their yields to decline. The hope among central bankers was that through this impact on long-term interest rates, quantitative easing would also bring about a portfolio rebalancing effect. In effect, central banks were betting that investors in search of higher yields would put their money elsewhere—perhaps in corporate bonds. The portfolio rebalancing effect could stimulate private investment and, as a result, the economy in general. In their initial phases, the QE programs were also intended to improve the function of financial and capital markets still reeling from the effects of the crisis.

From a macroeconomic perspective, central banks reverted to QE policies to move inflation closer to its targeted level (for most central banks, around 2 percent) and stimulate economic growth and employment. QE was conjured to prevent an exhaustion of monetary policy impact, since policy interest rates were already down to zero or in some cases even below—the *zero lower bound*. As early as 2002, Bernanke had rather confidently included QE actions as an option if interest rates ever became stuck at zero.[33] At the time, it was only a possibility in the United States and Europe, but only a few years later, it became the harsh reality.

In fact, many of the operations performed by central banks in recent years under the *nom de guerre* of "QE" aren't new, let alone revolutionary. In modern times, central banks have been continuously engaged in open-market operations, meaning the buying and selling of bonds and other securities to help manage bank reserves and the money supply. Open-market operations are used to get the federal funds rate to its desired level; that rate is the main determinant for short-term market interest rates. What *was* quite revolutionary is that the financial crisis led central banks to perform these operations on a massive scale never seen before in peacetime, and also that the operations were performed in only one direction. Central banks were buying on a massive scale, which resulted in an explosion of their balance sheets and a steep rise in bank reserves. All this buying of bonds and securities led to an ocean of liquidity, an evolution that has inspired constant commentary, analysis, and controversy.[34]

The COVID-19 pandemic accelerated the deployment of QE worldwide. The balance sheets of the four leading central banks in the advanced world—the Fed, the ECB, the BoJ, and the Bank of England— are quite revealing in this respect. If you take January 2008 as a starting date, the sum of these banks' balance sheets increased by $5 trillion over the next five years. These same four central banks increased their combined balance sheets by $8 trillion in *only eight months* following February 2020. The pandemic inspired *QE on steroids*, and the mystic hand of central bankers touched the world more than ever before.

The Fed also added an important policy lever to its toolkit just before QE interventions began. QE operations substantially increase bank reserves. This rise in reserves makes it difficult for the Fed to control the federal funds rate, its basic policy interest rate. In 2006, Congress permitted the Fed to start paying interest on banks' reserve balances starting in 2011. When the financial crisis hit, that start date was moved forward to October 2008. By altering the interest rate it paid on bank reserves, the Fed was positioned to control the federal funds rate even when bank reserves were plentiful. Increasing the rate paid on bank reserves makes placing the reserves with the Fed more attractive and redirects these reserves from elsewhere in the economic and financial systems. Reducing the Fed rate on reserves has the opposite effect.

Betting on QE

The buildup of the Fed's QE program developed in three stages.[35] The first, known as QE1, started in November 2008, when the Fed announced that it would buy $600 billion in government bonds and mortgage-backed securities. The main purposes of QE1 were to fend off the impending collapse of Fannie Mae and Freddie Mac, and to breathe new life into the ailing housing market and mortgage loans. Once it was understood that the intervention was insufficient to have real impact, the Fed decided in March 2009 to increase the program to "up to" $1.75 trillion.[36] Given the many uncertainties surrounding the effects of these purchases, the FOMC retained the option to stop the program before that limit was reached.

Despite the impressive size of the enlarged QE1 program, the economy continued to sputter, and deflation still seemed possible. In response, the Fed announced a second QE program in November 2010. While it was fairly subdued, internal criticism of Bernanke's QE path began to be more direct. For this QE2 program, the Fed committed to buy $600 billion in long-term securities between November 2010 and June 2011. Clearly, these asset purchases were becoming an integral part of the Fed's toolkit to carry out monetary policy and manage the economy. Despite its appeals to other US policymaking bodies, including the Congress and the president, to do their part in the fight against the crisis and its aftermath, the Fed board increasingly realized they were "the only game in town."[37] Several observers and Fed members, including St. Louis Fed president Jim Bullard, remarked that the strict time limitation that had been placed on the QE programs would reduce their effectiveness in influencing behavior in the markets.

In September 2011, the Fed announced another QE program, the Maturities Extension Program (MEP), that was immediately nicknamed "Operation Twist" by the press. The MEP is generally considered to have been part of QE2 in the United States. As the program's name indicates, it was meant to extend the average maturity of the assets kept in the Fed's portfolio. Under the MEP, the Fed initially intended to purchase $400 billion in Treasury securities with maturities of at least six years and sell an equal amount of securities with maturities of less than three years over a period of nine months. In June 2012, the Fed extended the program until the end of 2012; in total, $667 billion in shorter-term securities were replaced by longer-term securities.

The MEP was an attempt to reinforce the impact of QE without further pumping up the Fed's balance sheet, but as the Fed continued down the QE path, criticism mounted. Several board members, including Kansas City Fed president Thomas Hoenig, were concerned about the size of the Fed's balance sheet. Some members of Congress, mostly on the Republican side, voiced harsh criticism, sometimes focused on Bernanke himself. Sarah Palin, the Republican vice-presidential candidate in the 2008 election who is not exactly known for her interest in or knowledge of monetary policy, claimed the time had come for "Chairman Bernanke to cease and desist."[38] Republican Senator Bob Corker of Tennessee accused Bernanke of "throwing seniors under the bus," due to the negative effects of zero-interest rates on the savings accounts of the elderly.[39] A growing number of economists lobbied the Fed to seriously reconsider or even discontinue its QE programs,[40] voicing fears of inflation and concerns about financial stability.

Criticism also rolled in from abroad. Germany's long-standing and highly respected minister of finance Wolfgang Schäuble remarked, "I don't recognize the economic argument behind this measure...The Fed's decisions bring more uncertainty to the global economy."[41] During my tenure as Belgium's minister of finance, I got to know Schäuble. I brought up his quote during an informal conversation in 2015, and he answered that he "still stood by that criticism. The Fed and other central banks have acted courageously and correctly during the financial crisis. I believe, however, that they have continued too long on the road of massive interventions aimed at manipulating long-term interest rates. Not only are there major inflation risks, these policies also created too [many] distortions in financial markets and in the real economy."

Schäuble also argued that the Fed's policy drove down the dollar exchange rate in an artificial way and thus created problems for other countries in terms of competitiveness in international trade (in particular, the German car industry). This argument was echoed by a number of policymakers in emerging countries. Brazil's minister of finance, Guido Mantega, declared "an international currency war" was underway between countries trying to compensate for their loss of competitiveness due to the dollar's depreciation.[42] The Chinese vice minister of finance Zhū Guāngyào attacked the Fed's policies because he believed they created "excessive fluidity on the financial markets of emerging countries."[43] At the G20 Summit in Seoul on November 11 and 12 of 2010, President Barack Obama was grilled about the Fed's QE policy by many of the attendees.[44]

This foreign and domestic criticism made the situation more complicated for Bernanke and his Fed. The MEP was hitting its ceiling, since the Fed was running out of short-term securities. The economy was still weak, with an unemployment rate above 8 percent. The deepening euro crisis had cast a long shadow over economic prospects. Given these factors, Bernanke became convinced that *more* action, not less, was needed to stabilize the economy. In the Fed Board's internal deliberations, some members expressed their concerns.[45]

Despite strong opposition from Charles Plosser, president of the Philadelphia Fed, among others, Bernanke finally persuaded his colleagues to launch further monetary policy accommodations in a QE3 program. The Fed announced that it would buy $40 billion of mortgage-backed securities guaranteed by Fannie and Freddie and $45 billion of Treasury securities *per month*, further expanding its balance sheet by $85 billion on a monthly basis. Unlike the earlier QE programs, this QE3 was open-ended. The Fed specified that these monthly purchases would continue until two thresholds were reached, an unemployment rate of 6.5 percent and an inflation rate of 2.5 percent. The message was not that the Fed would *stop* its purchases when these thresholds were reached; instead, it would *reconsider* its policy stance in that event.

Wrong-Footed

In May and June of 2013, Fed chairman Bernanke, under pressure from further resistance among his board and the FOMC, hinted that the Fed might begin to moderate its asset purchases later in the year. The markets reacted vigorously to Bernanke's hints; long-term rates shot up, and equity markets tanked. Capital flew out of emerging markets as investors hustled to benefit from expected higher rates in the United States. Markets calmed down somewhat after Bernanke and several Fed governors known to be close to him (who were also critical of the QE operations), including Jeremy Stein, Jerome Powell, and New York Fed President William Dudley, went out of their way to argue that the Fed would continue its polices as long as the economy's performance remained weak. This "taper tantrum" episode unambiguously indicated that the Fed was in a delicate situation as a consequence of its unconventional monetary policies. Had the Fed largely, if not entirely, lost its ability to go against the financial markets?

The monthly purchases of $85 billion in assets continued, despite repeated rumors that the Fed was about to change course. The *Financial Times* referred to Bernanke as "the taper traitor" because he refused to start reducing the monthly interventions in September.[46] "At this point in my tenure," Bernanke reflected in his memoirs, "I didn't care about the commentary or about bond traders' anger at being wrong-footed."[47]

Bernanke's laconic attitude was also inspired by another development. In the autumn of 2013, Bernanke's successor as Fed chairman became a hot topic. Although President Barack Obama had praised him on several occasions, Bernanke was ready to leave. Janet Yellen, who had served as vice chair of the Fed board since 2010, became his successor in February 2014. Four years later, Yellen, who was not keen about serving under Donald Trump, who distrusted everything related to the Obama administration, was succeeded by Jerome Powell.

Before leaving the Fed, Bernanke wrong-footed commentators and the markets one last time. At the end of 2013, the Fed announced—against expectations—a reduction to $75 billion in the monthly pace of securities purchases. Yellen continued to unwind operations, and by October 2014, the Fed asset purchases halted. At that point, the Fed's balance sheet stood at $4.5 trillion, or 26 percent of GDP; prior to the financial crisis, it had hovered around $1 trillion. In a statement on September 17, 2014, the Fed explained its "exit strategy," emphasizing that it would continue to implement its monetary policy by targeting the federal funds rate. Things would go back to the "old normal," many thought…

Down and Up Again

From 2014 until the end of 2017, the Fed maintained its balance sheet around $4.5 trillion by rolling over securities as they matured. In September 2017, the Fed started to gradually reduce its balance sheet by ceasing to roll over maturing securities. At the peak of the balance sheet runoff, the Fed allowed $30 billion in Treasuries and $20 billion in mortgage-related securities to expire each month. At the end of the first quarter of 2019, the Fed's balance sheet total was still $3.9 trillion, with bank reserves of roughly $1.5 trillion. On March 20, 2019, the Fed, in reaction to a wave of volatility in the financial markets, announced that by September, it would halt the runoff of its balance sheet. Yet the balance sheet began to rise again, to close to $4.2 trillion, by the end of 2019. In October of that year, problems in the money markets inspired the Fed to restart its purchase of short-term bonds, at a rate of $60 billion a month. Bloomberg pointedly referred to the renewed asset purchases as "undoing the unwind."[48] It seemed that the ups and downs of financial markets were dominating US monetary policies more than its dual mandate of controlling inflation and unemployment.

Then everything changed again with the sudden arrival of the COVID-19 pandemic. Almost instantly, there was, the *Financial Times* claimed, a "clamour for cash as the economy hits an iceberg."[49] Equity markets tanked, losing up to 25 percent in a few weeks' time. Risk spreads in the bond market soared, and suddenly many emerging markets were facing a debt crunch. "Deluges of downgrades" rampaged through the financial markets.[50] Central banks acted swiftly and decisively, providing massive amounts of liquidity in an effort to stop a lethal credit crunch loop. The pandemic could provoke defaults that would cause bank losses and market panic, leading to a halting of credit flows and even more defaults—a vicious circle.

Along with a second reduction of the federal funds rate in March 2020, the Fed reinforced its QE interventions to counter the pandemic's devastating effect on the economy. The Fed announced that "in the coming months," it would make $700 billion in additional asset purchases ($500 billion in Treasuries and $200 billion in mortgage-backed assets), an initiative that was quickly reinforced by the launch of eleven specific refinancing facilities. The Fed also set up new dollar-swap facilities with other central banks to meet the soaring international demand for dollars. In just a few weeks' time, these QE actions pushed the Fed's balance sheet total from $4 trillion to $7 trillion—much higher than it had ever been during the financial crisis. As the Fed reopened the monetary spigots, Congress launched a $3 trillion crisis package with measures to support businesses and massive amounts of income support for families and individuals.

It's often forgotten when QE programs are discussed that these massive asset purchases bring in a lot of money for the US Treasury and thus improve the federal budget situation. The Fed funds all its operating costs from the interest it earns on the securities in its portfolio, and it remits most of the remaining income to the Treasury. Remittances from the Fed to the Treasury stood at $35 billion in 2007 but rose dramatically in later years. Between 2010 and 2017, the Fed's remittances more than doubled, to an average of $75 billion per year. In 2018, they declined to $62 billion, still substantially more than in the years prior to the financial crisis. What happens to these remittances in the future is of course dependent on how the Fed manages its balance sheet and what happens with interest rates.

The German Dilemma

While the financial crisis originated in the United States, Europe's banking system was at least as shaky as the American one. The ECB's first reactions to the crisis were consistent with the Fed's, and the ECB pulled out all the stops to keep the financial markets from freezing and interbank lending from drying up. Pure QE operations began in the middle of 2014, more than five years after the worst phase of the crisis. From day one of the crisis, the ECB was well aware of the necessity to keep bank credit flowing throughout the system.[51] After all, the nonfinancial sector of the European economy is much more dependent on bank lending than its American counterpart.[52]

The ECB immediately took on its lender-of-last-resort task by expanding its main liquidity-enhancing operations and launching several rounds of *long-term refinancing operations* (LTROs)—actions right out of the Thornton and Bagehot playbook. Next, it tried to resolve a sudden, steep drop in interbank activity caused by the escalation in uncertainty. The ECB organized several LTRO auctions with maturities ranging from six to thirty-six months and a Covered Bond Purchase Program (CBPP) intended to improve market liquidity and ease funding conditions for banks and enterprises.

At the end of 2009, Greece revealed that its fiscal deficit had been massively understated, setting off the euro crisis that complicated matters for the ECB. The damage wasn't limited to Greece; financing costs rose for Portugal, Spain, Ireland, and Italy as well. Article 123 of the Treaty on the Functioning of the European Union prohibits monetary financing of member states, so the ECB faced a delicate situation. The Security Markets Program (SMP) was seen as a way around this problem, since it allowed the ECB to purchase government bonds in the secondary market. Doing so meant crossing an important line, and it created havoc. Axel Weber, president of the German Bundesbank and a member of the ECB's Council, openly spoke out against the SMP program, stating that he considered it incompatible with the European Treaty on the monetary union.[53]

A discussion started surrounding the SMP operations that remains unsettled; its resolution is of the utmost importance for the future of the European Union and its common currency. German minister of finance Wolfgang Schäuble agreed with Weber, and repeatedly told me he was not in favor of such operations but that he also realized they were unavoidable if the EU and its euro were to survive. Schäuble also very publicly opposed negative interest rates and remained vocal on ECB policies even after he left his role as minister of finance in 2017. Along with several other leading German politicians, in September 2020, Schäuble argued the ECB's monetary policy needed to fundamentally change, and the asset purchases and negative interest rates had to stop.[54]

Schäuble's push for drastic changes to the ECB's monetary policy came after the German Constitutional Court (GCC), better known as *Karlsruhe*, after the German city where it is located, produced a highly critical ruling on the ECB's bond-buying schemes.[55] ECB governors, the Court ruled, had insufficiently accounted for the side effects of these schemes on savers and financial institutions. These rumblings from leading German politicians and the GCC reflect the fundamental German dilemma regarding the EU, which has only intensified over time. In terms of monetary policy, the EU does many things the Germans (and the Dutch) don't like, but they don't dare oppose them outright because they don't want to threaten the union overall. But how long can this duality last?

Despite mixed feelings, to say the least, on the German side, the ECB bought €218 billion in Greek, Irish, Portuguese, Spanish, and Italian securities between May 2008 and September 2012, when the SMP program ended. By that time, the Outright Monetary Transactions (OMT) program, another product of Draghi's "whatever it takes" remark, came online (Draghi succeeded Jean-Claude Trichet as president of the ECB on November 1, 2011). The OMT program was intended to allow the ECB to address distortions in government bond markets originating from what were called "unfounded" fears on the reversibility of the euro. Euro-area member countries had to request OMT interventions, and by doing so had to accept monitoring of their policies. This implied that ECB action was conditional, and remarkably, not a single formal request to activate the OMT program was ever made.

By the end of 2013, the euro economy had emerged from the recession, and the worst of the monetary union's crisis was over everywhere, except for Greece. Yet growth remained very weak, and inflation was stuck well below the 2 percent target rate. Draghi's ECB became convinced that more action was needed. In June 2014, the ECB instituted a negative deposit policy rate for the first time ever and launched targeted long-term refinancing operations (TLTROs). These were "targeted" in the sense that banks lending to households and companies could obtain more favorable financing conditions from the ECB. Negative deposit rates and TLTROs were meant to reinforce each other in the fight against a weak economy and stubbornly low inflation,[56] and the ECB launched second and third rounds of TLTROs in March 2016 and March 2019, respectively.

On the QE Track

Shortly after the negative deposit rate and the first round of TLTROs went into effect, Draghi and his colleagues concluded yet more action was needed. In September 2014, the ECB decided to embark on a trajectory of quantitative easing in the form of its Asset Purchase Program (APP). The ECB announced that it would buy not only government bonds and securities, but also asset-backed securities, covered bonds, and corporate sector bonds. The net average monthly purchases under the APP program varied: €60 billion from March 2015 to March 2016; €80 billion from April 2016 to March 2017; €60 billion again from April 2017 to December 2017; and €30 billion from January 2018 to September 2018. During the last three months of 2018, the average net monthly purchases sagged to €15 billion.

After a ten-month pause, the ECB's governing council decided to restart its APP interventions at a monthly pace of €20 billion as of November 1, 2019.[57] The ECB communicated that these net additional purchases would continue "for as long as necessary to reinforce the accommodative impact of its policy rates, and to end it shortly before its starts raising the key ECB interest rates."[58] The balance sheet of the ECB went from less than €1,000 billion at the start of the twenty-first century to €3,000 billion in 2012, and more than €5,000 billion toward the end of 2019. As time went on, it became increasingly difficult to reject the hypothesis that the ECB's policy decisions were inspired by the volatility of and the fragility within the financial markets rather than by concerns about inflation or the overall economic outlook.

The restart of the APP opened up a significant divide within the ECB's governing council. Draghi had a clear majority, but representatives of Germany, France, the Netherlands, and several smaller countries voted against it. In terms of economic weight within the euro area, more than 50 percent of the monetary union voted against Draghi's proposal. The final Draghi policy package was also savaged by a group of heavyweight former central bankers, such as Jürgen Stark, Otmar Issing, and Helmut Schlesinger from Germany; Hervé Hannoun, Christian Noyer, and Jacques de Larosière from France; and Nout Wellink of the Netherlands.[59] By the time Draghi was succeeded by former IMF Managing Director Christine Lagarde on November 1, 2019, perspectives on Draghi and his legacy had become quite polarized. To some, he was a hero who had almost singlehandedly saved Europe's monetary union from extinction, but to others, he was the symbol of monetary adventures that sooner or later would end in catastrophe.

Lagarde experienced a baptism by fire. She had hardly settled into her Frankfurt office when the COVID-19 pandemic hit Europe like a meteor. The enormity of the event obliged the new ECB president to prove that she was up to the task of leading, despite the differences of opinion and divisiveness within the institution's governing council. Under Lagarde's leadership, the ECB left policy interest rates unchanged, but doubled down on QE efforts in an attempt to stabilize the economy and financial markets reeling from a deep recession and massive uncertainty.[60] On March 12, it announced €120 billion in additional asset purchases and extra liquidity support for banks through additional LTROs. A week later, the Pandemic Emergency Purchase Program (PEPP) was introduced; through it, assets for a total amount of €750 billion would be purchased. The ECB also allowed banks to borrow at negative rates as long as they maintained credit flows to the economy.[61] In the course of April 2020, the ECB relaxed several collateral rules, especially those regarding corporate bonds, "to further mitigate the impact of rating downgrades."[62]

Early in June, the ECB announced that it would buy an extra €600 billion in bonds through the PEPP, bringing the total to €1,350 billion.

Lagarde argued that the extra stimulus was necessary since the euro area was "experiencing an unprecedented contraction...[with]...severe job and income losses and exceptionally elevated uncertainty."[63] At this point in time, the ECB was forecasting a contraction of the euro economy in 2020 by 8.7 percent, with the potential for it to rise to 12.6 percent if the pandemic continued. This move came only a few hours after the German government announced a €130 billion stimulus program— clearly echoing Lagarde's argument that under the pandemic's extreme circumstances, fiscal and monetary policy had to be closely coordinated.

Late in the autumn of 2020, the pandemic's second wave hit the EU. In response, the ECB stepped up its efforts to limit economic damage by raising the amount of bonds it would buy in the PEPP to a total of €1.85 trillion; extending the PEPP's end date from June 2021 to March 2022; and announcing its intent to reinvest all proceeds from bonds coming due until at least the end of 2023. If, however, the economy recovered more quickly than expected, Lagarde indicated that the PEPP "need not be used in full."[64] The ECB also tightened the rules on the availability of ultra-cheap loans (loans priced at -1 percent). Several ECB council members argued that these loans were too generous.

Larger Than Life
The BoJ pioneered QE as a tool to keep monetary policy alive and kicking while policy interest rates are stuck at the zero lower bound. Though the move had not yet been defined as QE at that time, it rescued Japanese banks that were drowning in losses from bubble-related securities and bought up trillions of yen of commercial paper in the late 1990s. By March 2001, the economy and banking sector were still in tatters, so the BoJ organized further liquidity injections for Japanese banks and began to purchase long-term government bonds in an effort to reduce long-term interest rates.

The self-inflicted problems that grew in Japan during and after the extraordinary bubble of the 1980s were followed up by the global financial crisis, which also hit Japan quite badly. Yet the BoJ waited until

October 2010—two full years after Lehman failed—to take significant countermeasures against the crisis. The BoJ first announced that it would purchase ¥5 trillion in assets and raised that figure to ¥20 trillion (equal to 4 percent of GDP) shortly thereafter. By February 2012, its asset purchasing program was further increased by ¥10 trillion as the BoJ reiterated its intentions to not raise interest rates and to continue the asset purchasing program as long as necessary, as long as the risk of financial imbalances did not increase significantly.

After the 2012 election of Prime Minister Shinzō Abe, Haruhiko Kuroda became the new governor of the BoJ. Kuroda, who had close ties to the Abe government, announced a first round of "quantitative and qualitative easing" (QQE1) in which ¥30 trillion in government bonds and ¥1 trillion in exchange-traded funds (equities) would be purchased each year. This revolutionary move was a sign of the degree of desperation at the BoJ: the institution felt obliged to start buying equity shares of private companies. As the clear and present danger of deflation reemerged in October 2014, the BoJ opted to move to QQE2, which involved increasing purchases of government bonds to ¥80 trillion and of exchange-traded funds to ¥3 trillion each year.

In September 2016, the BoJ came up with a new policy goal, yield curve control. While the interest payable on reserves at the central bank would remain at -0.1 percent, more government bonds would be purchased so the ten-year interest rate, or yield, would stay at zero. The central bank estimated that ¥80 trillion in yearly purchases would be sufficient to achieve this goal, but it was implied that, if necessary, it would purchase more to achieve the desired yield curve control. In addition, the BoJ also launched an "inflation-overshooting commitment," meaning the policies already introduced would remain in place until inflation exceeded the 2 percent target on an ongoing basis.

The Japanese central bank, like almost all other central banks in the advanced world, doubled down on its unconventional instruments after the COVID-19 pandemic began. In April 2020, the BoJ held 50 percent of all outstanding government bonds and ¥30 trillion of equities on its balance sheet, but it decided to increase its holdings of commercial paper and corporate bonds from ¥5 trillion to ¥20 trillion. It also relaxed its collateral rules and substantially extended the maturities of corporate bonds.

As a consequence of the policies pursued by the BoJ, by the end of 2020, its balance sheet total reached ¥700 trillion (more than $6 trillion), more than twice what it had been five years earlier. Its balance sheet had become larger than the nation's GDP—a record among the advanced countries of the world. In the middle of 2019, the Fed's balance sheet stood at 20 percent of GDP and the ECB's was just below 40 percent of GDP.

It's fair to say that no other country in the world has gone as far as Japan, which is still the third-largest economy in the world, in its use of unconventional monetary policy tools. This also includes *forward guidance*, the last of the four unconventional tools, which will be discussed in detail in the next section. That Japan was unable to achieve a significant turnaround in terms of its overall economic perspective says a lot about these policies.

Guiding Light

The fourth component of the unconventional monetary toolbox that major central banks initiated in the wake of the financial crisis and leaned into during the pandemic was forward guidance on their policies.[65] Forward guidance is a communication strategy that attempts to reduce uncertainty in the economic and monetary environment and the sensitivity of money markets to macroeconomic and political news. With forward guidance, central banks hope to influence consumers, producers, and investors as they make decisions on spending and investments. Forward guidance is a tool central bankers use by providing information on their own *future* courses to influence private sector decisions *in the here and now*.[66] It is an application of the hypothesis that rational expectations dominate the behavior of consumers, producers, and investors.

Since the concept of the central bank was introduced, central bankers have always sent out signals on how they saw monetary policy evolving over time, although they were often pretty veiled ones. It is only in relatively recent times, however, that forward guidance has become a specific tool for central bankers. Three types of forward guidance exist. The first is based on a state-contingent threshold, meaning that a certain policy (a zero-interest policy rate, for example) will be continued as long as the state of the economy is judged to be in need of that policy stance. The second type is tied to a calendar date—for example, a policy will be continued until "the end of the year." The third is open-ended, meaning that the policy has no calendar end date or state-contingent threshold.

The BoJ pioneered QE, and it did the same with forward guidance. In fact, the Japanese central bank began using forward guidance long before the term became broadly used. In April 1999, Masaru Hayami, then the governor of the BoJ, declared the central bank "will maintain the zero-interest rate policy until deflationary concerns are dispelled." Two years later, he announced, "The quantitative easing policy continues to be in place until the core CPI [consumer price index] registers stably zero percent or an increase." In February 2012, the BoJ announced that zero policy rates and asset purchases would be continued "until the Bank judges the 1 percent goal [for inflation] is in sight."[67] In October 2019, the BoJ told the markets that it "expects short- and long-term interest rates to remain at present or lower levels as long as needed to pay close attention to the possibility that the momentum toward achieving its price target will be lost."[68] These statements are just a taste of how forward guidance is used. It's not the purpose of this analysis to go into the details of every statement flavored with forward guidance, but following are some additional examples from the Fed and the ECB.

The Federal Open Market Committee announced on December 8, 2008, "Weak economic conditions are likely to warrant exceptionally low levels of the federal funds rate for some time." This statement was repeated in August 2009, with "for some time" replaced with "for an extended period." In August 2011, the FOMC announced that the federal funds rate would remain exceptionally low "at least through mid-2013," which a few months later became "at least through late 2014," and in September 2012 was rephrased as "at least through mid-2015." A new message came in December 2012—the federal funds rate would remain in the 0 to 0.25 percent range "at least as long as the unemployment rate remains above 6.50 percent, inflation between one and two years ahead is projected to be no more than a half percentage point above the Committee's 2 percent longer-run goal, and longer-term inflation expectations continue to be well anchored." By October 2014, the FOMC declared, "If incoming information indicates faster progress toward the Committee's employment and inflation objectives than the Committee now expects, then the increases in the target range for the federal funds rate are likely to occur sooner than currently anticipated." In December 2016, on the occasion of the first new target range increase, the FOMC announced that it expected "economic conditions will evolve in a manner that will warrant only gradual increases in the federal funds rate."[69]

The ECB began dabbling in forward guidance in July 2013, when Draghi stated, "The Governing Council expects the key ECB rates to remain at present or lower levels for an extended period of time." The ECB regularly repeated similar kinds of conditions for its policy course. In June 2018, it provided forward guidance on its asset purchase program by stating, "We anticipate that after September 2018, subject to incoming data confirming our medium-term inflation forecast, we will reduce the monthly pace of the net asset purchases to €15 billion until the end of December 2018 and then end net purchases." On the occasion of one of its last major Draghi-inspired policy decisions, the reduction of the deposit rate to -0.50 percent, the ECB stated it expected interest rates to remain at either present or lower levels until the inflation outlook would "robustly converge to a level sufficiently close to but below 2 percent within its projection horizon, and such convergence has been persistent."[70]

Forward guidance should be seen as a *reinforcer*, a tool by which central bankers can accentuate and deepen the impact of their basic policy positions through their decisions on interest rates, specific refinancing facilities, and quantitative easing.[71] Forward guidance can be of crucial importance at critical turning points in a central bank's overall policy stance, since at those moments substantial doubts about the seriousness of the turning point have the capacity to undermine the policy's effectiveness. Forward guidance can be a powerful tool when broad-based doubts about the way in which central banks will proceed in the future persist.

Yet forward guidance is not without risks. First, there is the risk of time inconsistency, because changing circumstances can lead to important deviations from the forward guidance path outlined. Second, forward guidance that implicitly reflects pessimism about future growth potential can become a self-fulfilling prophecy. Third, if it is particularly convincing, forward guidance stimulates the financing of longer-term assets by short-term debts because that strategy will be seen to have less risk.[72] Forward guidance can increase leverage in the system. It can also lead to herd behavior. It can cause investors to ignore other important signals coming from the financial markets and from the economy in general. The next chapter, an evaluation of the unintended consequences of the unconventional monetary policy toolkit, will cover these risks in more detail.

Chapter 5: Paying a Hefty Price

*How unconventional monetary policies became
increasingly self-defeating*

THE MOMENTOUS NATURE OF THE GLOBAL FINANCIAL CRISIS
and the COVID-19 pandemic inspired the major central
banks of the world to launch, stick to, and regularly reinforce
unconventional monetary policies. The unconventional toolbox involves
four primary levers: policy interest rates at zero or even below zero;
new targeted lending arrangements to deal with specific elements of
the financial turmoil; asset purchase programs or quantitative easing;
and forward guidance on future interest policy. Although the political,
economic, and institutional context has changed dramatically since
the nineteenth century, these policy innovations closely hewed to
crisis-fighting prescriptions set forth by pioneering economists Henry
Thornton and Walter Bagehot in their time.

Both Thornton and Bagehot believed that anything and everything
had to be done to avoid a financial collapse, and the Great Depression
proved their point. The devastation of the 1930s showed what would
happen if policymakers did not act decisively. *Central bankers unlearned
the crucial lessons of Thornton and Bagehot and stood by as the Great
Depression ravaged economies and led to nightmarish political and military
developments. They relearned the lessons of Thornton and Bagehot and acted
appropriately when the global financial crisis and the pandemic arrived.*

There remains no doubt, given the circumstances of both the financial crisis and the pandemic, that the courageous and innovative actions taken by central banks were absolutely crucial to avoid dramatic meltdowns with incalculable financial, economic, social, and political consequences. Whatever the shortcomings of monetary policy before the financial crisis, Ben Bernanke, Jean-Claude Trichet, Mario Draghi, Mervyn King, and many other central bankers deserve respect for their performance from 2007 to 2009. Yet central banks in the major countries and regions of the world continued using their unconventional toolboxes long after the acute phase of the financial crisis was over. In some cases, their use even accelerated. The longer these policies were pursued, the more it became obvious that some unintended consequences could not be ignored. The COVID-19 pandemic necessitated new and innovative steps to keep the system going, but that only accentuated the perseverance of these unintended consequences. *A new learning process for central bankers has begun,* and nobody knows where this process will lead.

Other than a few notable exceptions—Bundesbank President Jens Weidmann; Dutch central bank President Klaas Knot; Philadelphia Fed President Charles Plosser; Kansas City Fed President and FDIC Vice-chairman Thomas Hoenig;[1] former Bank of India Governor Raghuram Rajan; and Christian Hawkesby, the assistant governor of the Reserve Bank of New Zealand—most central bankers and their academic brothers-in-arms have consistently downplayed these consequences, arguing that the benefits of these monetary policies far outweighed the negative side effects. Interestingly, Draghi himself conceded during the last weeks of his ECB presidency that concerns over unintended negative consequences of super-easy monetary policy are "well placed," and added that the side effects of QE were "less visible" than those from rate cuts.[2] Lagarde, Draghi's successor, told the European Parliament she was "fully aware of the side consequences" of the ECB policy, but didn't elaborate further.[3] Economic research—as well as the glare of reality—contradicted their efforts at minimization.

These complicated and difficult-to-quantify issues are reminiscent of John Maynard Keynes's remarks on the long and the short term:

We do not know what the future will bring, except that it will be quite different from anything we could predict. I have said in another context that it is a disadvantage of the "long run" that in the long run we are all dead. But I could have said equally that it is a great advantage of the "short run" that in the short run we are all alive. Life and history are made up of short runs. If we are at peace in the short run, that is something. The best we can do is put off disaster, if only in the hope, which is not necessarily a remote one, that something will turn up.[4]

Did the policies pursued during and following the acute phases of these crises increase the risk of even more mayhem down the road? Have we purchased some tranquility, order, and "peace" in the short run (which is now more than ten years long) by accepting and fueling bigger risks down the road? One can interpret Keynes' quote as an argument in favor of policies that kick the can down the road, don't bother with longer-term perspectives, and just hope and pray that something will turn up. In some cases, this attitude might be somewhat justified, but in the case of unconventional monetary policies, that justification is increasingly unconvincing, to say the least. The harmful nature of a number of unintended consequences of these policies has become quite obvious and has shown a tendency to worsen over time.

I will detail these adverse consequences under the headings of:
- Butch Cassidy Syndrome
- Michael Jackson Syndrome
- David Copperfield Syndrome
- Semper Augustus Syndrome
- Savior-Turned-Bully Syndrome
- "26 = 3.8 Billion" Syndrome
- Zombie Syndrome
- Sloth Syndrome

Before digging into each we must express two notes of caution: first, there's no way to know what would have happened if central bankers had not pursued unconventional monetary policies or if they had stepped away from these policies much earlier.[5] Maybe things would have worked out better in the longer run, or maybe the meltdown and subsequent recession would have been much worse. We can't know for sure. But even if one gives the central bankers the benefit of the doubt for their policies since the financial crisis, the mostly unintended negative consequences of the unconventional monetary policy can't be denied.

Second, inflation has been intentionally left off the list of unintended consequences of the extensive use of the unconventional monetary toolbox for a simple reason. After a prolonged period of money creation in excess of real growth in the economy, a burst of inflation is expected. Centuries of monetary history in all corners of the world offer ample proof of this truth.

As unconventional monetary policy became standard practice for major central banks over the course of more than a decade, numerous inflation warnings have been flagged. Given the fact that consumer price inflation remained stubbornly low or trended into outright deflation, these warnings were ignored or even ridiculed. In fact, inflation was present the whole time, but it was restricted to asset prices (equities, real estate, art and other assets), rather than more closely watched consumer price indices.

Consumer price inflation didn't rear its ugly head because of various circumstances quite specific to the period of unconventional monetary policy dominance: the rise of China, demographic shifts, and information and computer technology-enhanced consumer power. However, all the while, underlying pressure was unleashed by massive monetary expansion. It was only a matter of time before CPI inflation came to pass, and the COVID-19 pandemic provided exactly that inflationary dynamic. Inflation is covered in greater detail in the next chapter.

Butch Cassidy Syndrome
In 1970, I was fifteen years old. The director of my high school had forbidden students from seeing movies in a theater without parental supervision and promised that those who violated the ban would be

punished severely. His edict made the theater irresistibly attractive to me, so I joined forces with four or five of my high school classmates to sneak into a local theater for our very first movie experience—a daring undertaking. The movie was *Butch Cassidy and the Sundance Kid*, starring Paul Newman as the former and Robert Redford as the latter. It was a great movie, and although I never saw it again, I can still vividly remember certain scenes and lines from the film. But then again, isn't every first experience unforgettable?

The real Butch Cassidy was born in 1866 as Robert LeRoy Parker and died in 1908 after a lifetime of stealing. The thief's story was somewhat sympathetic, so he became a true American legend through the actions of the gang he created, the notorious "Wild Bunch." Bringing Butch Cassidy and his Wild Bunch into the story of the consequences of the policies pursued by central bankers may sound far-fetched. Whatever shortcomings and behavioral handicaps central bankers may exhibit, acting as a "wild bunch" is certainly not among them. But there's a parallel between Butch Cassidy's Wild Bunch and modern central bankers who sit high on the unconventional policy horse. They are acting with the best of intentions for the overall well-being of markets and economies, but central bankers have been stealing from the future and from neighboring countries on a much more massive scale than the Wild Bunch were ever capable of.

First, consider the stealing from the future. A key component of the central bankers' unconventional toolkit has been to systematically hold down interest rates. Short-term market interest rates were held down by bringing the policy rates close to or even below zero and by announcing that they would stay there for a prolonged period of time (i.e., forward guidance). Long-term interest rates were held down through massive asset buying in the QE programs. As a consequence of these actions, *nominal* interest rates and *real* interest rates (i.e., the nominal rates corrected for inflation) have remained very low, or have gone negative in some advanced countries, for many years in a row.

Consistently low nominal and real interest rates have an impact on what economists call the *intertemporal choices* of consumers, investors, and even governments. Translated in layman's language, this means that consistently low interest rates make spending today, whether it's for consumption or investment purposes, more attractive than spending tomorrow, all other elements being equal.[6] *Not* spending today doesn't lead to substantial reward, since the compensation for that delay (i.e., the return you would get on the money saved) is minimal, given the low interest rate. Moreover, spending today is stimulated because the cost of borrowing is low, and low borrowing costs encourage debt accumulation.

These intertemporal choices are also made by governments. Only the interest costs of outstanding public debt figure into annual budgets. Very low or negative interest rates mean that the impact of new debt on the current budget is relatively small or close to zero, so governments take this as an opportunity to reduce pressure on controlling current expenditures and revenues. If interest rates start to increase someday, elected officials figure that they'll probably be out of office by then, and it will be someone else's problem. Never underestimate the incurable short-term bias evident in politics.[7] We will revisit this concept at the end of this chapter in a section on the Sloth Syndrome.

By making spending more attractive than saving, and by reducing the cost of credit and thus stimulating debt accumulation and less-prudent fiscal policies, the unconventional monetary policy toolkit steals from the future. By using QE policies, central bankers are "sucking future demand into the present,"[8] as one analyst rather colorfully phrased it. In 2014, Claudio Borio, chief economist of the BIS, warned unconventional monetary policies "steal growth and prosperity from the future."[9] William White, one of the very few to have explicitly warned of the financial crisis before it came to fruition, called out "a fundamental intertemporal inconsistency arising from the repeated use of monetary easing to stimulate demand."[10]

What is spent today cannot be spent tomorrow. Debt taken on to finance spending today will inevitably reduce spending tomorrow, as that debt must be repaid in the future. Princeton economist Atif Mian and his colleagues, who introduced the concept of "indebted demand," wrote that accommodative monetary policies "generate a debt-financed short-run boom at the expense of indebted demand in the future. When demand is sufficiently indebted, the economy gets stuck in a debt-driven liquidity trap, or *debt trap*."[11] This debt trap, among other things, makes it increasingly difficult for central bankers to walk away from their unconventional monetary policies.

Of course, one of the objectives of these unconventional monetary policies has been to create this intertemporal transfer in order to fill a perceived hole in overall demand.[12] Such policy actions reduce the danger of a recession in the present, but they increase the risk of problems with aggregate demand in the economy further down the line—unless the policies also raise the longer-term growth perspectives of the economies concerned. Higher structural growth *could* lead to higher incomes in the future, which would reduce the effect of debt repayments on aggregate demand, but that result is not expected. Economic theory and empirical research confirm that this result is highly unlikely to occur.

The growth effect of unconventional policies is limited. Empirical studies differ widely in terms of the quantitative growth effect in the short run, but there's broad consensus that the growth effect of these policies is temporary.[13] It's especially worrisome that one of the side effects of very low interest rates is suppression of corporate investment. Indebted demand reduces the attractiveness of investment, because smaller future demand has a negative impact on the profitability of investments. Indebted demand also hurts corporate pension schemes, which weakens future cash flows and further reduces investment potential in the future.

Very low interest rates encourage corporate leadership to reduce investment in another way. If rates are low, companies can borrow on a large scale to finance share buybacks, which raise share prices and thus increase the value of the share options held by those corporate leaders. But these actions also mortgage the future, because a lack of investment now in productive capital means a company will be less competitive in the future.[14] For the last decade, central bankers have pleaded for more structural reforms to stimulate economic growth and investment, largely because most realize that unless a new growth spurt comes along, the indebted demand trap created by unconventional monetary policies will be a serious problem in the future.

The dilemma goes beyond simply stealing from the future: these policies also lead to stealing from neighboring nations. Unconventional monetary policies usually lead to devaluation of the currency of the country or region where such policies are applied. Devaluation as a practical shortcut out of a recessionary or low growth state is probably the oldest trick in the economic policy playbook. Currency depreciation tends to strengthen international competitiveness (at least in the short run), encourage exports, and discourage imports, all of which will stimulate growth, investment, and job creation in the country where the depreciation occurs. But if all countries try to devalue their way out of their problems, nobody will gain anything. Worse yet, everyone stands to lose. Competitive devaluations are prototypical *beggar-thy-neighbor policies* that can lead to political animosity, trade wars, and even real wars among countries.[15]

Substantial evidence has shown that unconventional monetary policies (and QE in particular) lead to currency devaluation.[16] Despite the fact that central bankers have never specifically defined currency devaluation as an objective of their unconventional monetary policies, these policies have produced it nonetheless. During my tenure as Belgium's minister of finance, I spoke with several central bankers who didn't deny that they'd welcomed the effect QE policies had on exchange rates. (Usually ministers of finance like it just fine too.) It's fair to say, then, that this exchange-rate effect isn't really an *unintended* consequence of QE interventions. If demand is weak everywhere, actions that result in currency devaluation in one nation will cause reactions from nations experiencing currency appreciation. When a country tries to steal demand away from its neighbors, even if they're far away, it only succeeds in the (very) short term.

The international effects of unconventional monetary policies go beyond exchange rates alone.[17] They often lead to what Rajan called "competitive monetary easing."[18] When exchange rates rise due to unconventional monetary policies in use by the United States, the

European Union, Japan, and China, many other countries—especially those in emerging markets—feel the squeeze and are obliged to use unconventional monetary policies. As the COVID-19 pandemic raged, unconventional monetary policies were deployed worldwide more than ever before.

The capital inflows that often occur when one country uses QE policies tend to be destabilizing forces in other countries because they are mostly short term and speculative in nature. They flow in quickly on a massive scale, but they usually flow right back out just as quickly. When the leading economic regions of the world use unconventional monetary policies, they steal more than aggregate demand from their neighbors: they also steal away financial stability and mortgage the economic prospects of those neighbors. Central bankers who pursue unconventional monetary policies behave much like Butch Cassidy and his Wild Bunch, just in a more civilized and more subtle way.

Michael Jackson Syndrome

Michael Jackson is among the greatest legends in pop music, but other aspects of Jackson's actions and personality have cast a controversial shadow over his reputation and legacy. Among these less-desirable aspects was Jackson's habit of accumulating debt at a breathtaking pace. Throughout his lifetime, he was recklessly extravagant; despite having earned hundreds of millions of dollars during his career, Jackson was a debt addict. At the time of his death in 2009, Jackson's accumulated debt was estimated at $400 to $500 million, a record among celebrities who have gone down the debt drain.[19]

Michael Jackson is certainly not an ideal representative agent depicted in economists' models, but debt addiction has become a basic characteristic of the worldwide economic model. Given the heights that debt has reached in the last twenty or so years, the threat of the world drowning in debt is more real than ever before.[20] Back in October 1974, the magazine *Businessweek* published a cover story entitled "Debt Economy." Exactly four years later, it published another entitled "New

Debt Economy." Today, such a story might be called "Super Debt Economy" or "Debt Economy: Is There Really No Limit?"

At the end of 2020, the International Finance Institute warned of the "attack of the debt tsunami."[21] Two years earlier, esteemed *Washington Post* commentator Robert J. Samuelson wrote that the global debt burden's "numbers are so large as to be almost incomprehensible."[22] That incomprehensibility was worsened by the COVID-19 pandemic. The OECD estimated that as a consequence of the pandemic, at least $17 trillion would be added to public debt, sending public debt-to-GDP ratios through the roof in many countries.[23] As the pandemic raged on, mentions of "debt explosion" and "debt deluge" were commonplace in the press.

As discussed in Chapter 2, massive leverage was probably the most important driver behind the global financial crisis. Leverage is the expression of debt in terms of the underlying economic reality manifested through, for example, the evolution of GDP or bubble-free asset values. In the years leading up to the financial crisis, inflated asset prices hid the extent of the leverage "sickness." When asset prices started to fall, the sickness turned grave overnight. During and immediately after the financial crisis, it became clear that relentless increases in debt ratios worldwide had to end and needed to be reversed in order to avoid future crises. To put it in technical terms, the world needed a serious dose of *balance sheet de-leveraging*.

Unfortunately, in terms of debt, everything went back to business as usual after the financial crisis subsided. Worse yet, the debt engine shifted into a higher gear. "Global debt surges to highest level in peacetime," read a headline in the *Financial Times* in the autumn of 2019.[24] A few months later, the pandemic sent global debt levels even further into the stratosphere. In remarks made in 2016 on our collective debt addiction, British businessman and academic Adair Turner wrote,

> The [financial crisis] itself was caused by excessive real economy leverage and by multiple deficiencies in the financial system itself; but the main reason recovery has

been slow and weak is not that the financial system is still impaired, but the scale of the debt burden accumulated over the preceding decades…Once economies have too much debt, it seems impossible to get rid of it. All we have done since the 2007–2008 crisis is to shift it around, from the private to the public sector, and from advanced economies to emerging economies, such as China. Total debt to GDP, public and private combined, has continued to grow.[25]

Five years after the end of the crisis, Jaime Caruana, general manager of the BIS, concluded, "There is simply too much debt in the world today."[26] World Bank President David Malpass warned, in emerging countries, "the size, speed, and breadth of the latest debt wave should concern us all."[27] All of these perspectives predate the COVID-19 pandemic, which only made matters much, much worse.

Debt and leverage predate civilization—loans were provided for the planting of seeds as far back as 3000 BC—but never before has the world splurged on debt as in recent decades.[28] As documented in Chapter 2, leverage and debt accumulation accelerated dramatically in the decade prior to the financial crisis, and despite much rhetoric against the buildup, the world just kept on going. Between the end of 2007 and the end of 2017, the overall worldwide debt ratio (debt as a percent of GDP) increased from 179 percent to 217 percent. In nominal terms, overall debt, meaning private and public debt combined, increased from $110 trillion to more than $170 trillion, according to official BIS statistics.[29] The relative increase in debt ratios was largest in emerging countries, where private debt (households and companies) rose dramatically. In a wide-ranging analysis of debt in emerging countries, the World Bank Group concluded that overall debt climbed to $55 trillion by the end of 2018, a climb of 56 percentage points to 170 percent of GDP.[30] China holds more than a third of that $55 trillion in debt.

Some estimates of overall debt are even higher. According to the Institute of International Finance (IIF), a financial industry association, the total overall debt stood at $253 trillion or 322 percent of worldwide GDP at the end of the third quarter of 2019, the highest level on record. Again, this was *before* COVID-19 arrived.[31] The IIF report showed that overall debt in the emerging markets had more than doubled since 2010, and that state-owned enterprises had played a major role in that debt build-up. China dominated both of those developments.

In a November 2020 follow-up report, the IIF showed that the pandemic generated further debt accumulation at an unprecedented pace.[32] It projected that total global debt would increase during 2020 by $15 trillion and reach 365 percent of world GDP (45 percentage points higher than at the end of 2019). The report found the rise of debt levels in emerging markets particularly worrying.

Whatever the exact total may be, overall debt has reached astronomical numbers, certainly since the onset of the pandemic. In comments on the all-time highs in debt load, IMF Managing Director Kristalina Georgieva remarked,

> The bottom line is that high debt burdens have left many governments, companies, and households vulnerable to a sudden tightening of financial conditions…If investor sentiment were to shift, the more vulnerable borrowers could face financial tightening and higher interest costs—and it would be more difficult to repay or roll over debt. This, in turn, could amplify market corrections and intensify capital outflows from emerging markets…High debt is not just a risk to financial stability, it can also become a drag on growth and development efforts.[33]

Even before the pandemic, the IMF voiced great concern about rising corporate debt. Noting the huge increase in corporate debt ratios that has transpired since the financial crisis, it estimated in October 2019 that 40 percent of the corporate debt in eight countries—the United States, China, Japan, Germany, Great Britain, France, Italy, and Spain—would be at risk of default if a downturn half as serious as the financial crisis occurred.[34] The sum at risk represents at least $19 trillion. "A sharp, sudden tightening in financial conditions could unmask these vulnerabilities and put pressures on asset price valuations," two senior IMF officials commented.[35]

The IMF's worries about the evolution of worldwide corporate debt were echoed by the BIS in its 2019 annual report, which showed particular concern about the collateralized loan obligation (CLO) market that has exploded in volume since the financial crisis ended. It's not hard to see parallels between this CLO market and the collateralized debt obligations (CDOs) that contributed to the severity of the financial crisis. And again, this is where things stood before the pandemic made the situation much more perilous.

Central bankers' unconventional monetary policies have worsened the leverage and debt situation that brought about the worst financial crisis since World War II. According to Hans Mikkelsen, credit strategist at Bank of America, "The chosen solution to a debt crisis is more debt."[36] Fed Chairman Jerome Powell claimed during the pandemic that the Fed was "still putting out the fire," but they were doing so by pouring gasoline on it.[37] *Financial Times* commentator Gillian Tett remarked early in 2020, before the pandemic became widespread beyond China, that the policies amounted to "a deluge of central bank petrol."[38] Another *Financial Times* piece later that year stated, "Central banks…[got]… caught in a leverage trap of their own making."[39]

These statements are somewhat unfair, as Thornton and Bagehot agreed, and history has proven, that in a crisis, central bankers must pull out all the stops to avoid an implosion of the financial system and a true depression in the real economy. They undoubtedly made major mistakes in the years leading up to the financial crisis, but as lenders of last resort, central bankers acted as they should have once the crises began to spread. The suddenness and intensity of the pandemic obliged the central banks to double down on their usage of the unconventional monetary toolbox. But the fact remains when these unconventional monetary policies are extended over a prolonged period of time, an already precarious overall leverage and debt situation will worsen further.

Now, the world economy is more addicted to debt than ever before. The volume of credit creation and debt accumulation needed to produce a 1 percent increase in GDP rises every year. This dependency on higher and higher levels of leverage and debt ratios makes the world economy and its markets increasingly vulnerable, since sudden shocks become more likely in such an environment. The effects of these sudden shocks and stops also reverberate more quickly and intensely throughout the system, as everything is much more interconnected. Financial stability has been undermined by policies created to combat a crisis caused by high leverage and rising debt ratios—much like energetically digging a deep hole in the ground and then, after stumbling into the hole, deciding to dig an even deeper hole to get out of the first hole. In 1940, the legendary folk singer Woody Guthrie wrote a song called "The Jolly Banker," with the lyric, "If you show you need it, I'll let you have credit." The logic of central bankers' unconventional monetary policies is that credit is shoveled down everyone's throat, whether they need it or not.

How far can it go? Herbert Stein, chairman of the Council of Economic Advisors under US Presidents Nixon and Ford, once said before the Joint Economic Committee of the US Congress, "I recently came to a remarkable conclusion which I commend to you, and that is that if something cannot go on forever it will stop. So, what we have learned about these things is that the federal debt cannot rise forever relative to GDP."[40] His quote has subsequently been boiled down to an economics rule known as Stein's law—"If something cannot go on forever, it will stop." When Stein spoke these words in 1976, US federal debt stood at 33 percent of GDP. At the end of 2018, it reached 106 percent of GDP. In Japan, public debt was around 50 percent of GDP in 1976. At the end of 2018, it reached 238 percent of GDP.

It's worth contemplating what Stein would think of those enormous numbers, and what he'd think about a former Bank of Japan Policy Board member's reflection that "Japan may be entering a new norm."[41] In the same vein, consider the question posed at the end of 2019 by Kristalina Georgieva, "Is it possible that debt levels that were deemed too high in the past are acceptable?"[42] Well, maybe or maybe not. Nobody knows for sure.

David Copperfield Syndrome

I've discussed a long-gone legend, Butch Cassidy, and one who departed relatively recently, Michael Jackson. Next, I'll turn to a still-living legend: David Copperfield. I'm not speaking of the protagonist of the Dickens classic of the same name, but instead the magician David Seth Kotkin, better known by his stage name David Copperfield. Just as Copperfield makes things (and himself) disappear, unconventional monetary policies have made substantial amounts of people's savings disappear, if not literally than certainly in terms of the purchasing power of every dollar, euro, or yen they save. The mystic hand of central bankers has orchestrated an astonishing disappearing act: a clear-cut case of financial repression leading to a massive transfer of financial resources from savers to the government.[43]

Copperfield was born in New Jersey in 1956, but he has long made his home and his living in Las Vegas. *Forbes* magazine named Copperfield "the Houdini in the desert…the most commercially successful magician in history."[44] His mind-boggling illusions—including the disappearances of a Learjet, the Statue of Liberty, and an Orient Express dining car—have earned him twenty-one Emmy Awards and eleven Guinness World Records. The US Library of Congress named him a Living Legend in 2009. Perhaps central bankers are in line for some of these awards as well, given their gift for making money disappear.

I'll share an example from my own country, Belgium. Most Belgians are exemplary but conservative savers. Stashing money in a safe, traditional savings account is the most popular way to put money aside. By the end of 2019, a total of €300 billion—equal to roughly 70 percent of Belgium's GDP—was outstanding in Belgian savings accounts. A back-of-the-envelope calculation indicates that since the start of unconventional monetary policies, the real purchasing power loss for each euro in those savings account was at least 15 percent—a truly impressive figure.[45] This loss is attributable to the consistently low interest rates set by the ECB, which have placed strong downward pressure on credit and debit rates of financial institutions. That's nice for debtors who can take advantage of low debit rates, but it's terrible for savers. Interest rate policies applied since the financial crisis have been nothing less than a tax on savers and a subsidy for borrowers.

The same is true for Germany. Germans have a long-standing aversion toward debt. (Look no further than the German word *schuld*, which can mean debt, guilt, or blame.) As of December 2020, German citizens held a dazzling €2.4 trillion in savings accounts, and the loss of real purchasing power of the money held in those accounts is similar to the 15 percent registered in Belgium. So far, German banks have refrained from charging negative interest rates on savings accounts, but if negative central bank policy rates don't go away, banks and savings institutions will have no choice but to pass these negative rates on to the holders of savings accounts.[46] Such a move would really be a shock to Germans and Belgians alike. A few weeks before he left the ECB, the popular German tabloid *Bild* characterized Draghi as "Count Draghila" sucking the life out of German savers' hard-earned money.[47] The more serious weekly *Der Spiegel* articulated the sentiment a bit less aggressively: *"Wenn Sparen arm macht,"* which is best translated as "when saving makes you poor."[48]

Unfortunately, people with relatively modest savings suffer the most under these circumstances. Those who have more money are generally also more sophisticated in financial matters and have the means and know-how to move their money into vehicles that provide better yields. It's undeniable, then, that central banks' unconventional monetary policies also reinforce inequality. In the words of Karen Petrou, managing partner at Federal Financial Analytics, "Low interest rates are the scourge of the poor and the vulnerable…Most households have no hope of accumulating savings, they are better off being profligate…Low rates are tough on vulnerable households; negative rates are brutal."[49] I'll return to the inequality consequences of unconventional monetary policies later in this chapter.[50]

There are also negative intergenerational aspects to the savings dilemma. *Washington Post* columnist Allan Sloan summarized this as follows, "Having retirees who've saved for decades subsidize borrowers is a wealth transfer."[51] Chris Martenson, the co-founder of PeakProsperity.com, argued that the Fed's policies "throw granny under the bus because the program boils down to taking from savers and fixed-income recipients and transferring that purchasing power to other entities."[52] In Chapter 4's section "On the QE Track," I mentioned that a prominent group of former senior European central bankers heavily criticized Draghi's September 2019 stimulus package. In their argument, they noted that as a consequence of the unconventional monetary policies, "the young generations consider themselves deprived of an opportunity to provide for their old age through safe interest-bearing investments." They concluded that such policies "create serious social tensions."[53]

David Copperfield's entertaining illusions have brought him fame and fortune. It remains to be seen how central bankers' disappearing acts will work out for them. When central banks make saved money disappear, it's no illusion, and its consequences go beyond the financial, economic, and social arenas. In the spring of 2016, former German minister of finance Wolfgang Schäuble declared that Draghi bore significant responsibility for the rise of the far-right AfD party in German elections: "I'm not happy with low interest rates…I said to Mario Draghi…be very proud: you can attribute 50 percent of the results of a party that seems to be new and successful in Germany to the design of his policy."[54] Although Schäuble later walked back his comments, he maintained that the effects of the ECB's monetary policies will lead to greater popularity for extremist parties. All over the Western world, substantial parts of the electorate have deserted established centrist parties and politicians in favor of populists and extremists. Frustrations among frugal savers who feel they are being unfairly treated are part of the cause.

Semper Augustus Syndrome
It's only a small leap of logic to go from the illusions of David Copperfield to a centuries-old story about a moment in time when beautiful flowers

performed a magic act on human behavior. During the seventeenth century, the land now known as the Netherlands was one of the most prosperous countries in the world, and its capital, Amsterdam, was a center of wealth. The flower known as the tulip, which originated in Turkey, was a symbol of high status in Dutch society, as they were available in much more intense colors than other flowers of that era. Demand for tulip bulbs skyrocketed, and the rest, as they say, is history. A huge speculation developed as reduced supplies collided with feverish and even manic demand. Prices began a spectacular rise in 1634, and by the start of 1637, they had reached astronomical numbers—an average tulip bulb was valued at ten times the annual salary of a craftsman, and in one case, a bulb of the sought-after Semper Augustus variety was traded for twelve acres of prime land. But in February 1637, the tulip bubble (better known as the Tulip Mania) collapsed.

In the movie *Wall Street: Money Never Sleeps,* Gordon "greed is good" Gekko, masterfully performed by Michael Douglas, describes the tulip mania as "The greatest bubble story of all time...Back in the 1600s, the Dutch got speculation fever to the point that one could buy a beautiful house on the canal in Amsterdam for the price of one bulb...Then it collapsed...People got wiped out."

Some were wiped out, to be sure, but overall, damage to the Dutch economy was limited.[55] The main reason was that the speculative excesses of the tulip mania weren't driven by leverage and a glut of debt; the same was true of the dot-com bubble of the late 1990s. Other major financial excesses—the US stock market frenzy of the 1920s, the Japanese real estate and stock market bubble of the 1980s, and the bubbles leading to the 2007–2009 global financial crisis—were highly destructive because they were fueled by extreme leverage and debt.

Unconventional monetary policies have led to persistent, very low or negative short- and long-term interest rates. When adjusted for inflation, real interest rates in the advanced world have been in mostly negative territory for years now. This reality encourages debt accumulation and leverage, since the cost of debt is low. Forward guidance has indicated that these policies will continue, creating a frantic search for yield.[56]

When low-risk interest-bearing assets can't provide an acceptable return, investors start looking elsewhere. Of course, getting people to spend and invest in riskier assets is among the objectives of these unconventional monetary policies, but things can get out of hand. Debt-driven bubbles, modern versions of the Tulip Mania, are right around the corner in circumstances such as these.

With interest rates stuck at or close to zero, investors' relentless search for yield has produced a long list of potential bubble areas. For example, in the middle of 2019, the American financial magazine *Barron's* identified "ten market bubbles just waiting to pop: US government debt, US corporate debt, US leveraged loans, European debt, BoJ balance sheet and related equity holdings, unprofitable IPOs,[57] cryptocurrencies and cannabis, growth and momentum stocks, software and cloud stocks, and exchange-traded funds."[58] While it's questionable whether some items on this list are in fact bubbles, real estate developments in some countries and art investments could arguably be added to the list. Shortly after the publication of the *Barron's* list, bubble expert Robert Shiller, the 2013 winner of the Nobel Prize in economics and author of the book *Irrational Exuberance*,[59] remarked, "I see bubbles everywhere."[60]

Today, almost fifteen years after central banks began deploying their unconventional monetary policies, the signs of bubble-reinforcing circumstances and attitudes are everywhere: rising levels of debt and leverage; extremely low interest rates; strongly reduced credit spreads; continuously softening credit terms ("funding is even cheaper today than during the pre-crisis credit bubble," the *Financial Times* noted early in 2020);[61] feverish merger and acquisition activity; high levels of speculative IPOs and share buy-backs by companies; spectacular growth of shadow bank activities; equity valuations that are way out of line with historic price/earnings ratios;[62] exuberant venture capital investments; and unusual activity in unorthodox investment areas, like art and specific raw materials. Despite all these signs, recognition and acknowledgment of bubbles remains a delicate and complicated issue. In an October 2019 *Forbes* magazine article, Gary Mishuris wrote, "Even the best investors in the world, Warren Buffett and Charlie Munger, did not fully realize the extent of the bubbles that they were in during either the late 1990s, nor the run-up to the Great Financial Crisis."[63]

When central bankers intensified their unconventional policies following the spread of the COVID-19 pandemic, the disconnect between what was happening in the real economy and in the financial markets reached mind-boggling proportions. For example, on December 9, 2020, the vacation rental company Airbnb went public. Its share price immediately went through the roof, bringing its market valuation to $87 billion two days after the IPO—more than twice the market valuation of Marriott, the world's leading hotel group, despite the fact that Airbnb posted a net loss of $674 million in 2019. Shortly before the Airbnb IPO, the market capitalization of DoorDash, the restaurant delivery company that hemorrhages losses, shot to $70 billion. "The IPO frenzy continues," the *Financial Times* commented dryly.[64] The market value of the video conferencing service Zoom exceeded that of either Exxon Mobil or IBM. The striking discrepancies between the real-life experiences of ordinary people struggling through the pandemic and this kind of financial lunacy has generated tremendous unease and even anger within societies. The IMF reported its own tongue-in-cheek conclusion that the behavior of the markets was "reflecting in part investor expectations of continued policy support."[65]

Read recent IMF Global Financial Stability (GFS) Reports and you'll find warnings of bubble dangers all over the place, although these warnings are generally rather veiled. In the October 2019 GFS Report, the IMF cautioned, "Easy financial conditions are encouraging financial-risk taking and are fueling a further buildup of vulnerabilities in some sectors and countries…Against the backdrop of easy financial conditions, stretched valuations in some markets, and elevated vulnerabilities, medium-term risks to global growth and financial stability continue to be firmly skewed to the downside."[66]

After the pandemic began, these warnings gained even more relevance. In its October 2020 GFS Report, the IMF warned that in terms of global financial stability, "vulnerabilities are rising…in the nonfinancial corporate sector…and in the sovereigns sector…

Corporate liquidity pressures may morph into insolvencies…While the global banking sector is well capitalized, there is a weak tail of banks." The report went on to plead for "stepping-up prudential supervision to contain excessive risk-taking in a lower-for-longer interest-rate environment."[67] In a note to its clients in September 2020, Deutsche Bank was more explicit than the IMF: "We see an increasing risk of financial disruption down the road…[from]…the growing overvaluation of assets and mounting debt levels."[68]

There is strong evidence that unconventional monetary policies have significantly contributed to increased risk-taking behavior as investors search the world for yield.[69] Monetary policymakers now recognize this reality. Robert Kaplan, president of the Dallas Fed, remarked that he believed very low interest rates were "contributing to elevated risk evaluations, and I think we ought to be sensitive to that."[70] Yves Mersch, a member of the executive board of the ECB, expressed concern early in 2020 that "the increase in asset and housing prices is excessive and results from the exceptionally long period of extremely accommodative monetary policy…There is substantial empirical evidence that monetary policy encourages risk-taking in the financial system and that the risks of an asset price correction are increasing."[71]

One of the most amazing things to surface has been the phenomenon of negative-yielding debt. Bonds and other securities bearing a negative interest rate hardly existed before 2015, but by mid-2016, the volume of outstanding sub-zero debt climbed to $12 trillion. It fell to around $8 trillion before beginning to climb again as of early 2019. A new peak was reached toward the end of 2020, with negative-yielding debt representing a total of $18 trillion—27 percent of the world's investment-grade debt and more than 20 percent of world GDP. Bloomberg News interpreted this most remarkable phenomenon of a huge pile of negative-yielding debt as "a sign that demand for havens is just as intense as that for riskier assets."[72] Reputed investor and commentator James Grant of the Interest Rate Observer said of the trillions of dollars in subzero debt, "There has been nothing like it in 4,000 years."[73]

Despite the intense search for yield, investors are still rushing into negative-yielding bonds, or at least they're not running away from them. I am currently serving as the chairman of the Committee on Budgets of the European Parliament, and a hedge fund manager who came to meet with me in 2020 in that capacity made rather blunt comments to that effect: "We still buy bonds because we see central banks continue to buy bonds, so prices of bonds can be expected to go up further, offering a nice profit opportunity despite the negative yield effect."[74] JP Morgan Asset Management's messaging was blunt as well: "Central banks have recast themselves from the investor's foe to the investor's friend."[75] When central banks started to buy corporate bonds during the pandemic, Barnaby Martin, head of European strategy at Bank of America, noted that market demand for corporate bonds was exceptionally high because of the "liquidity backstop that central banks have put in place... [Investors]...feel that central banks have their back."[76] The safety net provided by central banks produces massive amounts of moral hazard: investors go for income, pure and simple, leaving all the risk up to the central banks. Unconventional monetary policies have undeniably led to systemic mispricing of credit risk—or more accurately, systemic *underpricing* of risk.

It's obvious that central banks have boxed themselves into a corner, since stopping or even substantially reducing asset purchase programs will lead to major selloffs in the bond market—when central banks purchases of bonds stop, bond prices will fall—and rising interest rates. "By their aggressive actions over the last decade," remarked Jim Reid, a research strategist at Deutsche Bank, "central banks have effectively trapped themselves into continually intervening in government bond markets. They're arguably beyond the point of no return."[77] Gillian Tett of the *Financial Times* concurred: "We are starting a new decade with a financial system and investor base that is hooked on central bank support to a greater degree than we have ever seen before."[78]

The pandemic only made matters worse. In the midst of it, Matt King, an analyst at Citibank, concluded, "The more central banks drive real yield down and valuations in risk assets up, the more they will need to keep buying just to keep them there."[79] If there ever was a catch-22 trap, this is it.

The Shadow World

The spectacular growth of shadow banking activities in the wake of the financial crisis has been both a consequence and a driver of the frantic search by investors for yield. Lehman Brothers and other big American investment banks all belonged to the shadow banking sector at the time of the financial crisis. The Financial Stability Board (FSB), established by a decision at the G-20 Summit in 2009, redefined the shadow banking phenomenon as *non-bank financial intermediation*, probably because the latter description sounds somewhat less suspicious.[80] The term *markets-based finance* has also gained traction as an alternative name for shadow banking.

Both markets-based finance and non-bank financial intermediation describe shadow banking activities well because, in the words of Bernanke, shadow banking "comprises a diverse set of institutions and markets that, collectively, carry out traditional banking functions—but to do so outside, or in ways only loosely linked to, the traditional system of regulatory depository institutions. Examples of important components of the shadow banking system include securitization vehicles, asset-backed commercial paper conduits, money market funds, markets for repurchase agreements, investment banks, and mortgage companies."[81] Of course, the breathtaking speed of innovation in the fintech sphere— that is, the newest computerized and communication technology applied to financial services—has created "a bonanza that will reshape finance" and that will significantly affect not only what transpires in the shadow banking sector but also in more traditional banking outfits.[82]

The growth of the shadows of the financial system has been spectacular. By the end of 2018, the broadest definition of the shadow bank sector—that it encompasses all institutions that are not central banks, insurance companies, pension funds, or public financial institutions—managed $114 trillion in assets, which constitutes a third of all financial assets worldwide.[83] A narrower definition places the number at $51 trillion. Investment group BlackRock is probably the largest of the shadow banks, with $7 trillion assets under management. Since 2010, shadow banking has grown by roughly 75 percent and traditional banking has grown by 35 percent, so the relative importance of shadow banking has increased substantially. The United States is still by far the most important shadow bank market, but China and also India are catching up fast, leading William White to conclude that the development of shadow banking in those nations "is now a major source of concern."[84] Activities in the shadow bank sector have spread to all financial activities, including mortgage, consumer, and corporate lending, as well as securitization and derivatives trading.

Since shadow bank activities are much less regulated—if at all—than the traditional banking sector (they operate, so to speak, in the shadows of the regulatory regime), extreme leverage and systemic risks can accumulate more easily. There are several links between shadow and traditional banks, including credit lines, investor relationships, and co-financing of transactions. Shadow bank activity also tends to promote market and asset price volatility, as most shadow bank vehicles offer investors the opportunity to withdraw money whenever they wish.

Most importantly, most shadow banks do not have direct access to central bank refinancing. This leaves them vulnerable to severe liquidity shocks, given that they often show extreme maturity mismatches between the asset and liability sides of their balance sheets. A lack of access to central bank funding can lead to fire sales of assets in times of trouble, which exacerbates the initial problems given the many links between shadow banks and the traditional financial sector.[85] Moreover, there is more room in the shadow banking system to "hide" loss-making positions than in the regulated banking sector.

This spectacular growth of the shadow banking system was spurred in part by the very low interest rate environment that has persisted due to continued use of unconventional monetary policies. But changes to the regulation of the traditional banking sector, especially the increase in capital requirements imposed after the financial crisis, was at least as great a contributor to the growth. Thus, it's unfair to blame central bankers alone for the risky rise of shadow banks (although many central banks do play significant regulatory roles).

There is no doubt, however, that the spectacular rise in shadow bank activities has played an important role in a relentless rise in leverage and debt worldwide. In the same context, shadow banking has also contributed significantly to the growth of a wide variety of complex derivatives-based strategies that aim for higher profits but inevitably create more risk in the markets.

When the COVID-19 pandemic struck, Tobias Adrian, head of the IMF's markets department, sounded the alarm bell when he noted, "Today's crisis is primarily a health crisis, but the size of it has led to an economic crisis, and that could in turn become a financial crisis."[86] The traditional banking sector has been much better capitalized and more strictly regulated due to regulatory changes made after the financial crisis, but it's obvious that when the next financial crisis eventually arrives, the shadow banking sector will probably be at its epicenter. According to Mark Sobel, chairman of the Official Monetary and Financial Institutions Forum, "Non-banks are the hole in the regulatory system we never dealt with."[87]

Savior-Turned-Bully Syndrome

As the story of negative consequences unfolds, there is room next to Butch Cassidy, Michael Jackson, David Copperfield, and beautiful seventeenth-century tulips for saviors and bullies, most certainly when they come together as one. Central bankers contributed to the negative environment that made the financial crisis such a terrible experience, but it can't be denied that once the crisis was underway, they assumed their role of lender of last resort straight from the Thornton and Bagehot playbook. When the pandemic struck, they once again stepped up and acted quickly and decisively to avert disaster.

Central bankers saved the world from destructive implosions of the financial system, and they also became the saviors of major parts of it. The policies they put in place during the financial crisis saved the banking sector from widespread bankruptcies and their major shareholders from financial extinction. Insurance companies and pension funds received substantial relief from central bank policies—particularly from their support of asset prices, as these assets figured prominently on their balance sheets. However, once the acute phase of the crisis was over, these branches of the economy began to perceive central bankers' insistence on continuation of a low interest rate environment in a different and less sympathetic way. To banks, insurance companies, and pension funds, central bankers have transformed in a few years' time from saviors into bullies.

Banks are *maturity transformers*. The money at their disposal comes from four sources: their shareholders' capital, the deposits they receive from the public, the proceeds from sales of debt securities, and the short-term wholesale funding they raise in the market. Apart from their shareholders' capital, most of these funding resources are short term. Deposits, for example, can be withdrawn at any moment, and the same is true for most of the short-term wholesale funding. Yet significant differences exist among banks in terms of the relative importance of each of these funding categories. European banks rely much more heavily on client deposits than their American counterparts.

Banks use the funding they attract to extend loans, to invest in (mostly government) bonds, and to hold portfolios of other assets, such as derivatives and liquid assets. Most of these redeployments of funding resources are for the longer term. Thus, banks are first and foremost maturity transformers: they transform short-run money in longer-run investments. This transformation is the major contribution, and a very important one, that banks make to economic growth and overall welfare. However, the *maturity mismatch* inherent in banking activities also makes them vulnerable to liquidity shortages—particularly in the case of a bank run, which central banks must attend to as lenders of last resort.[88]

Initially, banks benefited from the low interest rate environment. Since their funding was largely short term, the cost of that funding could be adjusted downward quickly. The redeployments were mostly longer term, so they were more resilient against the drop in interest rates—only new loans carried the lower rates. Thus, the intermediation margin of banks—the difference between the interest received on their loan portfolios and other assets and the interest payable on their funding amalgam—initially improved. However, the longer (very) low interest rates stick around, the smaller this margin advantage becomes. Under the pressure of sharpened competition on the funding and redeployment sides, the impact on the intermediation margin eventually turned negative. When policy rates are negative, the margin risks becoming a millstone around the necks of banks, for two reasons.

First, it's hard for banks to impose negative rates on their deposit holders. There is substantial opposition to such a move in society at large, and people would withdraw their deposits from banks if it did happen. It's better to stick money under a mattress than leave it in a bank that literally takes some of it away—exactly what happens with negative interest rates. Since they are afraid of the public's reaction to a negative interest rate on deposits, banks are confronted with a zero lower bound on deposits.

Second, as lending rates on new loans declined—competition certainly played a role in this—many banks compensated for the loss in revenue by increasing lending volumes. An overall push toward more lending, which is contagious across the sector, led to the loosening of lending standards and the stimulation of lending for mergers and acquisitions, share buybacks, and real estate. Some have described this as financial institutions *gambling for resurrection*.[89] Given this, banks are increasingly vulnerable to shocks, whether from a weakened economy, a depression-like situation like the one caused by the pandemic, or a sudden rise in interest rates.[90] This last factor hits banks very hard, since it reverses the advantage they enjoyed early on in the low interest rate period.

The unconventional monetary policies of major central banks of the world hits banks even harder because of the tremendous increase in competition brought about by the digital revolution. All the technology giants—Google, Apple, Facebook, Amazon, Microsoft, Tencent, and Alibaba—and an endless stream of fintech start-ups have made deep inroads into banks' traditional lines of business. The bullying of the central banks—that is, consistently very low interest rates and negative policy rates that weigh heavily on their profitability—make it more difficult for them to react appropriately to new competitors. For banks, it's a double whammy.

If banks are suffering under the consequences of unconventional monetary policies, what about insurance companies and pension funds, institutions that are already under pressure as the population ages? In 2015, the OECD noted that for these institutions, "the outlook is troubling as their solvency positions will deteriorate unless they have actively adopted risk management strategies."[91] Like every other company, the balance sheets of these institutions have two sides, assets and liabilities. The return on the assets on their balance sheets must be high enough for them to fulfill their obligations on their liability side. The liabilities of insurance companies are the claims they face and the payouts they owe to their clients; for pension funds, they are the benefits their clients have a right to. Quite often, the claims and benefits are guaranteed, a complicating factor if and when the return on assets consistently falls under downward pressure.

Investment-grade bonds and securities have long since been the pillars on which the business models of insurance companies and pension funds used to be built. Such bonds made up a large part, if not even a major part, of the asset allocation of these institutions. The returns on these bonds were an important contributor to the revenue insurance companies and pension funds needed, but since the 2007–2009 global financial crisis and the subsequent persistence of unconventional monetary policies, the returns to these bonds melted away like snow before the sun. COVID-19-induced monetary policy action only reinforced this development. The impact of the unconventional monetary policy measures has obliged insurance companies and pension funds to adjust their asset allocation with the aim of getting to higher returns. In an early warning, the OECD showed great concern about "the extent to which pension funds and insurance companies have, or might become, involved in an excessive 'search for yield' in an attempt to match the level of returns promised to beneficiaries or policyholders."[92] Inevitably, a higher exposure to riskier and less liquid assets followed.[93]

Insurance companies and pension funds are now much more active in venture capital, private equity, equity and derivative trading, corporate credit, and real estate than ever before. Higher valuations in bond and equity markets can and did save the day for the present, but remember Stein's law—this cannot and will not go on forever. As a consequence of their changed asset allocation positions, insurance companies and pension funds are much more vulnerable to an economic downturn or to changes of sentiment in the markets. According to Rick Rieder, chief investment officer of BlackRock, "Pension funds can't match their liabilities with where rates are today, so they have to hope that equity markets will continue to rally."[94]

This increased vulnerability is a consequence of unconventional monetary policies. At the same time, it makes continuation of those policies almost a necessity. The celebrated bond trader Bill Gross noted in 2017, "Central banks may be trapped in QE forever."[95] It's reminiscent of a line in "Hotel California," a classic pop song by the legendary band Eagles. "You can check out anytime you like, but you can never leave."

"26 = 3.8 Billion" Syndrome

The list of unintended consequences of the unconventional monetary policy toolkit is long: stealing wealth, income, and jobs from the future and the neighbors; stimulating the accumulation of leverage and debt; punishing savers; contributing to a frantic search for yield (and thus spurring major asset bubbles); a spectacular expansion of shadow banking; and bullying the traditional financial sector. Atop that impressive list are three more consequences with far-reaching impact: an increase in wealth inequality; the structural weakness of productivity growth through the impact of "zombie" companies and banks; and disincentivizing political decision-makers to set sound policies and create structural reforms.

While poverty rates have declined worldwide, *inequality* has been on the rise.[96] Poverty and inequality are not the same thing, and it's important to avoid simplistic, erroneous conclusions when it comes to the matter of inequality.[97] There's also an important qualifier that must be noted—while inequality *within* countries is on the rise, inequality *among* countries is declining in a relatively spectacular way.[98] Of course, the pandemic and its dire social and economic consequences have had an important and, unfortunately, negative impact on inequality in many countries. While the impact of the pandemic must not be underestimated, the matters at hand are the consequences of the unconventional monetary measures used to combat the consequences of the pandemic and the financial crisis.[99]

Even before the pandemic, inequality was already a major issue, especially after the financial crisis. People were understandably enraged when stories surfaced about the fabulous salaries, bonuses, and commissions people working in finance received for setting up irresponsible or sometimes fraudulent financial constructs that ended in disaster. As it became clear that many wealthy individuals and businesses successfully avoided paying their fair share of taxes, the discontent grew.[100] All this anger and frustration gave birth to the Occupy Wall Street movement and other grassroots organizations focused on inequality, and it has driven many voters to get behind populist and extremist parties and politicians.

The recent attention paid to inequality isn't surprising, given that the twenty-six richest people in the world hold as much wealth among them as the 3.8 billion people who make up the poorer half of the world's population.[101] In the United States, the three richest people—Bill Gates, Jeff Bezos, and Warren Buffett—own as much wealth as the poorer half of the US population.[102] Inequality is unavoidable, and in a well-functioning market economy, it is even desirable, but there are limits to arguments in defense of inequality.[103] In most discussions regarding the drivers of inequality, issues like globalization, technological innovation, and tax policies are generally cited.[104] Should unconventional monetary policies be added to this list? That would be a real game changer, since monetary policy is generally considered to contribute to income *equality* given its mandate to dampen the consequences of the business cycle's ups and downs.

There are two sides to the story regarding unconventional monetary policies and equality. First, there's no denying the fact that central bankers and the policies they pursued were crucial in preventing both the financial crisis and the pandemic from progressing into total economic calamities. Income and wealth inequality would have been much worse had that come to pass, as a prolonged depression hits the lower ends of the income and wealth distribution the most. Furthermore, the unconventional monetary policies contributed to the recovery from the financial crisis in terms of economic activity and job creation, and they also kept inflation (and deflation) at bay. But as previously discussed, the impact of these policies on economic growth tends to diminish considerably as time goes on, which brings us back to the dangers of growing inequality.

Second, the impact of the unconventional monetary policies on asset prices is undeniable. Housing prices, equity notations, and bond prices, as well as all the other assets that have been frantically sought after in investors' quest for yield, have all gone up substantially over the last decade. For example, while the real economy tanked during the pandemic, high-tech stocks climbed dramatically in value. In the United States, financial wealth is much more unevenly distributed among households and individuals than in Europe.[105] Since equities and bonds are commonly held by wealthier people, increases in their value tend to widen wealth inequalities. In Europe, only small fractions of citizens own bonds (4.6 percent), publicly traded shares (8.8 percent), and mutual funds (9.4 percent), but almost every household holds deposits (97.2 percent).[106]

Which of these two sides dominates the distributional effects of unconventional monetary policies? There's no straightforward answer to this question. Studies performed by central banks tend to see the first effect (more activity, more jobs, more income) dominating the second, which makes it easier for them to reject the claim that their policies increase inequality.[107] Yet some academic studies show the opposite.[108] The answer, then, is nuanced.[109] Unconventional monetary policies helped reduce income and wealth inequality by avoiding major financial collapses and by stimulating recovery. Yet the effect of these policies on asset prices increased wealth inequality, since those who already had more assets became proportionally richer.

That being said, as the growth effect tends to fade away over time, the impact of continued low interest rates and asset purchase programs on asset prices dominates the impact of these policies on inequality. An abrupt asset price collapse would work in the other direction, of course, but then again, such a collapse would negatively impact the economy and would once again worsen conditions for the poorer segment of society. But most of all, you cannot underestimate the effect of *sentiment* in this context. Among the general public, the consensus is that unconventional monetary policies create advantages for certain groups (investment bankers, real estate owners, and so on) that are already considered privileged. These feelings of unjustness and unfairness are destructive forces, harming social cohesion and feeding political extremism.[110]

Zombie Syndrome

The Zombie Syndrome is next to last in the list of unintended consequences of unconventional monetary policies. Paul Krugman, winner of the 2008 Nobel Prize in Economics, framed the argument back in 1990, when he claimed, "Productivity isn't everything, but in the long run, it is almost everything."[111] There are echoes of the insights of the father of modern economics, Adam Smith, in Krugman's assertion that a country's ability to improve the standard of living of its population depends almost entirely on its ability to raise the output per worker or the output per hour worked, as these yardsticks are the most sensible measures of productivity. So how are unconventional monetary policies related to the evolution of productivity? More specifically, how do these policies negatively impact productivity? This story is all about the walking dead—in the words of *The Economist,* "the corporate undead."[112]

First, let's examine the data. Productivity is seemingly on a long-run downward path in advanced countries. For the OECD as a whole, productivity, as measured by the compound annual growth rate of real GDP per hour worked, declined from 3 percent between 1971 and 1996 to 2 percent between 1997 and 2004. Between 2005 and 2016, it sagged even further, to 0.8 percent.[113] This downward pattern in productivity is quite similar across the United States, Japan, and European nations. Several factors are at work here, but the role of unconventional monetary policies in this negative evolution of productivity is well documented.[114] Zombies play a central role in the fall of productive growth.

The concept of zombie firms was first used in an analysis of Japan's "lost decade" of stagnation. Productivity came to a standstill when distressed banks failed to foreclose on unprofitable and highly indebted companies, known as "zombie firms."[115] The broad definition is a company that is unable to cover its debt-servicing costs from current profits for a period of at least three consecutive years. A narrower definition adds the condition of meager potential for future growth.[116] According to the broad definition, the share of companies that qualify as zombies rose steadily from 4 percent of all firms in the late 1980s to 15 percent in 2017. By the narrower definition, the share of zombie companies rose from 3.5 percent in the mid-1990s to 8 percent in 2016. Over the same period, the probability of remaining a zombie firm after the three-year term rose dramatically.[117]

Data on the evolution of the volume and quality of corporate debt corroborate these zombie statistics. Not only has total corporate debt and business sector credit increased substantially since the financial crisis, the overall quality of debt and credit has significantly deteriorated at the same time, particularly in the United States, China, and major European nations, such as Italy, Spain, and the United Kingdom. The IMF has estimated that the share of speculative-grade debt among total corporate sector debt is close to 50 percent in China and the United States, and even higher in those three European countries.[118] In early 2020, the ratio of net debt to operating profits stood at 2.2 across the S&P 500—more than twice the level of the ratio in 2008.[119] The COVID-19 pandemic forced many companies to run down their cash reserves and increase debt to the point where solvency became an issue. Almost overnight, this massive increase in corporate leverage and indebtedness became a systemic risk.

Credit quality is also under pressure. This is especially true in Europe, where bank loans still make up 80 percent of all corporate external financing; in the United States, they stand at 20 percent.[120] The European Commission estimated that by mid-2019, European banks were still carrying close to €800 billion in non-performing loans.[121] In November 2020, the ECB warned that under a severe—but not at all unlikely—scenario, European banks would have to face an additional €1.4 trillion in non-performing loans, a truly mind-boggling figure.[122] Banks, especially the weaker ones, often *extend and pretend* loans in order to avoid a restructuring that might end in a capital shortfall. In effect, zombie companies are kept alive by zombie banks. In the Savior-Turned-Bully Syndrome section, I referred to this phenomenon as *gambling for resurrection*, but it is sometimes called *evergreening*.

Do unconventional monetary policies contribute to the zombification of companies? The answer is yes, for two main reasons. First, very low interest rates stimulate debt accumulation, and over time, they also lead to a weakening of the conditions imposed on borrowers. It's remarkable that the growth in the relative share of zombie companies in the overall corporate economy began to increase significantly when central banks shifted to a pattern of consistently low policy interest rates. When long-term interest rates dropped as well following the financial crisis, thanks to the central banks' asset purchase programs, the increase in the share of zombies accelerated. This tendency was intensified by the pandemic-induced acceleration in the use of unconventional monetary policies. Second, weaker banks in the EU were greatly assisted by the ECB's asset purchases, which mainly consisted of government bonds. The resulting increase in value of these bonds strengthened the banks' balance sheets, especially those that held large portfolios of assets in countries where the economy was particularly weak, such as Greece, Portugal, Spain, Ireland, and Italy. This *back-door recapitalization* allowed weaker banks to continue and reinforce their extend and pretend strategies.

Amidst the rise in the relative importance of zombie companies, four effects stand out:

- First, given that credit has flowed increasingly to riskier borrowers in the corporate sector, the system is much more vulnerable to shocks, such as a sudden uptick in interest rates or a pandemic. Even a relatively mild recession could have serious consequences.

- Second, given their persistent trouble with debt servicing, it's reasonable to assume zombie companies are less productive and weigh negatively on overall productivity.

- Third, zombie companies create *congestion effects*. Their continued existence requires the usage of personnel and capital, and these factors of production cannot be reallocated to other activities. In an environment of rapidly changing technologies and intense competition, the congestion effect of zombie companies is a drag on productivity and the growth potential of the economy.

- A fourth effect of the increasing presence of zombie companies is that it makes the entry of new firms more difficult, because the factors of production become frozen into less productive or totally unproductive activities. Fewer entries mean less competition and a drag on productivity and growth potential.

Recent research has brought another interesting point to light indirectly related to the zombie syndrome, but which also has important consequences for competition and productivity.[123] Low interest rates normally stimulate investment, but persistently very low interest rates also produce a strategic effect in the sense that they inspire industry leaders to invest more aggressively in order to keep potential competitors at bay. Potential competitors—let's call them followers— are disincentivized to invest as the gaps between them and the leaders in the market widen. Put another way, consistently low interest rates make it increasingly difficult for followers to achieve the high payoffs associated with market leadership. Low interest rates, then, become a disincentive for investment. The strategic effect of persistently low interest rates reduces competition, leads to more concentrated industries, and weighs down productivity gains. It's no coincidence that over time, a clear correlation appears between interest rates going down and staying down and increases in industry concentration and market power.[124] This increased market power has counterproductive economic implications and also important political and cultural consequences.[125]

Zombification of the corporate landscape was a major issue *before* the COVID-19 pandemic, but after it hit, the situation went from bad to worse. Governments all over the world had to intervene on an enormous scale to avoid the tsunami of bankruptcies that were possible due to the draconic measures taken to fight the spread of the coronavirus. An article in *The Economist* in September 2020 reported, "A combination of furlough schemes to reduce wage bills, state-backed loans to provide liquidity and laws, or other measures to stop bankruptcies have prevented a wave of company failures."[126] BIS researchers predict that governments and central banks have a delicate task ahead as they "seek to shore up companies that would be viable in less extreme circumstances, while at the same time not excessively dampening corporate dynamism by protecting weak and unproductive ones."[127]

Sloth Syndrome

If you perform an internet search for "laziest animal," chances are high that either *koala* or *sloth* will appear near the top of the list. Koalas are known for their laziness, as they are awake only two to six hours each day. Sloths ("the group of arboreal neotropical xenathran mammals," according to Wikipedia) behave similarly and are particularly known for their extremely slow pace. What do these animals have in common with central bankers and their policies? While I admit to some degree of hyperbole here, politicians have arguably behaved like sloths when making decisions influenced by central bankers' relentless pursuit of unconventional monetary policies.

Of course, life in the political arena can be pretty much the opposite of slow; indeed, it is often quite demanding and exhausting. I can testify to this, since the four years I served as minister of finance in the Belgian government demanded a lot of me in terms of physical and mental resilience. In my current role as chairman of the Committee on Budgets of the European Parliament, the discussions are often intense, and the job requires a lot of time and energy. Yet the fifteen or more hours a day that politicians work isn't completely devoted to efforts in the long-term interest of society. Politics demands a lot of effort that isn't for the common good, and if that sounds like an understatement, that's because it is. Many of the battles and electorally inspired turf wars that are unavoidable in a democracy have little to do with benefiting the electorate, and unfortunately, short-term electoral considerations edge out higher ideals more often than not.

While persistent *Sturm und Drang* is commonplace in modern, social media-driven political life, central bankers have conveniently provided many elected officials with an excuse to step away from policies that are desperately needed. Because they know that central bankers' monetary policies can bail them out, politicians and governments in advanced countries abdicate their decision-making responsibilities and move at a sloth's pace, if at all. Monetary policy, so to speak, is a drug to which most politicians surrender without too much resistance.

Easy financing conditions and low to negative interest rates are a terrible environment for fiscal discipline. The more attractive borrowing becomes, the more frequent it will be, in both the private and public sectors. This a clear case of moral hazard.[128] If government borrowing becomes a free lunch, politically speaking, incentives to improve public finances tend to disappear. Excessive deficits and buildup of debt becomes almost natural. "Politicians," University of Chicago economist John Cochrane argued, "will take the cheap money as long as markets are happy to provide it."[129] The unconventional toolbox of central banks has been crucial to markets' readiness to keep on providing cheap money.

Unconventional monetary policies weaken the drive to push through structural reforms that could lift the structural growth potential of the economy. In statements and interviews, central bankers frequently make the case for fiscal discipline and ask that governments place more emphasis on public investment. While they plead for structural reforms of labor markets, education, job training, and taxation, their persistent use of unconventional monetary policies generates exactly the opposite outcome. Central bankers' policies disincentivize politicians to pursue the very reforms that central bankers champion—a clear-cut catch-22. Accommodative monetary policies are not and never will be an alternative to structural reform in the real economy, no matter what fanciful theories (for example, the Modern Monetary Theory) may allege.

The extent of the Sloth Syndrome goes even further than the situation I just described. Unconventional monetary policies regularly generate asset bubbles—sometimes, enormous ones. Such bubbles create the illusion of abundant revenues for governments. Consider the situation in Spain and Ireland in the period before and during the financial crisis. Revenues generated by the enormous real estate bubble that the two countries experienced in the years leading up to the crisis caused their budget deficits to disappear, and their debt-to-GDP ratios declined substantially. Both were hailed as laudable examples of fiscal discipline in the euro area. Unfortunately, when the bubble burst, government revenues sharply declined, and the huge sums expended to clean up the ensuing banking and financial mess generated large deficits and quickly escalated debt-to-GDP ratios.

The eight syndromes detailed in this chapter explain how the unintended consequences of the unconventional monetary policies that central bankers have consistently deployed over the past fifteen years have backfired and muted the positive effects of those policies on inflation, growth, and financial stability. Over time, they have eroded financial stability, economic growth, job creation, income equality, productivity, and the quality of political decision-making, and in the end, inflation shot upward anyway. Just as Thornton and Bagehot described long ago, these unconventional tools are very effective in a crisis. But the monetary drug is also highly addictive, and a detox is long overdue.

The trillion-dollar/euro/yen/etc. question: where do central bankers go from here? The next chapter will reexamine the policy framework used by central bankers—in particular, the 2 percent inflation target that has been of primary importance for more than two decades. The framework is obsolete and too narrow, and an update is in order. The epilogue will grapple with how to address the problems generated by these unconventional monetary policies in the short term. No matter which solution comes to pass, we'll remain on a trajectory loaded with uncertainty and unexpected pitfalls.

Chapter 6: The 2 Percent Obsession

Why central banks need a new policy framework

THOSE WHO CANNOT REMEMBER THE PAST ARE CONDEMNED to repeat it." This well-known quote from writer and philosopher George Santayana is applicable to central bankers and their travails. During the 1920s and 1930s, they obviously didn't remember, or didn't take seriously, the lessons taught by nineteenth-century economic savants Henry Thornton and Walter Bagehot on the importance of the central banks' role as lenders of last resort in a crisis. The Great Depression was a direct consequence of this unlearning on the part of central bankers. By the time the global financial crisis came about in 2007, central bankers had relearned the lessons of Thornton and Bagehot and applied them rigorously, and a twenty-first century repeat of the Great Depression or worse was avoided. Early in 2020, as the world economy nosedived again as a result of the COVID-19 pandemic, central bankers once again acted swiftly and decisively, following a modern version of Thornton and Bagehot's playbook. Their continually expanding application of the unconventional monetary toolbox made it evident that, more than ever before in human history, the mystic hand of central bankers was everywhere.

Both the financial crisis and the pandemic obliged the central bankers to pull out all the stops and launch a battery of unconventional monetary policies to prevent calamities. Yet continuous use of that unconventional toolbox for more than a decade has led to eight unintended and unfortunately negative consequences. Moreover, after being declared dead by many analysts and economists, the consumer price inflation beast has reared its ugly head once more. Clearly, new lessons must now be learned. Given the magnitude of these unintended negative consequences and other considerations that will be covered in detail in this chapter, there is a sense of urgency to learn those lessons and adjust policies accordingly. So where are the central banks today, and what direction should they follow in the future?

First, consider the present situation. Things don't look promising. While most of their interventions were necessary at one time, in addition to facing troubles from a rise in inflation, central bankers are caught in a *triple trap*: a financial market trap, a fiscal trap, and an expectations trap. The pressure from these traps leads central bankers to think that they cannot back off these policies, or at least that it's too early to do so right now. This attitude of kicking the can down the road is based on the hope that, to paraphrase Keynes, "something" will turn up that allows a return to a more orthodox situation. Even if this hope would be remotely justified, the consequences of unconventional monetary policies in place now are creating an increasingly heavy burden on the economy and on democratic values and institutions.

Like Pavlov's Dog

The first trap that has ensnared central bankers is a *hold-up by the financial markets*. Ironically, central bankers created the conditions necessary to make this hold-up a reality and to allow financial markets to conquer the commanding heights of monetary policy. Bernanke and the Fed walked away from an initial attempt to normalize monetary policy in 2013 because of pressure from the markets. Market pressure again led the Fed to reverse normalization efforts in the second half of 2019, and turmoil in the US bond market in March 2020 pushed the Fed to enact drastic policy action. The September 2019 policy package that Draghi struggled to pass through the ECB council was also driven by pressure from the markets. Each time the markets tank or face a calamity, or when uncertainty rises for whatever reason, everyone expects the central banks to step in decisively—which they have, time and again.

Central banks focus on policy objectives like price stability, the overall state of the economy, and financial stability. When turmoil erupts in the financial markets and threatens these objectives, policy actions are warranted, but it's almost always rather uncertain how likely these threats really are. Being careful and proactive is commendable in some circumstances, but if central bankers respond automatically each time, like Pavlov's salivating dogs, a codependency develops.[1] Mohamed El-Erian, one of the most eminent market analysts, has described central bankers as "the markets' best friends,"[2] making investors "enormously confident in the willingness of systematically important central banks— namely, the Federal Reserve and the European Central Bank—to inject liquidity at the *first* [italics mine] sign of serious market stress, regardless of how much further they have to venture into the domain of experimental unconventional policy."[3] Equity strategist Chris Wood concurred with El-Erian's opinion: "It is the Fed which follows the markets, not the other way around."[4]

The clear pattern of financial market dominance of monetary policy interventions is impossible to ignore. This phenomenon is best known as the Greenspan put or the Bernanke put, or more generally, *the Fed put*. Research has proven the existence of this put and its causal nature— market gyrations, especially in the stock market, drive policy decisions, rather than the other way around. This causal relationship first clearly emerged in the mid-1990s.[5] Given the parallels between the various leading central banks, it's fair to say that in addition to a Fed put, there's also an ECB put, a BoJ put, and certainly a Bank of China put. In short, the financial markets worldwide have fully and happily adjusted to the puts of the central banks of the world.

This financial market trap is of course of major importance. The modern world is riddled with uncertainty and disorder, and financial markets tend to react instantly. Intense geopolitical tensions between the

United States and China; Europe's manifold hurdles on the road to further integration (or the first steps toward disintegration, given the Brexit saga); the sudden rise in inflation; China's mounting economic problems and internal strife; the continuous threat of jihadist and other extremist terrorist acts; climate change; worldwide demographic upheaval; the threat of major cyberattacks; geopolitical hotspots like the South China Sea; the eternally turbulent Middle East; several "frozen" conflicts that can turn hot at any moment (Ukraine, the Nagorno-Karabakh region, and so on); and the unpredictable behavior of autocrats like Russia's Vladimir Putin, Turkey's Recep Tayyip Erdoğan, and North Korea's Kim Jong-un, are just a few factors that incite turmoil in financial markets at any time.

New surprises are just around the corner: unexpected shocks are now the rule, rather than the exception. Moreover, the COVID-19 pandemic and the health insecurities it provoked have added a new dimension to the uncertainty and fear that can paralyze individuals, companies, governments, and markets. Today, black swans are no longer a rare breed. Financial markets have evolved in such a way that they are often the *sources* of shocks and black-swan events. For example, the prominent role of exchange-traded funds (ETFs) or trackers and the growing use of algorithmic high-speed trading have added a high degree of uncertainty regarding market function and have increased the risk of sudden disorderly market developments. The shadow banking system is a fertile breeding ground for sudden shocks and black-swan events as well.

While their efforts began with the best intentions, central bankers are now the prisoners of their own policies. The financial market trap that has ensnared central bankers is a direct consequence of statements like "whatever it takes," "will do everything necessary," and "we can do even more." The enormous mountain of negative-yielding debt persists only because the market expects central banks to continue their interventions and buy bonds and other securities on a regular basis. If central banks discontinue these purchases, long-term interest rates will inevitably increase. Central bankers intervene in the equity markets *because* the balance sheets of insurance companies and pension funds are loaded with equities and related assets in an attempt to maintain a return on assets that is high enough to satisfy their liabilities.

Catch-22

On to the *fiscal trap*: if central bankers step back from their unconventional policies, they risk making the bleak outlook for public finances even worse in most countries. This phenomenon is known as the danger of *fiscal dominance* of monetary policy. The delicate relationship between fiscal and monetary policies, a long-standing dilemma of macroeconomics,[6] is especially thorny in the euro area, a monetary union with fiscally autonomous member states. This fact inspired ECB Executive Board Member Isabelle Schnabel to remark, "The euro has been built on the principle of *monetary dominance*."[7]

Further deterioration of public finances is sure to inspire more tension in financial markets, if not total upheaval. If very low or negative short-term interest rates or asset purchase programs are discontinued, the cost burden of debt on the budgets of many countries would create tremendous pressure. Letting deficits escalate as a consequence of this higher interest burden is probably not an option, given the high debt ratios many countries already face—especially in light of the costly measures taken to keep businesses and citizens afloat during the COVID-19 pandemic.[8]

The tax increases or expenditure cuts needed to compensate for an increased cost burden of debt would be substantial; so substantial, in fact, that they may not be possible in most democratic countries. Drastic deficit-reducing initiatives would provoke fierce opposition, particularly from rent-seeking interest groups that would stand to lose their advantages. (These groups are usually quite successful in transforming their hardly altruistic opposition into public resentment.) As recent history has shown, these phenomena strengthen populist and extremist political parties and weaken democratic institutions.

Of course, central bankers are not responsible for national budgets and debt levels: that responsibility resides with elected politicians. To a certain extent, central bankers can argue that politicians have betrayed them. As indicated in the introduction of this book, this was the motivator of the sentiments Mario Draghi vented at Christine Lagarde's dinner in Washington in 2017. For central bankers, this is a classic catch-22. Their policies created an opportunity and the time needed for politicians to act on budget deficits and to enact structural reforms that would improve growth and employment potential and labor market flexibility. On the other hand, the cheap money that flowed from central bankers' policies allowed politicians to abdicate responsibility for the policy changes central bankers hoped for. I characterized this as the Sloth Syndrome in Chapter 5.

As if all this wasn't enough, central bankers face a third trap that is also at least partially of their own making: *the expectations trap*. Politicians and citizens have come to expect central bankers to keep inflation under control; ensure financial stability; arrange smooth financing of budget deficits and outstanding debt; avoid recessions (and unemployment); and provide an engine of economic growth. Even if central bankers do indeed have a mystic hand, this combination of objectives is totally unrealistic and a recipe for disappointment. The expectations trap is a hardship brought about by politicians' and other policymakers' abandonment of their own responsibilities, leaving central bankers as "the only game in town." Most, though not all, central bankers have eagerly attempted to live up to that image.

Unelected Power

The traps central bankers find themselves in today have created a situation that is both unstable and unsustainable, because it is fundamentally *undemocratic* and *counterproductive*. The magnitude of the unintended negative consequences discussed in Chapter 5 will only intensify over time. If the unconventional monetary policies continue, the result will be disappointing levels of economic growth, employment opportunity, productivity gains, income equality, financial stability, and policy reform on the part of elected governments. It's unfair to blame central bank policies for an intensification of anxiety and frustration in Western societies, but these policies do contribute to a rise in societal upheaval.

Right now, the mystic hand of central bankers is felt everywhere, but the results of their actions suffer from decreasing and sometimes negative returns to scale. The mystic hand of central bankers will become an increasingly destructive hand that must be shackled, something politicians on the extreme left and right would happily fulfill. More moderate and sensible politicians will feel increased pressure to curtail the degrees of freedom provided to central bankers. In the past, however, politicization of central banks has been a recipe for disaster, and there's no reason to think things will be any different in the future.

The present situation has a decidedly undemocratic touch, since it has caused an immense broadening of the role central banks play throughout society. The mystic hand of central bankers now reaches much further and deeper into the economic and societal fabric than ever before. For example, central bankers now have a decisive impact on equity values and thus on corporate strategies and investment. When they systematically buy government bonds, they are implicitly making political choices. Buying corporate bonds entails choices in the corporate sphere, and buying mortgage-backed securities favors the real estate sector of the economy.

By increasing asset values, central bankers favor the rich and the well-to-do, which fuels resentment among the rest of the population. Perhaps the most important factor of all is that the firepower of central banks to pursue such policies is viewed as limitless—despite the undeniable decreasing returns to scale.[9] If central bankers continue to make the same kinds of choices they have been making for the past decade and a half, justification of their independence will become untenable. Jens Weidmann, president of the German Bundesbank and member of the ECB Council, is acutely aware of this danger; he remarked, "The more widely we interpret our mandate, the greater the risk that we will become entangled with politics and overburden ourselves with too many tasks."[10] In Germany, for well-understood historical reasons, the independence of the central bank is an essential topic among the public at large.

In his far-ranging book *Unelected Power*, written prior to the COVID-19 pandemic, Paul Tucker, the former deputy governor of the Bank of England, summarized this evolution succinctly when he argued central banks

> have emerged as institutions standing at the intersection of three crucial manifestations of the modern administrative state. Through their balance-sheet operations (quantitative easing and credit easing) that alter the size and shape of the state's consolidated balance sheet, they are part of the *fiscal state*. Through their role as the lender of last resort, they are part of the *emergency state*. And...they are now unequivocally part of the *regulatory state*. Arguably, no other unelected policymakers occupy a similar position.[11]

The German Constitutional Court's criticism of the ECB's unconventional monetary policies was grounded in a similar reasoning.

Adam Tooze, director of the European Institute at Columbia University, addressed the same issues when he referred to "the giant increase in power and responsibility that has accrued to the Fed and its counterparts around the world in reaction to COVID-19...Formal mandates have rarely been adjusted, but there has clearly been a huge expansion in reach...In the American case, where the extension has been most dramatic, it amounts to a hidden transformation of the state..."[12] Sebastian Mallaby, senior fellow at the Council on Foreign Relations, concluded, "The Fed has emerged as the biggest agent of big government, a sort of economics superministry."[13] Moreover, the major justification for the independence of central bankers—preventing politicians from engaging in inflationary adventures via misuse of the printing press—seems to have disappeared.

The democratic legitimacy of the additional power and authority that central banks have acquired, precisely because they are now regarded as the "only game in town," is a crucial societal issue that calls into question the role of technocratic meritocracy in modern society, now more than ever in the aftermath of the COVID-19 pandemic. Medical technocrats, such as virologists, played a central role in decisions on fighting the pandemic. In many instances, the line between their duty to inform and advise democratically elected leaders and their advice, effectively replacing the decision-making of those elected leaders, was quite unclear.

How far can technocratic discretion go? Did epidemiologists and other medical advisors go too far during the COVID-19 pandemic? Or should elected politicians step aside and let technocrats take over in emergencies? Are the actions that modern central bankers have taken defensible given the constraints of the mandate that elected politicians have given them? If so, what is the role—if one exists—of democratic oversight on central bankers' actions? If the explosive issue of democratic legitimacy is not carefully considered by elected leaders—the representatives of the citizens' will—there is a risk that in the medium to longer term, central bankers will be perceived as "members of a cosmopolitan elite, capable of moving what appear to be unimaginably vast sums of money within and across countries in defense of the interests of a powerful and unrepentant financial sector, all to support the status quo."[14]

It's no coincidence that Christine Lagarde publicly championed integrating concerns about climate change into the ECB's monetary policy actions when she stated, "The ECB is at the service of the European people."[15] In the same vein, Fed Chairman Jerome Powell stated during a presentation given in the summer of 2020 that the American central bank's new policy framework would include inequality considerations—making the Fed the first central bank to explicitly do so.[16] These initiatives by the leadership of major central banks are at least partially inspired by their need to strengthen the democratic legitimacy of their institutions, given how unconventional monetary policies often replace normal democratic decision-making. It remains to be seen how these new approaches will blend into the primary tasks of central banks.[17]

The Japanese example shows that the situation of being trapped in a policy conundrum and nevertheless continuing with the same policy mix can go on for a prolonged period of time, since in the country of the rising sun experiments with unconventional monetary policy tools started during the 1990s. Government debt equal to more than 250 percent of GDP and a central bank balance sheet total equal to more than 100 percent of GDP—much higher ratios than in the US or the euro area—are more the numbers that one expects for a country submerged in a huge and endless financial and fiscal crisis. Not so for Japan, at least so far. The mystic nature of what central banking is all about undoubtedly contributes to the fact that unconventional monetary policies can keep the boat floating for a long time despite mounting evidence of the undemocratic and counterproductive nature of that policy mix.[18]

That said, central banks' continued use of the unconventional monetary policy toolbox is untenable. If more stable and sustainable policies are not implemented, economic and political disorder will ensue as result of the cascade of unintended consequences coupled with the surge in inflation. What path should central bankers follow in the future? In order to determine this, we must first consider the generally acknowledged objective of monetary policy: stabilizing the economy at, or close to, an inflation rate of 2 percent annually. This analysis requires a close examination of the characteristics of inflation today.

The 2 Percent Obsession

The need to bring inflation up to 2 percent annually has been central bankers' consistent defense for their relentless use of the unconventional monetary toolbox.[19] Yet when it comes to inflation, the world has changed a lot since the 1980s. Consider the numbers: among advanced countries as a whole, the percentage change in consumer prices averaged 10 percent during the 1980s.[20] In the decade that followed, the percentage halved on average to 5 percent. In the first decade of the twenty-first century, average consumer price inflation fell even further to 3 percent. Between 2010 and 2020, it dropped below 2 percent.

In the decades after World War II, central banks had good reason to focus on the threat of price increases eventually getting out of control. From the mid-1960s until the early 1980s, a time known as the "Great Inflation," annual increases in price levels in advanced countries sometimes reached 20 percent or more.[21] This generated widespread fears that intensifying inflation could both undermine the economy and lead to social and political instability. It's rather ironic that one of the sternest warnings about the destructive consequences of inflation was voiced more than half a century earlier by none other than John Maynard Keynes.[22] In the postwar period, Keynes was the intellectual hero of the economists—the early Keynesians—who advocated for the policies that eventually unleashed the Great Inflation.

During the Great Inflation, most, but not all, central bankers earned a reputation as, in the words of central banking legend Paul Volcker, "knee-jerk inflation fighters."[23] (Volcker led the final assault on the inflation dragon in the late 1970s.) Since the global financial crisis (and in Japan since the 1990s), the opposite has been true. Deflation has replaced inflation as the central bankers' major policy concern, as they worry about the debt-deflation nexus possibly degenerating into a deep depression.[24] In this topsy-turvy world, the overall price level in the economy no longer needs to be pushed down; instead, it has to be pushed up.[25] ECB Executive Board Member Isabelle Schnabel summarized the overarching concern of most present-day central bankers succinctly: "Too low, rather than too high, inflation remains the main predicament of our times."[26] A few months after Schnabel's strong statement, the inflation outlook changed rather dramatically.

Along with the fight against recurring episodes of financial instability, the 2 percent inflation target is the inspiration behind central bankers' systemic policy of continuous monetary accommodation. In the wake of the battle to get the beast under control during the Great Inflation period, inflation targeting became the primary goal of central banking in the early 1990s.[27] There was broad consensus that controlling inflation was the greatest contribution central bankers could make to economic welfare and human progress. To put it in more technical terms, central bankers were tasked with firmly anchoring inflationary expectations at a sufficiently low, but not too low, level.

Inflation targeting began in New Zealand in 1990, and throughout the 1990s, Canada, the UK, Australia, Sweden, Poland, Israel, Brazil, and Chile followed in the same track. The BoJ, the ECB, and the Fed don't identify as inflation targeters per se, but over time they adopted many of the main elements of inflation targeting. The ECB's official objective is to get inflation "below but close to 2 percent." Bernanke publicly spoke of the 2 percent target in 2012, and a year later the BoJ made the same move. Either explicitly or implicitly, 2 percent became the magic number—the obsession, so to speak—for inflation targeting.

It's interesting that the 2 percent objective has been so stubbornly pursued, given the lack of success it has yielded. In Japan, the United States, and the euro area, inflation has remained (for the most part) below 2 percent since the financial crisis and has often flirted with outright deflation. Fed Chairman Jerome Powell referred on one occasion to a "persistent undershoot of inflation from our 2 percent longer-term objective."[28] At the end of October 2020, the annualized rate of consumer price inflation stood at 0.5 percent in China, 1.2 percent in the United States, -0.4 percent in Japan, and -0.3 percent in the euro area.[29] Given the amount of monetary stimulus that has been injected into the financial and economic systems almost continuously for years, this is rather astonishing. While little inflation in the prices of goods and services has surfaced during the past fifteen or so years, inflationary tendencies in asset prices have regularly developed impressive bubbles. Thus, policies inspired by the 2 percent inflation target have more often than not resulted in destabilizing financial booms and busts.

Isn't it time to question the policy target of 2 percent inflation?[30] It appears that the enigmatic 2 percent inflation rate is not a realistic or constructive guideline for monetary policies. Central bankers have proven that they know how to bring inflation down; their ability to push it up, however, is in doubt. By consistently missing the 2 percent target, central banks lose credibility. After all, many factors that lie beyond the reach of monetary policymakers have led to structurally lower inflation rates, including developments in the labor markets, demographic changes, the boom of the sharing economy, technological advancement, and globalization. Economists often refer to these phenomena as positive supply shocks, and most of them will persist. Evidence clearly shows that inflation targeting becomes problematic when the economy is hit by supply shocks.[31]

In recent years, up to the end of 2020, inflation remained systematically low on a global scale.[32] Stubbornly pursuing unconventional and very accommodative monetary policies to boost it to 2 percent while nonmonetary factors structurally push down on inflationary forces in the economy makes no sense. The plot thickens when the unintended consequences of these policies negate their positive contributions, which is exactly what has happened.

The New Inflation Normal
During the 1980s and 1990s, many formerly communist or strongly state-led economies, including China, India, and the nations that made up the Soviet Union, began to liberalize and in so doing boosted the reach of globalization, unleashed powerful competitive forces, and substantially increased the flow of cheaper products. This U-turn in the economic environment of large parts of the world added nearly 1.5 billion people to the global workforce in a short period of time. Harvard labor economist Richard Freeman termed this phenomenon The Great Doubling, since it effectively doubled the size of the workforce around the world.[33] This was part of a more general globalization of markets involving not only labor but also product and capital markets, which led to an erosion of pricing power for many companies. Global conditions, and especially the growth of global value chains, came to play a much larger role in economic processes, including inflation.[34]

The massive change to the supply side of the world labor market significantly and structurally diminished the bargaining power of unions in the developed world, reducing wage cost pressure on prices. It's striking that wage increases have followed productivity gains much more closely since the early 1990s in advanced economies, and have significantly reduced the instance of price increases as a consequence of wage cost increases.[35] The doubling of the global workforce had the greatest impact among blue-collar workers, but subsequent advances in data analysis, artificial intelligence, cloud computing, and information and communication technologies have substantially reduced the bargaining power of white-collar workers in advanced nations as well. A marked shift from full-time employment to temporary and part-time work contracts also made labor markets more flexible and reduced wage pressure. Last, a massive boom in e-commerce enhanced competitive forces in the retail business through the "Amazon effect," and also reinforced the fundamental changes in the labor market.[36]

The labor market was also influenced by structural demographic changes—specifically, the aging population.[37] Economic research has shown a clear negative relationship between inflation and the old-age dependency ratio, which is calculated as the ratio of population aged sixty-five and older to the population aged fifteen to sixty-four. The higher the old-age dependency ratio becomes, the lower inflation tends to be.[38] This demographic change and the pension reforms necessitated by it often led to reductions in the net-after-tax pension, which stimulated a steady increase in the share of the workforce that is fifty-five years old or older.[39] In Japan, for example, 4 million people older than sixty-five years of age returned to the workforce between 2003 and 2018. Similar trends are occurring in the United States and the euro area. This influx of older workers exerts downward pressure on wages and prices.[40]

The aging of society also contributes to structurally lower inflation rates due to the saving, investment, and consumption channel. Older people tend to consume and invest less than younger people. Consider the costs faced by the younger generations to build a family and acquire a place to live and furnishings for it in an environment with much higher asset prices (which are caused, in large part, by unconventional monetary policies). When older people make up a larger share of the population, less upward pressure on the prices of goods and services will exist. As life expectancies increase across the board, many older people increase their saving efforts in order to be financially prepared for a longer period of retirement. Lower inflationary trends are also influenced by the easy financing conditions that are currently in force and investors' frantic search for yield, inspired by the low interest rates that created easy financing conditions. Yield seekers divert resources to new initiatives that often burn through a lot of capital in search for market share and monopolistic positions, and place more downward pressure on prices.

Yet another development contributing to downward pressure on the price level of goods and services is the boom in the "sharing economy," loosely defined as crowd-based markets allowing the exchange of privately owned goods and services. Uber and Airbnb are perhaps the best-known examples of the sharing economy that have brought idled goods and services (privately owned rooms, homes, and apartments for rent, and cars for transportation) to the market. The effect of the sharing economy on pushing down prices was shown in a recent analysis of Airbnb's entry into the Texas rooms-for-rent market.[41]

It was never carved in stone that conditions that kept consumer price inflation low would remain unchanged.[42] For example, while the shorter-term consequences of the aging population lead to deflation, the longer-term effects of the demographic change may lead to the opposite effect because of shortages in labor markets.[43] Another example is the fact that increases in broad measures of the money supply have been much higher since the start of the COVID-19 pandemic than they were following the global financial crisis. Historical linkages between money supply and inflation may have weakened, but they certainly haven't disappeared.

During the first half of 2021, potentially powerful inflationary forces resulted from massive spending and borrowing engineered to prop up economic recovery in the wake of the drastic measures taken to fight the pandemic and substantial increases in pandemic-related uncertainty. The European Union, China, and many other economies went into spending and borrowing overdrive as a result of the pandemic, but US President Joe Biden's massive initiatives to stimulate the economy and improve physical and social infrastructure have dwarfed their efforts. In total, Biden's ambitious economic package approaches $6 trillion.

At least four other phenomena have reinforced the inflationary pressures unleashed by this spending and borrowing spree. First, pandemic-related safety measures and uncertainty caused major disruptions in supply chains; bottlenecks in production and deliveries; and significant shortages of critical resources like microchips and precious metals. Second, the pandemic also led to substantial increases in enforced savings that were suddenly unleashed once restrictions were rescinded. Third, the maturation of China's forty-year-long transition has diminished downward pressure on consumer prices. Fourth, quasi-monopolistic market structures created by major tech companies have enhanced their pricing power considerably.

Given these developments, the substantial rise in consumer price inflation that surfaced in the United States the spring of 2021 is not surprising. As this book went to press in July 2021, the true nature of this rise in inflation remained under debate. Is the inflationary genie really out of the bottle, or, as central bankers have argued, is this only a temporary uptick in consumer price inflation?

Giant Wisdom

As the inflation problem has reemerged, discussions of the 2 percent inflation target have taken on another dimension, but the essence of the discussion basically remains the same. To understand why, we must establish a comprehensive definition of price stability. Alan Greenspan provided a coherent definition for price stability in the mid-1990s, during his term as Fed chair. Price stability, Greenspan argued, is "that state in which expected changes in the general price level do not effectively alter business or household decisions."[44] Greenspan's take is similar to an argument developed by the late Martin Feldstein, former president of the National Bureau of Economic Research, who pointed out that price stability allows contracts, commercial deals, accounting rules, tax laws, and the like to be expressed in nominal terms without worry of unexpected movements in inflation or the value of money, which is the same thing.[45]

Obviously, high or very volatile annual inflation rates don't fit this definition of price stability, because high or volatile inflation dramatically affects private spending and investment decisions. But is it possible to argue that an inflation rate of 2 percent, or close to it, as the ECB's dogma goes, is the only inflation rate that passes the Greenspan/Feldstein test? Are there solid scientific and empirical findings that prove that 2 percent is superior to, say, 1 percent or 3 percent? The short answer is no, as described by Paul Volcker in his memoirs,[46] and I humbly concur with Volcker's learned opinion.

> I puzzle about the rationale…I know of no theoretical justification…[but]…I do know some practical facts. No price index can capture, down to a tenth of a quarter of a percent, the real change in consumer prices. The variety of goods and services, the shifts in demand, the subtle changes in pricing and quality are too complex to calculate precisely from month to month or year to year…Concerns are being voiced that consumer prices are growing too slowly—just because they're a quarter or so below the 2 percent target! Could that be a signal to "ease" monetary policy, or at least to delay restraint, even with the economy at full employment? Certainly, that would be nonsense.[47]

Here, Volcker is *not* arguing that the case for the 2 percent inflation target is completely invalid, but he *is* saying that there's no reason for it to be the rule in perpetuity.

Harvard economist Jeffrey Frankel, who served on the US Presidential Council of Economic Advisers from 1983 to 1984 and again from 1996 to 1999, is in complete agreement with Volcker. "Why should central bankers keep banging their heads against the wall of a desired inflation rate? To be sure, monetary authorities should be transparent about their expectations for long-run inflation, as well as for real GDP growth and unemployment. Rather than doubling down on their oft-missed 2 percent target, however, perhaps the Fed and other central banks should quietly stop pursuing it aggressively."[48] Both Volcker and Frankel believed that trying to reach that 2 percent inflation target at all times might be counterproductive; recent experience has borne that fact out.

Volcker rounded out his plea against the 2 percent obsession by taking on the argument made by many central bankers and economists that in the twenty-first century, fear of deflation has reinforced a mandate to push inflation toward an annual rate of 2 percent. "Deflation," Volcker wrote, "is indeed a serious matter if extended over time. It has not been a reality in this country [the United States] for more than eighty years… Only once in the past century, in the 1930s, have we had deflation, serious deflation. In 2008–2009, there was cause for concern. The common characteristic of those two incidents was collapse of the financial system."[49] Volcker concluded by upending the deflation/unconventional monetary policies nexus: "The lesson, to me, is crystal clear. Deflation is a threat posed by a critical breakdown of the financial system…The real danger comes from encouraging or inadvertently tolerating rising inflation and its close cousin of extreme speculation and risk taking, in effect standing by while bubbles and excesses threaten financial markets. Ironically, the 'easy money,' striving for a 'little inflation' as a means of forestalling deflation, could, in the end, be what it brings about."[50]

Volcker has not been alone in his criticism of what Gillian Tett of the *Financial Times* defined as "our modern terror of deflation."[51] In a panel discussion, Raghuram Rajan referred to the deep-seated fear of deflation as "the deflation bogeyman."[52] Daniel Gros, director of the Centre for European Policy Studies (CEPR), warned, "Central bankers throughout the developed world have been overwhelmed by the fear of deflation. They shouldn't be. The fear is unfounded, and the obsession is damaging…Developed-economy central banks should overcome their irrational fear of a deflationary spiral."[53] Both Rajan and Gross acknowledged that deflation can be harmful, but stressed that the current economic environment reduces the danger.

After exhaustive analysis of the history of major deflationary periods and their costs, researchers at the BIS concluded that serious questions should be asked regarding "the prevailing view that goods and services price deflations, even if persistent, are always pernicious" and "it is critical to understand the driving forces" of deflationary episodes before jumping to alarmist conclusions.[54] The analysis also stressed the importance of distinguishing between drops in the prices of goods and services and drops in the prices of assets, such as equities and real estate; the latter type was shown to be more harmful to the economy. During the Great Depression, for example, falling asset prices caused most of the damage.

The Conjoined Twins

Central bankers need a solid framework in place to enable timely and consistent policy actions. This is critical to maintain the credibility of their institutions and strengthen the impact of their decisions. The framework is the core of the institutional technology required for central bankers, along with other regulatory and supervisory authorities, to establish the trust necessary for the monetary and financial system to function well. Whether it's explicit or implicit, the 2 percent annual inflation rate target has been the dominating characteristic of the framework used in developed countries since the 1990s. It's now clear that this framework is inadequate, obsolete, and too narrow.

It's obsolete because, given the dynamics of the inflation process in modern society, the 2 percent inflation target is unattainable through monetary policy actions alone. It's too narrow, because a mountain of evidence has proven that the pursuit of price stability in the sphere of goods and services in a numerically fixed way is counterproductive. Chapter 5 described in detail the various unintended consequences created by unconventional monetary policies, and these in turn were primarily designed to attain the 2 percent inflation target. As Volcker indicated, very accommodative polices designed to get the inflation rate at the 2 percent target fuel financial booms, and massive credit expansion feeds relentless increases in asset prices. These booms heighten financial and economic risks in the longer term.[55] Unconventional monetary policies have contributed to the development of a financial cycle in which self-reinforcing processes in funding conditions, asset prices, and risk-taking generate expansions followed by contractions. This cycle has become the major determinant of the ebbs and flows of the business cycles.[56]

So, what would be a better policy framework for modern central bankers? Again, I find myself in agreement with Paul Volcker, who concluded that the basic lesson of twenty-first-century monetary policy is that central bankers should emphasize "price stability and prudent oversight of the financial system" at the same time.[57] They must focus not just on price stability, but also on financial stability as an explicit policy objective.[58] Of course, central bankers should *always* consider financial stability, but since the 2 percent obsession has dominated central bankers' policy framework, financial stability has been an *ex post,* rather than an *ex ante,* consideration. This isn't surprising, given Greenspan's "cleaning up after the crisis" approach that has continued to set the tone long after his departure from the Fed.[59] The financial crisis revealed just how costly this cleanup strategy can be, especially when the system is riddled with massive financial imbalances and leverage.

Price stability and financial stability are conjoined twins or, as Claudio Borio of the BIS succinctly put it, "joined at the hip. They are fundamental properties of a smoothly functioning monetary system. They are both ways of safeguarding the value of money, by protecting against default, erosion of purchasing power, or a dysfunctional payments system."[60] Bundesbank president Jens Weidmann concurred: "Monetary policymakers cannot look away when their actions contribute to the build-up of financial imbalances that pose a long-term risk to price stability. Here too the rule applies: monetary policy has to consider its unintended side effects and constantly weigh up benefits and costs."[61]

History has shown time and again that it is impossible to have price stability in the longer term without also having financial stability. The events of the twenty-first century so far have proven that price stability is a *necessary* condition to have financial and macroeconomic stability, but it is not a *sufficient* condition. Dangerous financial imbalances can lurk under a veil of tranquility projected by low and stable consumer price inflation, and over time they can become extremely destructive. If financial stability considerations are not considered when monetary policy is devised, longer-term economic growth perspectives and price stability, whether it's in an inflationary or deflationary direction, will be placed in jeopardy. If more attention had been paid to history, unpleasant surprises like the 2007–2009 global financial crisis would have been less severe or perhaps could have been avoided altogether.[62]

A Kuhnian Moment

The framework for central bankers must change in two respects. First, the 2 percent obsession must become a thing of the past. The Fed missed an opportunity to make this change during a recent review of its monetary strategies. At the end of 2020, Fed Chair Jerome Powell announced that in the future, the central bank would pursue a "flexible form of average inflation."[63] He didn't explicitly mention the 2 percent target, but his rhetoric made clear that 2 percent is still the magic number; if a period passes where inflation is below 2 percent, the Fed will shift the strategy to achieve a period in which inflation is higher than 2 percent. This new strategy not only leaves the deeply flawed 2 percent inflation targeting intact, it also raises a lot of additional questions and problems, like the role of expectations, the asymmetry in objectives (shortfalls in employment will be compensated, overheating not), and the neglect of financial stability.[64]

Price stability will always be the central banker's most important objective, but going after a specific numeric target, whether it's an average or not, makes no sense. At one time, there was reasoning behind it, but that is in the past. ECB President Christine Lagarde is well aware that the 2 percent target is obsolete. In September 2020, she declared, "We need to thoroughly analyze the forces that are driving inflation dynamics today and consider whether and how we should adjust our policy strategy in response."[65] The Greenspan/Feldstein definition of price stability referenced earlier specifies that it should be determined with thoughtful judgment and keen observation of what is going on in the economic and financial system at the given time. Price stability can occur at an annual inflation rate of 2 percent, but depending on the circumstances, the equilibrium rate may be higher or lower. This is not a plea for complete discretion for central bankers; instead, it is a plea for thoughtful and circumstantial interpretation of guidelines, just like a Taylor rule or any other rule or model routinely used by central bankers.

The second adjustment the framework requires involves integrating the variables and parameters that affect financial stability into the policy decision-making process. This adjustment requires a step back in time, because in the past, close examination of monetary and credit aggregates was essential to designing monetary policy. These aggregates have all but disappeared from econometric models used at central banks, and they are rarely even mentioned in central bankers' statements or speeches. Their absence can be explained, most likely, by the fact that some previous policies that heavily focused on stabilization of monetary aggregates led to disappointment.[66] Former Bundesbank and ECB official Otmar Issing was on to something when he lamented, "How long will we have to wait until the neglect of money and credit in monetary theory and policy will be understood as the major source of macro policy mistakes?"[67]

When they are carefully interpreted, monetary and credit aggregates can be leading indicators that financial (in)stability is on the horizon. These include money supply aggregates like M1, M2, and M3; credit-to-GDP ratios; loan-to-value ratios; and debt service-to-income ratios.[68] Credit-to-GDP ratios in particular must be scrutinized in order to safeguard financial stability.[69] Intrinsic asset values—that is, the real value of an asset as opposed to its inflated value as a consequence of unconventional monetary policies—are of particular importance.[70]

When monetary and credit aggregates and asset prices are considered, close attention must be paid to the ways in which financial markets change, especially in new or rapidly growing markets. If in the last fifteen years more attention had been paid to the movement and interactions of monetary and credit aggregates and asset prices—for example, the fact that inflated asset values can give a misleading picture of the loan-to-value ratio—a lot of economic misery could have been avoided or at least muted.[71] It's hard to deny that these aggregates have proven to be significant indicators of risks to financial stability.

Further research is needed to refine these parameters and fully understand their meaning and policy relevance, and this research will not be easy. It will take rigor to avoid the trap of focusing on certain numbers or targets, like the 2 percent obsession. Solid approximations are better than settling on a specific number. Evaluation of monetary and credit aggregates and the evolution of asset prices will always be matters of contextual interpretation. Again, this is not a plea for total discretion, but instead for thoughtful integration of these considerations into a policy narrative that starts from prescribed rules and models. It's also a plea to systematically and seriously take all factors into account in order to arrive at the best policy possible.

These two fundamental changes to the framework won't come easily. Most central bankers are undeniably very intelligent and well-trained people, but humility is a rare character trait among them. During my terms as Belgium's minister of finance and as a member of the European Parliament, it was always striking to me that during discussions on the framework of monetary policies, top representatives of the ECB invariably changed their tone and spoke more sharply and impatiently than when other matters were under discussion. Despite all their talk about transparency and accountability, an attitude of "never apologize, never explain" among central bankers remains constant.[72]

The landmark work of Thomas Kuhn, the scientific philosopher who introduced the term "paradigm shift," revealed that they seldom come easily.[73] The paradigm shift that central banking needs will be particularly challenging, given the way the fraternity of central bankers approach their work. It requires a good dose of humility and openness of mind to admit that the old ways have become ineffective or perilous. But it is undeniable that they must.

A Complicated Craft

Despite all the progress that has been made in understanding the ins and outs of economic and financial reality and of monetary policy issues, central bank policy making will always be at least as much an art as it is a science. Thus, the mystic hand of central bankers will remain so. The question is, how much of it will be left to discretion and how much will depend on rule following? Should central bankers rigidly follow rules related to either the target(s) of monetary policy or its instruments, or should they have total discretion and set monetary policy as required by the unique characteristics of a specific moment in time?

To any careful student of monetary policy theory and practice, going all the way back to Thornton and Bagehot and moving all the way forward to recent times, it should be crystal clear that there is no room for simplification in responsible central bank policymaking. Barry Eichengreen, a professor of economics at the University of California, Berkeley, noted, "Whenever there was an effort to reduce the art of central banking to a simple formula, be it an exchange rate target under the gold standard or an inflation target more recently, other problems, such as threats to financial stability, have had an awkward tendency to intrude. They will undoubtedly do so again."[74] Central banking has always been a complicated craft, and although no one knows where developments in skill and technology—for example, artificial intelligence—might eventually lead, a complicated craft it will remain.[75]

Even among those known for their belief that central bankers must obey strict monetary rules—like John Taylor, father of the Taylor rule(s), and the late Milton Friedman, who came up with the *k-percent rule* for money supply growth—the truth is more nuanced than is often suggested.

In 2015, Taylor stated he did not "want to chain the Fed to an algebraic formula…Having a rules-based policy for your instruments does not mean that you follow a formula."[76] Three years earlier, he wrote, "The distinction between rules and discretion is more a matter of degree."[77]

Taylor also argued, "Simply having a specific numerical goal or objective is not a rule for the instruments of policy; it is not a strategy; it ends up being all tactics."[78] He concluded, "In reality, rules or strategies are simply ways to help central bankers improve monetary policy as they operate and communicate with markets and citizens in a democracy and interact in a global monetary system…There are many ways that policymakers can internalize the principles of a clear and consistent strategy as they formulate their day-to-day decisions."[79]

In his program for monetary stability, designed in 1960, Friedman wrote that the line between monetary policies based on obedience to specific rules and more discretionary policy regimes is a blurry one. "Reasonable rules," Friedman noted, "are hardly capable of being written that do not leave some measure of discretion."[80] Over time, Friedman became increasingly open to the idea that monetary policy should account for the evolution of the real economy, thereby recognizing the utility of a Taylor rule, and that targeting a single monetary aggregate had become very difficult. Moreover, Friedman acknowledged central bankers had been quite successful at stabilizing the economy through the use of monetary policy—an implicit acceptance of the need for intelligent discretion in determining monetary policy actions.[81]

The rules developed by Taylor and Friedman are focused on instruments central bankers use to conduct monetary policy: for Taylor, the policy interest rate, and for Friedman, some aggregate of the money supply. This instrument-rule approach can be contrasted with the "constrained discretion" approach followed by those who adhere to inflation targeting.

Bernanke, the central banker who arguably had the most influence on the development and persistence of unconventional monetary policies, laid out the characteristics of constrained discretion in 2003.[82] According to his view, monetary policy should be guided by two principles: first, a strong commitment to keep inflation low and stable, and second, subject to the first principle, monetary policy should strive to limit cyclical swings in economic activity. In the United States, the latter principle boils down to the second part of the Fed's dual mandate: to maximize employment. Constrained discretion allows central bankers to deploy *all* instruments available, including interest rate changes, QE policies, and forward guidance.

I propose a variant of the constrained discretion approach. In it, price stability and financial stability are explicit goals of monetary policy, fully recognizing that policy actions can instigate financial instability, which will in turn threaten price stability. I believe there is room for central bankers to use a variety of instruments to come as close as possible to the realization of its objectives. In most countries, the central bank shares the responsibility for the nation's financial stability with one or more macroprudential authorities. Regular consultations and careful coordination of policy actions with these other constituencies would greatly enhance the impact of those actions. While there is no question that central bankers' actions have greatly contributed to financial instability over the last two decades, it would be wrong to hold them solely responsible for all the troubles.

A better framework for monetary policy involves continuous and careful analysis, interpretation, solid judgment, and the courage to make decisions that go against popular sentiments or desires. Policymaking has always been and will always be at least as much an art as it is a science. Unexpected shocks to our financial and economic system are inevitable, and despite the undeniable progress that has been made in the scientific study and quantification of monetary policy, I agree with Martin Feldstein's conclusion that "science cannot replace judgment, because there are too many things we simply do not understand. And finally, no matter how good the science gets, there are problems that inevitably depend on judgment, on art, on a feel for financial markets."[83]

Epilogue

THE GLOBAL FINANCIAL CRISIS OF **2007–2009** AND THE COVID-19 pandemic were deep and unexpected shocks in societies worldwide. Central banks stepped in to prevent these shocks from devolving into devastating social, economic, and political consequences. After exhausting their short-term interest rate policy space by bringing these rates near (and even below) zero and installing new refinancing facilities, most central banks went all in on unconventional monetary policies—most notably, an array of QE programs. QE-inspired interventions pumped up the balance sheets of central banks to levels never seen before in peacetime. The often complicated and revolutionary nature of most of these interventions and their utterly strange effects— zero or even negative interest rates!— reinforced the public image of central bankers as being extraordinary people. The "mystic hand" possessed by central bankers, it seemed, enabled them to perform acts that were beyond the average person's comprehension.

Very low nominal and real interest rates have been pervasive for the past fifteen years, leading many observers to accept this situation as *the new normal*. Yet this extensive and long-term use of unconventional monetary policy tools has created at least eight unintended negative consequences. These policies silently steal demand from the future and from neighboring countries. They lead to debt accumulation and extreme leverage. They penalize savers. They stimulate the development of financial bubbles and their aftermath. They place undue strain on banks, insurance companies, and pension funds. They exacerbate wealth inequality. They suppress productivity and the growth potential of the economy. They disincentivize politicians to enact desperately needed structural reforms. Worse yet, each of these negative consequences tend to intensify over time. The decisions that central bankers make have direct long-term effects on the citizens of their nations and the citizens of others, despite not being elected to their positions.

The 2 percent inflation target most central banks use as a reference number for price stability has been an important driver behind the rationale for extension of these policies. In reality, the effect has been much like using a shotgun to kill a fly—the 2 percent target has rarely been achieved, and the attempt has involved a lot of collateral damage. In advanced countries, consumer price inflation hovered closer to 1 percent or zero (and sometimes has strayed into deflation) before it began to creep up substantially in early 2021. By invariably missing their target time and again, central banks have undermined the one asset they can't afford to lose—their credibility. In modern economies, the determinants of inflation are beyond the grasp of monetary policy, making the struggle for the 2 percent target an unattainable and counterproductive fight that produces harmful side effects.

The long recovery from the financial crisis has taught a powerful lesson: central bankers must include financial stability concerns in their policy-determining framework. Price stability and financial stability are conjoined twins—we cannot have one without the other. To incorporate financial stability considerations, central banks must closely monitor monetary and credit aggregates and the divergence between intrinsic asset values and their market prices—no matter how hard it may be to do so in real time. Asset price inflation must be a primary concern for monetary policymakers.

Monetary policy is important for financial stability, but so are also prudential and regulatory policies.[1] These are not solely the responsibility of central banks, however; other constituencies bear responsibility as well, and central bankers must work closely with them when formulating their policies. In the past, monetary policy and prudential and regulatory oversight were often viewed as substitutes—expansionary monetary policies should, the argument went, be flanked by stricter oversight and regulation. Yet this simply does not work in practice. The two are complementary.

We have learned that cleaning up after a crisis is worse than preventing it in the first place. Central bankers should be *leaning against the wind instead of cleaning up after the storm.* They won't be able to head off every financial storm—they never have, and they never will—but taking a broader perspective will allow them to prevent situations from getting completely out of hand, as was certainly the case prior to the financial crisis.

What does this mean for the immediate future? Excuses can always be found for not starting policy corrections, but barring a new major shock on the scale of the financial crisis or the COVID-19 pandemic, monetary policy should move toward higher short- and long-term interest rates—particularly now that rising consumer price inflation has become a reality. This is absolutely *necessary*; if not, societies will soon be overwhelmed by the unintended negative consequences of unconventional monetary policies. To bring longer-term interest rates into a more appropriate range, central banks must rethink their QE policies and balance sheet positions. Short-term interest rates can be raised more directly through traditional refinancing and deposit rates of the central banks.

That said, changing demographics and globalization have had a downward effect on equilibrium, or "natural" rates of interest. The normalization I believe is necessary is *not* simply a return to the interest rates in place prior to the financial crisis. Instead, a logical sequence of normalization begins with stabilization of the balance sheets of central banks, followed by gradual moderate rises in policy interest rates, and eventually, reductions in the balance sheet totals of the central banks. This last phase is the most delicate of all.

The monetary and fiscal responses to the COVID-19 pandemic—unavoidable and necessary as they were—have driven tensions and disequilibria in the financial and economic system to extremes. The need to normalize monetary policy is urgent; first because unconventional monetary policies are actively generating instability and uncertainty, and second because there must be policy space for the future. A resilient nation must have adequate policy space to combat major shocks that come along unexpectedly. Destructive black swan events happen, and in the span of the last twenty years, they've become a lot less rare (for example, the September 11 terrorist attacks, the 2007–2009 global financial crisis, and the COVID-19 pandemic). In calmer periods, we must seize the opportunity to move to policy stances that allow more room to move in the event of the next crisis. The question is not what to do in an emergency, because clearly, central bankers have figured that piece out. Instead, the question is what to do (and not do) under normal conditions. Long-term usage of expansionary monetary policies is akin to driving a car with only a gas pedal and no brake. It's time to sober up and gradually turn off the money spigot.

Normalization will take time. The necessary shifts in monetary policy will inevitably lead to protest and turbulence—and significant capital losses for many bond investors and equity holders—even if they are carried out with finesse. Moving too quickly will almost surely lead to chaos, panic, and further destabilization of markets and the economy— which would ultimately require new rounds of unconventional monetary interventions. It will take a lot of strategy, delicacy, courage, and principled determination on the part of central bankers to steer the ship on a new course and stay on it. The road to normalization will be a bumpy one, and it's critical that political leaders keep their distance from central bankers, and not make their already difficult work more complicated with impossible demands and counterproductive interventions.

A look back at history will show the rationale for moving carefully and slowly. Our most recent brush with the economic state we currently face—long-lasting, low, nominal interest rates, ballooning central bank balance sheets—was during World War II. Outstanding public debt ascended dramatically, and the balance sheets of central banks exploded as nations figured out how to finance their war efforts. In the years that followed, balance sheets shrunk, primarily as a result of percentage of GDP, but also due to cautious budgetary policies.[2] Central banks did little to reduce their asset positions nominally, but economic growth and rising GDP allowed for gradual normalization of central banks' balance sheets. Yet even then, a negative impact on economic growth was unavoidable.

Economic growth is critical. Hiroshi Nakaso, former deputy governor of the BoJ, pointed out two lessons learned from the evolution of the Japanese economy over the last three decades: "One is how important financial stability is, and the second is the importance of a growth strategy."[3] The essential nature of economic growth is underscored by the fact that ballooning central bank balance sheets almost always occur alongside ballooning debt levels—particularly public debt. High debt levels resulting from significant fiscal deficits and overburdened central bank balance sheets are inexorably intertwined.[4] Robust economic growth is the key to normalized central bank balance sheets and reduced sovereign debt levels. Ignoring these truths will lead to defaults, devaluations, disruptive deflation, and the financial, economic, social, and political chaos that will ensue. And here we are, in a tough spot, all around the world.

The most worrisome part of this top spot was summarized in a Bloomberg News headline in 2019: "The way out for a world economy hooked on debt? More debt."[5] Nations around the world have become debt junkies, weakening the overall health and resilience of the world economy. In advanced and emerging countries alike, economic growth has become dependent on larger and larger injections of debt.[6] The unconventional monetary policies pursued by central bankers have been central to this debt explosion.[7] We now face a dual challenge: we must untie the knots that unconventional monetary policies and sky-high debt levels have formed, and we need a new growth model to achieve that objective. We cannot achieve this without significant structural reforms.

There are two intermediate objectives for these structural reforms. First, the right incentives to obtain maximal employment must be put in place—for example, attending to taxation and regulatory hurdles that limit employment possibilities for the young and the elderly. Educational and job-retraining initiatives and reduction of wage costs are essential, particularly in advanced countries with significant numbers of less-educated, inexperienced, and difficult-to-employ citizens. Mechanisms to support the low-earned net wage will help provide all citizens with a decent, real, disposable income. An increase in employment levels among the active labor force to 80 percent or higher will benefit both the newly employed and society in general, as it will lower crime rates and help reduce budget deficits and public debt, thanks to increased revenue from income taxes and decreased expenditures for unemployment. Furthermore, high employment levels stimulate positive sentiments and expectations among investors, producers, and consumers, setting a virtuous cycle in motion.

The second intermediate objective is to stimulate innovation and productivity-enhancing investments through a refocusing of competition laws, corporate tax regimes, patent laws, and depreciation rules. Most countries must revise their corporate tax laws to discourage debt stockpiling—for example, substantially reducing the tax deductibility of interests to be paid on loans and putting in place tax incentives to strengthen equity capital. These measures will produce a much more resilient corporate sector.

Reforms must place much more focus on stimulating competition and avoiding quasi-monopolistic market situations. Monopolies place a brake on innovation, retard economic growth, and contribute to income and wealth inequalities.[8] Most countries will also need to place special attention on increased and more efficient public investment in order to increase productivity.[9] Of course, the specifics on what structural reforms are needed depend on the status of present policies, and thus they will differ from country to country.

Massive opposition to most structural reforms, mostly from organized interest groups at risk of losing specific advantages, is seemingly unavoidable.[10] In my own experience as Belgium's minister of finance from 2014 to 2018, I found the pursuit of such structural reforms to be a Herculean task. For example, during discussions on a reform of the corporate tax system that focused on lowering base rates, scrapping specific deductions, and simplifying the entire system, an endless parade of sector organizations and interest groups stepped forward to give lip service to agreeing with the rationale for reforms, but insisted that the benefits of the removal of their pet-tax advantage would be outweighed by the damage it would do to their business interests.

Resistance to structural reforms comes from entrenched corporate entities as well as countless other organized special-interest groups, including labor unions, medical associations, government workers, teachers' associations, and literally hundreds of other groups that exist to protect the advantages of its members at all costs—at the expense of the rest of society. The smaller the interest group is, the larger (in relative terms) the advantage will be for each member, and the stronger the incentive will be for each member to fight to retain the advantage. Organized interest groups are specialists in hiding their selfish objectives behind a veil of altruism and sincere concern for society.

Over time, the crusades of special-interest groups stifle the overall growth capacity of the economy by focusing on distribution of the pie rather than enlargement of it.[11] To unlock the full growth potential of the economy, the power of organized interest groups must be restrained. Rapid changes in the technological and regulatory environments will only intensify special-interest groups' resistance to reform.

The economy's growth potential is also dependent on reducing government debt levels. An elaborate review of different analyses on the topic concluded, "The empirical evidence overwhelmingly supports the view that large government debt has a negative impact on the growth potential of the debt-burdened economy. In many cases, this impact gets stronger as debt increases."[12]

To see an example of the critical need for substantive structural reforms to break the vicious circle created by debt-fueled economic growth, look no further than Japan. It was in an emergency situation long before any other country, plagued by the negative consequences of unconventional monetary policies and a spectacular rise in public debt levels since the 1990s. After Shinzō Abe won his second term as prime minister in 2012, he launched his "three arrows" approach to economic policy: Japan would double down on aggressive monetary expansion and substantial further fiscal stimulus, but it would also introduce a program of fundamental structural reforms throughout the Japanese social and economic system in order to lift the potential growth capacity of the nation's economy. On the first two arrows—monetary expansion and fiscal stimulus—the government delivered, but the structural reform arrow missed the target. Results were meager, at best, as the promised turnaround into robust economic growth and escape from rising debt levels and unconventional monetary policies never materialized.

Another lesson from Japan is that accumulation of public debt and relentless increases in central bank balance sheet totals can go on for an interminably long time. Yet there's little comfort to be found in this example, for at least two reasons. For one, Japan's extremely homogeneous population makes it hard to compare with other countries. Second, the unintended negative consequences of unconventional monetary policies increase over time, making corrective actions more imperative as time passes.

Despite frequent arguments to the contrary, there is little choice but to normalize monetary policies within a policy framework that has been adapted to the realities of the twenty-first century. In order for it to work, it must be carried out with a combination of unshakeable strategic resolve and careful consideration of the imperatives of the moment. And it must begin immediately, or financial instability and stalled growth will become fundamentals of our economic model. The disruptions and dislocations that central banks' unconventional monetary policies have caused will increase, and the necessary room to make policy maneuvers will shrink even further. It's impossible to predict when the next conflagration will arrive, but when it does, it will happen all of a sudden, and with massive force. All we can do now is remove the matches, gasoline, and tinder that are lying around.

If the unconventional monetary policies central banks have pursued for the past fifteen years continue, periods of turmoil, disorder, and paralyzing uncertainty will occur with increasing frequency. Crises will become more severe, and the room to adequately react in terms of policy simply won't be there. The return of inflation will become structural. Societies will become more fragile and destabilized. Popular revolt against the powers that be, including the central banks, will intensify, threatening not only the well-being and welfare of large segments of the population, but also the foundations of democratic societies. History has shown that nothing good will come of it.

Acknowledgments

MONETARY ECONOMICS AND CENTRAL BANK POLICIES FIRST began to fascinate me during my student days. Emiel Van Broekhoven, my mentor at the University of Antwerp during the second part of the 1970s, and long afterward, had a major hand in this. At a moment when Keynesianism was still alpha and omega in macroeconomics, he laid out for me the very different world of classical monetary economics. Emiel convinced me of the necessity to read and fully absorb the original contributions of great historical economists like Adam Smith, Knut Wicksell, John Maynard Keynes, and Milton Friedman.

As a journalist and editor, I spoke to literally hundreds of economists about the never-ending debate between the different schools of thought in macroeconomics and their impact on policymaking. In my time spent working in the banking sector and for private companies, the day-to-day relevance of central bank policies became very clear to me. The 2007–2009 global financial crisis and the COVID-19 pandemic had a huge impact on the evolution of the debate among economists, central bankers, and other policymakers.

During my time as Belgium's minister of finance, from 2014 to 2018, I had the opportunity to discuss many of the topics touched on in this book at length with fellow ministers of finance within Europe (Eurogroup, Ecofin, and so on), and also at forums, such as the annual meetings of the IMF and the World Bank, and numerous *ad hoc* events. In these meetings and discussions, we were often joined by central bankers from around the world, as well as leading figures from the world of private finance and economists working in academia and at think tanks. In my role as chairman of the Committee on Budgets of the European Parliament, I was often visited by many people from the financial world anxious to influence regulation and legislation under consideration. Many of these discussions touched on central bank policies at some point during the conversation.

Special thanks with respect to this manuscript go to Geert Noels, the perfectly harmonious biker/economist, and to Jan Smets, Pierre Wunsch, Tom Dechaene, and Jef Boeckx of the Belgian National Bank. I also extend many thanks to Frank Smets and Peter Praet of the ECB, and Klaas Knot, the president of the Dutch central bank.

The list of people who in one way or the other contributed to my thinking on central banks is long: Sven De Neef, my chief of staff as minister of finance of Belgium; Anthony de Lannoy, my assistant chief of staff who later served as executive director of the IMF; Willem Vanlaer, my assistant at the University of Hasselt; Marianne Collin; Herman Daems; Max Jadot; Johan Thijs; Marc Raisière; Jos Clijsters; Vincent Van Dessel; Jean-Laurent Bonnafé; Vittorio Grilli; Koen Hofman; Ivan Van de Cloot; Joep Konings; Servaas Deroose; Michael Bloomberg; André Sapir; Alan Greenspan; Nouriel Roubini; Axel Weber; Ashoka Mody; Raghuram Rajan; Amir Sufi; Anil Kashyap; Austan Goolsbee; Edmund Phelps; Daron Acemoglu; and Deirdre McCloskey.

I extend very special thanks to three colleagues of mine from my time as the Belgian minister of finance. First, Wolfgang Schäuble, the longtime German minister of finance, is a man of extraordinary courage, a rigorous thinker, and a most exemplary statesman. The second former colleague I must thank is Jeroen Dijsselbloem, the Dutch minister of finance who masterfully managed the Greek crisis in the euro area as president of the Eurogroup of ministers of finance. The third is Paschal

Donohue, the Irish minister of finance who has served since July 2020 as president of the Eurogroup; Paschal was always up for a challenging exchange of views.

Of course, I must thank my co-author Stijn Rocher, the young, brilliant, and somewhat eccentric economist who made working at the cabinet of the ministers of finance so much fun more often than not. The whole crew of hardworking men and women who toiled with me when I served as minister of finance deserves to be mentioned here—particularly the two stern and resourceful guardians of the secrets of the temple, Ann Pincket and Ellen Slegers. The same goes for the people with whom I worked so closely as a member of the European Parliament: the same Ellen, Ferry, Katrien, Caroline, Jan, Luc, and Gilles.

I dedicate this book to two of the most fascinating people I have ever met: Milton Friedman and Paul Volcker. The latter I interviewed only once, but that was more than sufficient to make me realize what a giant he was, literally and figuratively. I interviewed Milton Friedman three times in the preparation of my book on the Chicago School, the last time three months before his death. Volcker and Friedman, two men of genius, were humble and friendly, and at the same time intellectually ferocious.

Last but not least, I thank my wife, Danielle; my children, Matthias, David, Frederik, and Laura; their partners; my stepchildren, Nathalie and Isabelle; their partners; and, most of all, my beloved grandchildren, Jacob, Stan, Lucy, Martha, Emma, and Frances. I owe them all many hours of my time, the time I spent focused on this manuscript. I promise to make it up to them.

Bibliography

Acemoglu, Daron, 2009, "The Crisis of 2009: Structural Lessons for and from Economics," *mimeo,* January, author's personal website (accessed November 15, 2019).

Acharya, Viral, 2019, "Creating Zombies and Disinflation—A Cul de Sac for Accommodative Monetary Policy," presentation at the Indian Institute of Technology, Bombay, October 20 (accessed February 4, 2020).

Acharya, Viral; Eisert, Tim; Eufinger, Christian; & Hirsch, Christian, 2019, "Whatever It Takes: The Real Effects of Unconventional Monetary Policy," *The Review of Financial Studies,* September.

Acharya, Viral & Plantin, Guillaume, 2019, "Monetary Easing, Leveraged Payouts, and Lack of Investment," NBER working paper, Cambridge, MA, National Bureau of Economic Research, no. 26471.

Acharya, Viral & Richardson, Matthew, eds., 2009, *Restoring Financial Stability: How to Repair a Failed System,* Hoboken, NJ, John Wiley & Sons.

Acharya, Viral; Richardson, Matthew; Van Nieuwerburgh, Stijn; & White, Lawrence, 2011, *Guaranteed to Fail. Fannie Mae, Freddie Mac and the Debacle of Mortgage Finance,* Princeton, NJ, Princeton University Press.

Adalet McGowan, Müge; Andrews, Dan; & Millot, Valentine, 2017, "The Walking Dead? Zombie Firms and Productivity Performance in OECD Countries," OECD Economics Department working paper, OECD, no. 1372.

Admati, Anat & Hellwig, Martin, 2013, *The Bankers' New Clothes: What's Wrong with Banking and What to Do About It,* Princeton, NJ, Princeton University Press.

Adrian, Tobias & Shin, Hyun Song, 2008, "Financial Intermediaries, Financial Stability and Monetary Policy," *Federal Reserve Bank of New York Staff Reports,* Fed New York, no. 346.

Aguado, Iago, 2001, "The Credit-Anstalt Crisis of 1931 and the Failure of the Austro-German Customs Union Project," *Historical Journal,* no. 44.

Ahamed, Liaquat, 2010, *Lords of Finance: The Bankers Who Broke the World,* London, Windmill Books.

Ahrend, Rudiger, 2010, "Monetary Ease: A Factor Behind Financial Crises? Some Evidence from OECD Countries," *Economics. The Open Access,* Open Assessment E-Journal, p. 4.

Ahrend, Rudiger; Cournede, Boris; & Price, Robert, 2008, "Monetary Policy, Market Excesses, and Financial Turmoil," OECD working paper, Paris, OECD, March.

Alesi, Lucia & Detken, Carsten, 2018, "Identifying Excessive Credit Growth and Leverage," *Journal of Financial Stability,* April.

Alesina, Alberto & Summers, Larry, 1993, "Central Bank Independence and Macroeconomic Performance: Some Comparative Evidence," *Journal of Money, Credit, and Banking,* 25, no. 2.

Andrews, Dan & Petroulakis, Filippos, 2019, "Breaking the Shackles: Zombie Firms, Weak Banks and Depressed Restructuring in Europe," ECB working paper, European Central Bank, no. 2240.

Angeloni, Ignazio, 2020, "Issues Arising from the New 'Powell Doctrine,'" *Project Syndicate,* September 14.

Arrow, Kenneth & Debreu, Gerard, 1954, "Existence of an Equilibrium for a Competitive Economy," *Econometrica,* 22.

Asso, Pier Francesco; Kahn, George; & Leeson, Robert, 2010, "The Taylor Rule and the Practice of Central Banking," Federal Reserve Bank of Kansas City research working paper, no. 10-05.

Awuzu Pereira Da Silva, Luiz, 2019, "The Inflation Conundrum in Advanced Economies and a Way Out," speech at the University of Basel, Switzerland, May 5.

Bagehot, Walter, 1873, *Lombard Street: A Description of the Money Market,* New York, John Wiley & Sons Inc. (1999 edition).

-------, ed. St. John-Stevas, Norman, 1965–1986, *Collected Works,* fifteen volumes, London, *The Economist.*

Bagus, Philippe & Howden, David, 2011, *Deep Freeze: Iceland's Economic Collapse,* Auburn, Alabama, Ludwig von Mises Institute.

Bair, Sheila, 2012, *Bull by the Horns: Fighting to Save Main Street from Wall Street and Wall Street from Itself,* New York, The Free Press.

Ball, Laurence, 2018, *The Fed and Lehman Brothers: Setting the Record Straight on a Financial Disaster,* Cambridge, UK, Cambridge University Press.

Ball, Laurence; Gagnon, Joseph; Honohan, Patrick; & Krogstrup, Signe, 2016, *What Else Can Central Bankers Do?* Centre for Economic Policy Research, Geneva Reports on the World Economy, no. 18.

Banerjee, Ryan & Hofmann, Boris, 2018, "The Rise of Zombie Firms: Causes and Consequences," *BIS Quarterly Review,* September.

-------, 2020, "Corporate Zombies: Anatomy and Life Cycle," BIS working paper, Bank for International Settlements, no. 882.

Baring, Sir Francis, 1797, *Observations on the Establishment of the Bank of England and on the Paper Circulation of the Country,* New York, Augustus M. Kelley, 1967 edition.

Barwell, Richard, 2013, *Macro Prudential Policy: Taming the Wild Gyrations of Credit Flows, Debt Stocks, and Asset Prices,* New York, Palgrave Macmillan.

Basu, Kaushik, 2013, "Two Policy Prescriptions for the Global Crisis," *Project Syndicate,* April 23.

Bauer, Michael & Rudebusch, Glenn, 2016, "Why Are Long-Term Interest Rates So Low?" *FRBSF Economic Letter,* Federal Reserve Bank of San Francisco, no. 36, December 5.

Bayoumi, Tamim, 2019, *Unfinished Business: The Unexplored Causes of the Financial Crisis and the Lessons Yet to be Learned,* New Haven, CT, Yale University Press.

Becker, Bo & Ivashina, Victoria, 2015, "Reaching for Yield in the Bond Market," *Journal of Finance,* vol. 70, no. 5.

Beckworth, David, 2014, "Inflation Targeting. A Monetary Policy Regime Whose Time Has Come and Gone," Mercatus Center Research Papers, July 10.

Bernanke, Ben, 2000, *Essays on the Great Depression,* Princeton, NJ, Princeton University Press.

-------, 2002(a), "On Milton Friedman's Ninetieth Birthday," remarks at the Conference to Honor Milton Friedman, University of Chicago, Illinois, November 8.

-------, 2002(b), "Deflation: Making Sure 'It' Doesn't Happen Here," speech at the Washington, DC, Economists Club, November 21.

-------, 2003, "'Constrained Discretion' and Monetary Policy," speech before the Money Marketeers of New York University, New York, February 3.

-------, 2005, "The Global Savings Glut and the US Current Account," *Homer Jones Lecture,* St. Louis, MO, Federal Reserve Bank of St. Louis.

-------, 2013, "The Crisis as a Classical Financial Panic," speech delivered at the Fourteenth Jacques Polak Annual Research Conference, Washington, DC, Board of Governors of the Federal Reserve System.

-------, 2015(a), *The Courage to Act: A Memoir of a Crisis and Its Aftermath,* New York, W.W. Norton and Company.

-------, 2015(b), "Monetary Policy and Inequality," brookings.edu, Brookings Institution, June 1.

-------, 2020, "The New Tools of Monetary Policy," *American Economic Review,* April.

Bernanke, Ben; Geithner, Timothy; & Paulson, Henry, 2019, *Firefighting: The Financial Crisis and Its Lessons,* New York, Penguin Books.

Blanchard, Olivier, 2008, "The State of Macro," NBER working paper, National Bureau of Economic Research, no. 14529.

Blanchard, Olivier & Summers, Lawrence, eds., 2019, *Evolution or Revolution? Rethinking Macroeconomic Policy After the Great Recession,* Cambridge, MA, The MIT Press.

Blinder, Alan, 2013, *After the Music Stopped: The Financial Crisis, the Response, and the Work Ahead,* New York, Penguin Press.

Blot, Christophe; Creel, Jérôme; & Hubert, Paul, 2020, "Financial Stability Risks and Policy Options," *Monetary Dialogue Papers,* European Parliament, Economic and Monetary Committee, February.

Bordo, Michael, 2014, "Exiting from Low Interest Rates to Normality: An Historical Perspective," Hoover Institution Economics working paper, Stanford University, Palo Alto, CA, no. 14110.

Bordo, Michael; Eitrheim, Oyvind; Flandreau, Marc; & Qvigstad, Jan, eds., 2016, *Central Banks at a Crossroads: What Can We Learn from History?* New York, Cambridge University Press.

Bordo, Michael & Filardo, Andrew, 2005, "Deflation and Monetary Policy in a Historical Perspective," *Economic Policy,* vol. 20, no. 44.

Borio, Claudio, 2014, "The Financial Cycle and Macroeconomics: What Have We Learned?" *Journal of Banking and Finance,* August.

-------, 2017, "Through the Looking Glass," OMFIF City Lecture, The Official Monetary and Financial Institutions Forum, London, September 22.

-------, 2019(a), "Vulnerabilities in the International Monetary and Financial System," speech given at the OECD-G20 High Level Policy Seminar, Paris, September 11.

-------, 2019(b), "Central Banking in Challenging Times," SUERF Annual Lecture, SUERF/BAFFI CAREFIN Centre Conference, Mila, Algeria, November 8.

-------, 2020, "The COVID-19 Economic Crisis: Dangerously Unique," National Association for Business Economics, Perspectives on the Pandemic Webinar Series, July 2.

Borio, Claudio & Disyatat, Piti, 2010, "Unconventional Monetary Policies: An Appraisal," BIS working paper, Bank for International Settlements, no. 292.

Borio, Claudio; Disyatat, Piti; Juselius, Mikael; & Rungcharoenkitkul, Phurichai, 2017, "Why So Low for So Long? A Long-Term View of Real Interest Rates," BIS working paper, Bank for International Settlements, no. 685.

-------, 2018, "Monetary Policy in the Grip of a Pincer Movement," BIS working paper, Bank for International Settlements, no. 706.

Borio, Claudio; Erdem, Magdalena; Filardo, Andrew; & Hofmann, Boris, 2015, "The Costs of Deflations. A Historical Perspective," *BIS Quarterly Review*, Bank for International Settlements, March.

Borio, Claudio & Lowe, Philip, 2002, "Asset Prices, Financial and Monetary Stability: Exploring the Nexus," BIS working paper, Bank for International Settlements, no. 114.

Borio, Claudio & White, William, 2003, "Whither Monetary and Financial Stability? The Implications of Evolving Policy Regimes," BIS working paper, Bank for International Settlements, no. 147.

Boyes, Roger, 2009, *Meltdown Iceland: Lessons on the World Financial Crisis from a Small Bankrupt Island*, London, Bloomsbury Publishing.

Brown, Brendan, 2018, "What Is Wrong with the 2 percent Inflation Targeting," in Godart-van der Kroon, A. & Von Lamthen, P. eds., *Banking and Monetary Policy from the Perspective of Austrian Economics*, New York, Springer International Publishing.

Brunner, Karl, 1981, "The Art of Central Banking," Center for Research in Government Policy and Business, Graduate School of Management, University of Rochester, working paper, GPB, no. 81-6, June.

Brunnermeier, Markus; James, Harold; & Landau, Jean-Pierre, 2016, *The Euro and the Battle of Ideas*, Princeton, NJ, Princeton University Press.

Brunnermeier, Marcus & Koby, Yann, 2018, "The Reversal Interest Rate," NBER working paper, National Bureau of Economic Research, no. 25406.

Buti, Marco, 2020, "Economic Policy in the Rough. A European Journey," *CEPR Policy Insight*, Center for Economic Policy Research, 98.

Buttiglione, Luigi; Lane, Philip; Reichlin, Lucrezia; & Reinart, Vincent, 2014, *Deleveraging? What Deleveraging?* Geneva Reports on the World Economy 16, London, CEPR Press.

Caballero, Ricardo, Hoshi, Takeo; & Kashyap, Anil, 2008, "Zombie Lending and Depressed Restructuring in Japan," *American Economic Review*, vol. 98, no. 5.

Calomiris, Charles, 2009, "Financial Innovation, Regulation, and Reform," *Cato Journal*, Winter.

Carr, Edward, 1939, *The Twenty Years' Crisis, 1919-1939: An Introduction to the Study of International Relations*, London, Macmillan, 1946 edition.

Caruana, Jaime, 2014, "Debt: The View from Basel," BIS Papers, Bank for International Settlements, no. 80.

Cassel, Gustav, 1920, "Further Observations on the World's Monetary Problem," *Economic Journal,* March.

-------, 1928, *Postwar Monetary Stabilization,* New York, Columbia University Press.

Cavallo, Alberto, 2018, "More Amazon Effects: Online Competition and Pricing Behaviors," NBER working paper, National Bureau of Economic Research, no. 25138.

Cecchetti, Stephen, 2007, "Why Central Bankers Should Be Financial Supervisors," *Vox,* CEPR Policy Portal, November 30.

Cecchetti, Stephen & Kharroubi, Enisse, 2012, "Reassessing the Impact of Finance on Growth," BIS working paper, Bank for International Settlements, no. 381.

-------, 2015, "Why Does Financial Sector Growth Crowd Out Real Economic Growth," BIS working paper, Bank for International Settlements, no. 490.

-------, 2018, "Why Does Credit Growth Crowd Out Real Economic Growth?" NBER working paper, National Bureau of Economic Research, no. 25079.

Cecchetti, Stephen; Moharty, M.S.; & Zampolli, Fabrizio, 2011, "The Real Effects of Debt," BIS working paper, Bank for International Settlements, no. 352.

Chandler Jr., Alfred, 1977, *The Visible Hand: The Managerial Revolution in Business,* Cambridge, MA, Harvard University Press.

Chen, Qianying; Filardo, Andrew; He, Dong; & Zhu, Feng, 2015, "Financial Crisis, US Unconventional Monetary Policy and International Spillovers," BIS working paper, Bank for International Settlements, no. 494.

Chen, Qianying; Lombardi, Marco; Ross, Alex; & Zhu, Feng, 2017, "Global Impact of US and Euro Area Unconventional Monetary Policies," BIS working paper, Bank for International Settlements, no. 610.

Chernow, Ron, 2004, *Alexander Hamilton,* New York, Penguin Press.

Cieslak, Anna & Vissing-Jørgensen, Annette, 2018, "The Economics of the Fed Put," working paper, faculty.haas.berkeley.edu (accessed March 24, 2021).

Claessens, Stijn; Pozsar, Zoltan; Ratnovski, Lev; & Singh, Manmohan, 2012, "Shadow Banking: Economics and Policy," *IMF Staff Discussion Notes,* Washington, DC, International Monetary Fund, SDN 12/12, December 4.

Coggan, Philip, 2020, *More: The 10,000-Year Rise of the World Economy,* London, The Economist Books.

Collins, Chuck & Hoxie, Josh, "Report: Billionaire Bonanza 2018: Inherited Wealth Dynasties in the Twenty-First Century United States," *Institute for Policy Studies,* Washington, DC, October 30.

Colciago, Andrea; Samarina, Anna; & de Haan, Jakob, 2019, "Central Bank Policies and Income and Wealth Inequality: A Survey," *Journal of Economic Surveys*, 33(4).

Cour-Thimann, Philippine & Winkler, Bernhard, 2013, "The ECB's Non-Standard Monetary Policy Measures: The Role of Institutional Factor and Financial Structure," ECB working paper, European Central Bank, no. 1528.

Cowen, David; Sylla, Richard; & Wright, Richard, 2009, "Alexander Hamilton, Central Banker: Crisis Management During the US Financial Panic of 1792," *Business History Review*, vol. 83, no. 1.

Crowe, Christopher & Meade, Ellen, 2007, "The Evolution of Central Bank Governance around the World," *Journal of Economic Perspectives*, Fall.

Cui, Wei & Sterk, Vincent, 2018, "Quantitative Easing," CEPR discussion paper, Centre for Economic Policy Research, no. 13322.

Currie, Lauchlin, 1934, "The Failure of Monetary Policy to Prevent the Great Depression of 1929–1932," *Journal of Political Economy*.

Darvas, Zsolt, 2018, "Global Income Inequality Is Declining—Largely Thanks to China and India," bruegel.org, Brussels, Bruegel, April 19.

Davies, Glyn, 2002, *A History of Money from Ancient Times to the Present Day*, Cardiff, UK, University of Wales Press, 3rd edition.

Davies, William, 2017, "The Big Mystique," *London Review of Books*, Vol. 39, No. 3, February 2.

Debreu, Gerard, 1959, *The Theory of Value: An Axiomatic Analysis of Economic Equilibrium*, New York, John Wiley & Sons.

de Guindos, Luis, 2019, "International Spillovers of Monetary Policy and Financial Stability Concerns," speech at The ECB and Its Watchers XX Conference, Frankfurt, March 27.

Dell'Ariccia, Giovanni; Rabanal, Paul; & Sandri, Damiano, 2018, "Unconventional Monetary Policies in the Euro Area, Japan, and the United Kingdom," *Journal of Economic Perspectives*, Fall.

Dellemotte, Jean, 2009, "Adam Smith's 'Invisible Hand': Refuting the Conventional Wisdom," *L'Economie Politique*, no. 44.

De Loecker, Jan & Eeckhout, Jan, 2018, "Global Market Power," NBER working paper, National Bureau of Economic Research, no. 24768.

de Larosiere, Jacques, 2020, "Negative Interest Rates Cannot Save Indebted Countries," *Financial Times*, July 20.

Del Negro, Marco; Giannone, Domenico; Giannoni, Marc; & Tambalotti, Andrea, 2018, "Global Trends in Interest Rates," FRBNY staff reports, Federal Reserve Bank of New York, no. 866, September.

den Haan, Wouter, ed., 2013, *Forward Guidance: Perspectives from Central Bankers, Scholars, and Market Participants,* VoxEU.org eBooks, Centre for Economic Policy Research.

Derman, Emmanuel, 2004, *My Life as a Quant,* Hoboken, NJ, John Wiley & Sons.

de Rugy, Véronique & Salmon, Jack, 2020, "Debt and Growth: A Decade of Studies," *Mercatus Center Policy Briefs,* George Mason University, April 15.

de Soyres, François & Franco, Sebastian, 2019, "Inflation Dynamics and Global Value Chains," policy research working paper, Washington, World Bank Group, no. 9090, December.

Divine, Robert, 1967, *Second Chance: The Triumph of Internationalism in America During World War II,* New York, Atheneum Press.

Dobbs, Richard; Lund, Susan; Woetzel, Jonathan; & Mutafchieva, Mina, 2015, *Debt and (Not Much) Deleveraging,* McKinsey Global Institute, February.

Donovan, Donal & Murphy, Antoin, 2013, *The Fall of the Celtic Tiger,* Oxford, UK, Oxford University Press.

Douthat, Ross, 2020, *The Decadent Society: How We Became the Victims of Our Own Success,* New York, Avid Reader Press.

Dowd, Kevin, 2009, *Measuring Market Risk,* Hoboken, NJ, John Wiley & Sons.

Drehmann, Mathias; Juselius, Mikael; & Korinek, Anton, 2017, "Accounting for Debt Service. The Painful Legacy of Credit," BIS working paper, Bank for International Settlements, no. 645.

ECB, 2006, *A Journey from Theory to Practice. An ECB Colloquium Held in Honor of Otmar Issing,* Frankfurt, March.

-------, 2016, "Public Investment in Europe," *ECB Economic Bulletin,* European Central Bank, issue 2.

-------, 2017, "Domestic and Global Drivers of Inflation," *ECB Economic Bulletin,* Frankfurt, European Central Bank, issue 4.

-------, 2019, *Financial Stability Report,* Frankfurt, November.

Ehrmann, Michael; Gaballo, Gaetano; Hoffmann, Peter; & Strasser, Georg, 2019, "Can More Public Information Raise Uncertainty? The International Evidence on Forward Guidance," ECB working paper, European Central Bank, no. 2263.

Eichengreen, Barry, 1992, *Golden Fetters: The Gold Standard and the Great Depression, 1919–1939,* New York, Oxford University Press.

-------, 2011, *The Rise and Fall of the Dollar and the Future of the International Monetary System,* New York, Oxford University Press.

-------, 2014, "The Rules of Central Banking Are Made to be Broken," *Financial Times,* August 22.

-------, 2015, *Hall of Mirrors: The Great Depression, the Great Recession, and the Uses—and Misuses—of History*, New York, Oxford University Press.

-------, 2019, "Critics of QE Should Consider the Alternatives," *The Guardian*, June 11.

Eichengreen, Barry & Mitchener, Kris, 2003, "The Great Depression as a Credit Boom Gone Wrong," BIS working paper, Bank for International Settlements, no. 137.

Eisinger, Jesse, 2007, "Overrated," Portfolio.com, September.

El-Erian, Mohamed, 2020(a), "Central Banks Are Now the Markets' Best Friends," *The Guardian*, January 10.

-------, 2020(b), "The Pandemic's Complex Cocktail," *Project Syndicate*, October 6.

Emminger, Otto, 1934, "Die Englischen Währungsexperimente der Nachkriegszeit," *Weltwirtschaftliches Archiv*, September.

Epstein, Gerald, 2005, "Central Banks as Agents of Economic Development," Political Economy Research Institute working paper, University of Massachusetts, Amherst, no. 104.

Estrada, Javier, 2008, "Black Swans and Market Timing: How Not to Generate Alpha," *Journal of Investing*, Autumn.

-------, 2009, "Black Swans, Market Timing, and the Dow," *Applied Economic Letters*, 16.

Farrell, Greg, 2010, *Crash of the Titans: Greed, Hubris, the Fall of Merrill Lynch, and the Near-Collapse of Bank of America*, New York, Crown Business.

Fed Kansas City, 2003, *Monetary Policy and Uncertainty. Adapting to a Changing Economy*, Jackson Hole Symposium, August.

-------, 2005, *The Greenspan Era. Lessons for the Future*, Jackson Hole Symposium, August.

Feldstein, Martin, 1997, "The Costs and Benefits of Going from Low Inflation to Price Stability," in Romer, Christina & Romer, David, eds., *Reducing Inflation: Motivation and Strategy*, Chicago, University of Chicago Press for the NBER.

Ferguson, Niall; Schaab, Andreas; & Schularick, Moritz, 2014, "Central Bank Balance Sheets: Expansion and Reduction Since 1900," ECB Forum on Central Banking, Sintra, ECB, May.

Fetter, Frank, 1965, *The Development of British Monetary Orthodoxy 1797–1875*, Cambridge, MA, Harvard University Press.

Fiedler, Salomon & Gern, Klaus-Jürgen, 2020, "Financial Stability in the Euro Area," Monetary Dialogue Papers, European Parliament, Economic and Monetary Committee, January.

Filardo, Andrew & Nakajima, Jouchi, 2018, "Effectiveness of Unconventional Monetary Policies in a Low Interest Rate Environment," BIS working paper, Bank for International Settlements, no. 691.

Filardo, Andrew, 2019, "The Reaction Function Channel of Monetary Policy and the Financial Cycle," BIS working paper, Bank for International Settlements, no. 816.

Filardo, Andrew; Hubert, Paul; & Rungcharoenkitkul, Phurichai, 2019, "The Reaction Function Channel of Monetary Policy and the Financial Cycle," BIS working paper, Bank for International Settlements, no. 816.

Fisher, Irving, 1933, "The Debt-Deflation Theory of Great Depressions," *Econometrica,* October.

Fisher, Stanley, 2016, "US Monetary Policy from an International Perspective," speech at the 20th Annual Conference of the Central Bank of Chile, Santiago, November 11.

FitchRatings, 2019, "Shadow Banking Implications for Financial Stability," FitchRatings, May 21.

Forbes, Kristin, 2019, "Has Globalization Changed the Inflation Process?" BIS working paper, Bank for International Settlements, no. 791.

Frankel, Jeffrey, 2019, "Why Central Bankers Should Forget About 2 Percent Inflation," *The Guardian,* July 26.

Freeman, Richard, 2007, "The Great Doubling: The Challenge of the New Global Labor Market," in Edwards, J. Crain, M. & Kallenberg, A., eds., *Ending Poverty in America: How to Restore the American Dream,* New York, The New Press.

Friedman, Benjamin, 2008, "Chairman Greenspan's Legacy," *The New York Review of Books,* March 20.

Friedman, Milton, 1948, "A Monetary and Fiscal Framework for Monetary Stability," *American Economic Review,* June.

-------, 1960, *A Program for Monetary Stability,* New York, Fordham University Press.

-------, 1968, "The Role of Monetary Policy," *American Economic Review,* March.

-------, 1970, "The Counter-Revolution in Monetary Theory," IEA Occasional Paper, London, Institute of Economic Affairs, no. 33.

-------, 1997, "John Maynard Keynes," *Economic Quarterly,* Federal Reserve Bank of Richmond, Spring.

Friedman, Milton & Schwartz, Anna, 1963, *A Monetary History of the United States, 1863-1960,* Princeton, NJ, Princeton University Press.

FSB, 2020, *Global Monitoring Report on Non-Bank Financial Intermediation 2019,* Basel, Switzerland, Financial Stability Board, January.

Gagnon, Joseph & Sack, Brian, 2018, "QE: A User's Guide," *PIIE Policy Brief,* Washington, Peterson Institute for International Economics, October.

Gajewski, Pavel, 2015, "Is Ageing Deflationary? Some Evidence from OECD Countries," *Applied Economics Letters,* vol. 22, no. 11.

Galbraith, John Kenneth, 1954, *The Great Crash 1929,* New York, Houghton Mifflin.

-------, 1990, *A Short History of Financial Euphoria,* London, Penguin Books.

Garber, Peter, 2000, *Famous First Bubbles: The Fundamentals of Early Manias,* Cambridge, MA, MIT Press.

Gennaioli, Nicola; Shleifer, Andrei; & Vishny, Robert, 2015, "Neglected Risks: The Psychology of Financial Crises," NBER working paper, National Bureau of Economic Research, no. 20875.

George, Eddie, 1994, "The Pursuit of Financial Stability," *Bank of England Quarterly Bulletin,* February.

Georgieva, Kristalina, 2019, "How to Use Debt Wisely," Speech at the 20th Annual Research Conference, IMF, Washington, DC.

Gern, Klaus-Jörgen; Jannsen, Nils; Kooths, Stefan; & Wolters, Maik, 2015, "Quantitative Easing in the Euro Area: Transmission Channels and Risks," *Intereconomics,* Review of European Economic Policy, vol. 50, no. 4.

Giannini, Curzio, 2011, *The Age of Central Banks,* Cheltenham, UK, Edward Elgar Publishing.

Goldgar, Anne, 2008, *Tulipmania: Money, Honor, and Knowledge in the Dutch Golden Age,* Chicago, University of Chicago Press.

-------, 2018, "Tulip Mania: The Classical Story of a Dutch Financial Bubble Is Mostly Wrong," *The Conversation,* Boston, February 12.

Goldin, Ian; Koutroumpis, Pantelis; Lafond, François; Rochowicz, Nils; & Winkler, Julian, 2019, *The Productivity Paradox: Reconciling Rapid Technological Change and Stagnating Productivity,* Oxford, Oxford Martin School & Arrowgrass.

Goodfriend, Marvin, 1988, "Central Banking Under the Gold Standard," Carnegie-Rochester Conference Series on Public Policy, no. 19.

Goodhart, Charles, 1988, *The Evolution of Central Banks,* Boston, MIT Press.

-------, 1999, "Myths About the Lender of Last Resort," *International Finance,* 2:3.

Goodhart, Charles & Pradhan, Manoj, 2020, *The Great Demographic Reversal: Aging Societies, Waning Inequality, and an Inflation Revival,* London, Palgrave Macmillan.

Gourinchas, Pierre-Olivier & Obstfeld, Maurice, 2012, "Stories of the Twentieth Century for the Twenty-First," *American Economic Journal: Macroeconomics,* 4(1).

Graeber, David, 2011, *Debt: The First 5,000 Years,* New York, Melville House.

Greenspan, Alan, 2003, "Monetary Policy Under Uncertainty," in Fed Kansas City.

-------, 2007, *The Age of Turbulence. Adventures in A New World,* New York, The Penguin Group.

Greenwood, Robin & Scharfstein, David, 2013, "The Growth of Finance," *Journal of Economic Perspectives,* Spring.

Greider, William, 1989, *Secrets of the Temple: How the Federal Reserve Runs the Country,* New York, Simon & Schuster.

Gros, Daniel, 2016, "The Deflation Bogeyman," *Project Syndicate,* April 8.

-------, 2020, "The Dangerous Allure of Green Central Banking," *Project Syndicate,* December 18.

Haberler, Gottfried, 1976, *The World Economy, Money, and the Great Depression, 1919–39,* Washington, DC, American Enterprise Institute for Public Policy Research.

Haldane, Andrew, 2009, "Why Banks Failed the Stress Tests," speech at the Marcus-Evans Conference on Stress Testing, London, February 9–10.

Hall, Thomas & Ferguson, David, 1998, *The Great Depression: An International Disaster of Perverse Economic Policies,* Ann Arbor, University of Michigan Press.

Hammond, Gill, 2011, "State of the Art of Inflation Targeting," *Centre for Central Banking Studies Handbook,* London, Bank of England, no. 29.

Hartmann, Philip; Huang, Haizhou; & Schoenmaker, Dirk, eds., 2018, *The Changing Nature of Central Banking,* Cambridge, UK, Cambridge University Press.

Hartwell, Christopher, 2020, "Financial Risks in Europe: The End of the Beginning," Monetary Dialogue Papers, European Parliament, Economic and Monetary Committee, January.

Hawtrey, Ralph, 1933, *The Art of Central Banking,* London, Longmans, Green & Co.

Hayek, Friedrich, 1976, *Law, Legislation and Liberty: Volume 2: The Mirage of Social Justice,* Chicago, University of Chicago Press.

Heider, Florian; Saidi, Farzad; & Schepens, Glenn, 2019, "Life Below Zero: Bank Lending Under Negative Policy Rates," *Review of Financial Studies,* 32(10).

Helpman, Elhanan, 2018, *Globalization and Inequality,* Cambridge, MA, Harvard University Press.

Henriques, Diana, 2011, *Bernie Madoff: The Wizard of Lies,* New York, Times Books.

Hesse, Henning; Hofman, Boris; & Weber, James, 2017, "The Macroeconomic Effects of Asset Purchases Revisited," BIS working paper, Bank for International Settlements, no. 680.

Hetzel, Robert, 1987, "Henry Thornton: Seminal Monetary Theorist and Father of the Modern Central Bank," *Economic Review,* Federal Reserve Bank of Richmond, July/August.

Hirschman, Albert, 1977, *The Passions and the Interests: Political Arguments for Capitalism Before Its Triumph,* New Haven, CT, Yale University Press.

Hofmann, Boris & Bogdanova, Bilyana, 2013, "Taylor Rules and Monetary Policy," *BIS Quarterly Review,* September.

Holston, Kathryn; Laubach, Thomas; & Williams, John, 2017, "Measuring the Natural Rate: International Trends and Determinants," *Journal of International Economics,* 108.

Honohan, Patrick, 2019, "Should Monetary Policy Take Inequality and Climate Change into Account?" PIIE working paper, Peterson Institute for International Economics, October, no. 19–18.

Hoover, Herbert, 1952, *The Memoirs of Herbert Hoover: The Great Depression, 1929–1941,* New York, Macmillan.

Hoshi, Takeo & Kashyap, Anil, 2004, "Japan's Financial Crisis and Economic Stagnation," *Journal of Economic Perspectives,* Winter.

-------, 2015, "Will the US and Europe Avoid a Lost Decade? Lessons from Japan's Postcrisis Experience," *IMF Economic Review,* vol. 63, no. 1.

Humphrey, Thomas, 1989, "The Lender of Last Resort: The Concept in History," *Economic Review,* Federal Reserve Bank of Richmond, March/April.

-------, 2014, "Averting Financial Crises: Advice from Classical Economists," *Econ Focus,* Federal Reserve Bank of Richmond, fourth quarter.

Hutchinson, John & Smets, Frank, 2017, "Monetary Policy in Uncertain Times: The ECB Monetary Policy Since June 2014," *The Manchester School,* 85.

International Finance Institute, 2020(a), *Global Debt Monitor: Sustainability Matters,* IIF, Washington, DC, January 13.

-------, 2020(b), *Global Debt Monitor: Attack of the Debt Tsunami,* IIF, Washington, DC, November 18.

Irwin, Douglas, 2014, "Who Anticipated the Great Depression? Gustav Kassel Versus Keynes and Hayek on the Interwar Gold Standard," *Journal of Money, Credit, and Banking,* February.

Irwin, Neil, 2013, *The Alchemists: Three Central Bankers in a World on Fire,* New York, Penguin Books.

Issing, Otmar, 2013, "A New Paradigm for Monetary Policy?" *International Finance,* no. 16:2.

-------, 2020, "The Danger of Following the Fed," *Project Syndicate,* October 2.

James, Harold, 2009, *The Creation and Destruction of Value: The Globalization Cycle,* Cambridge, MA, Harvard University Press.

-------, 2012, *Making the European Monetary Union,* Cambridge, MA, The Belknap Press of Harvard University Press.

Jimenez, Gabriel; Ongena, Steven; Peydró, José-Luis; & Saurina, Jesus, 2014, "Hazardous Times for Monetary Policy. What Do Twenty-Three Million Bank Loans Say About the Effects of Monetary Policy on Risk-Taking?" *Econometrica,* vol. 82, no. 2.

Jokipii, Terhi; Nyffeler, Reto; & Riederer, Stéphane, 2020, "The BIS Credit-to-GDP Gap and Its Critiques," *Project Syndicate,* December 8.

Jones, Joseph, 1934, *Tariff Retaliation: Repercussions of the Hoover-Smoot Bill,* Philadelphia, University of Philadelphia Press.

Jordà, Òscar; Schularick, Moritz; & Taylor, Allen, 2011, "When Credit Bites Back: Leverage, Business Cycles, and Crises," NBER working paper, National Bureau of Economic Research, no. 17621.

-------, 2015, "Leveraged Bubbles," *Journal of Monetary Economics,* no. 76.

-------, 2016, "Macrofinancial History and the New Business Cycle Facts," NBER working paper, National Bureau of Economic Research, no. 22743.

Jordà, Òscar; Marti, Chitra; Nechio, Fernanda; & Tallman, Eric, 2019, "Why Is Inflation Low Globally?" *FRBSF Economic Letter,* Federal Reserve Bank of San Francisco, July 15.

Juselius, Mikael & Takáts, Elöd, 2018, "The Enduring Link Between Demography and Inflation," BIS working paper, Bank for International Settlements, no. 722.

Juselius, Mikael; Borio, Claudio; Disyatat, Piti; & Drehmann, Mathias, 2016, "Monetary Policy, the Financial Cycle, and Ultra-Low Interest Rates," BIS working paper, Bank for International Settlements, no. 561.

Kahneman, Daniel, 2011, *Thinking, Fast and Slow,* New York, Farrar, Straus, and Giroux.

Kanbur, Ravi, 2020, "An Age of Rising Equality? No, but Yes," *Project Syndicate,* September 21.

Kaufman, Henry, 2009, *The Road to Financial Reformation: Warnings, Consequences, Reforms,* Hoboken, NJ, John Wiley & Sons.

Kelly, Kate, 2009, *Street Fighters: The Last 72 Hours of Bear Stearns, the Toughest Firm on Wall Street,* New York, Penguin Group.

Keynes, John Maynard, 1924, *A Tract on Monetary Reform,* London, Macmillan & Co Limited.

-------, 1936, *The General Theory of Employment, Interest, and Money,* London, Macmillan & Co Limited.

Keys, Benjamin; Mukherjee, Tammoy; Seru, Amit; & Vig, Vikrant, 2010, "Did Securitization Lead to Lax Screening? Evidence from Subprime Loans," *Quarterly Journal of Economics,* February.

Khan, Lina, 2017, "Amazon's Antitrust Paradox," *Yale Law Review,* 126(3).

Kimball, Roger, 1998, "The Greatest Victorian," *The New Criterion,* October.

Kindleberger, Charles, 1973, *The World in Depression, 1929–1939,* Berkeley, University of California Press (1986 edition).

Kindleberger, Charles & Aliber, Robert, 2005, *Manias, Panics, and Crashes: A History of Financial Crashes,* Hoboken, NJ, John Wiley & Sons.

King, Mervyn, 2012, "Twenty Years of Inflation Targeting," The Stamp Memorial Lecture, London, School of Economics and Political Science.

-------, 2016, *The End of Alchemy: Money, Banking, and the Future of the Global Economy,* New York, W.W. Norton & Company.

Kirkegaard, Jacob, 2019, "Yes, We Are Probably All Japanese Now," *Monetary Dialogue,* European Parliament, September.

Kirti, Divya, 2017, "When Gambling for Resurrection Is Too Risky," IMF working paper, International Monetary Fund, 17/180.

Kliesen, Kevin, 2019, "Is the Fed Following a 'Modernized' Version of the Taylor Rule?" Part 1 & 2, *Economic Synopses,* Federal Reserve Bank of St. Louis, no. 2 and 3.

Knight, Frank, 1941, "The Business Cycle, Interest, and Money," *Review of Economics and Statistics,* May.

Koenig, Evan; Leeson, Robert; & Kahn, George, eds., 2012, *The Taylor Rule and the Transformation of Monetary Policy,* Stanford University, Palo Alto, Hoover Institution Press.

Koo, Richard, 2009, *The Holy Grail of Macroeconomics: Lessons from Japan's Great Recession,* Hoboken, NJ, John Wiley & Sons.

Kose, Ayhan; Nagle, Peter; Ohnsorge, Franziska; & Sugawara, Naotaka, 2019, *Global Waves of Debt: Causes and Consequences,* Washington, DC, World Bank Group.

Kuhn, Thomas, 1962, *The Structure of Scientific Revolutions,* Chicago, University of Chicago Press.

Kurlantzick, Joshua, 2016, *State Capitalism: How the Return of Statism Is Transforming the World,* Oxford, UK, Oxford University Press.

Kurz, Mordecai, 2018, "The Darker Side of Information Technology," *The Milken Institute Review,* April 27.

Kuttner, Kenneth, 2018, "Outside the Box: Unconventional Monetary Policy in the Great Recession and Beyond," *Journal of Economic Perspectives,* Fall.

Kydland, Finn & Prescott, Edward, "Rules Rather than Discretion: The Inconsistency of Optimal Plans," *Journal of Political Economy,* vol. 85.

Lagarde, Christine, 2020, "The Monetary Policy Review: Some Preliminary Considerations," speech at the ECB and Its Watchers XXI Conference, September 30.

Laidler, David, 1981, "Adam Smith as a Monetary Economist," *Canadian Journal of Economics,* May.

Lakner, Christoph, 2019, "A Global View of Inequality," *Policy Research Talk,* Washington, DC, World Bank, September 16.

Leeson, Nick, 2016, *Rogue Trader: The Original Story of the Banker Who Broke the System,* London, Sphere.

Lenza, Michele & Slacalek, Jiri, 2018, "How Does Monetary Policy Affect Income and Wealth Inequality? Evidence from Quantitative Easing in the Euro Area," ECB working paper, European Central Bank, October, no. 2190.

Levy, Mickey & Plosser, Charles, 2018, "The Murky Future of Monetary Policy," Hoover Institution Economics working paper, Stanford University, Palo Alto, CA, 20119.

Lo, Stephanie & Rogoff, Kenneth, 2015, "Secular Stagnation, Debt Overhang, and Other Rationales for Sluggish Growth, Six Years On," BIS working paper, Bank for International Settlements, no. 482.

Lonergan, Eric & Greene, Megan, 2020, "Dual Interest Rates Give Central Banks Limitless Fire Power," *Project Syndicate,* September 3.

Lui, Ernest; Mian, Atif; & Sufi, Amir, 2019, "Low Interest Rates, Market Power, and Productivity Growth," mimeo (accessed on Sufi's website, January 15, 2020).

Mackay, Charles, 1841, *Extraordinary Popular Delusions & The Madness of the Crowds,* London, Wordsworth Editions.

Mallaby, Sebastian, 2020, "The Age of Magic Money," *Foreign Affairs,* July/August.

Margo, Robert, 1993, "Employment and Unemployment in the 1930s," *Journal of Economic Perspectives,* 7(2).

Martin, Justin, 2000, *Greenspan: The Man Behind the Money,* Cambridge, MA, Perseus Publishing.

McCloskey, Deirdre, 2006, *The Bourgeois Virtues: Ethics for an Age of Commerce,* Chicago, University of Chicago Press.

-------, 2010, *Bourgeois Dignity: Why Economics Can't Explain the Modern World,* Chicago, University of Chicago Press.

-------, 2016, *Bourgeois Equality: How Ideas, Not Capital or Institutions, Enriched the World,* Chicago, University of Chicago Press.

McCullough, David, 1992, *Truman,* New York, Simon & Schuster.

McDonald, Lawrence & Robinson, Patrick, 2009, *A Colossal Failure of Common Sense: The Inside Story of the Collapse of Lehman Brothers,* New York, Random House.

McKay, Alsidair; Nakamura, Emi; & Steinsson, Jon, 2016, "The Power of Forward Guidance Revisited," *American Economic Review,* no. 106.

McNamara, Christian, 2016, "Temporary Guarantee Program for Money Market Funds," Yale Program on Financial Stability, Intervention Case Study, January 28.

McWilliams, Douglas, 2018, *The Inequality Paradox: How Capitalism Can Work for Everyone,* London, Harry N. Abrams.

Mehrling, Perry, 2011, *The New Lombard Street: How the Fed Became the Dealer of Last Resort,* Princeton, NJ, Princeton University Press.

Mehrotra, Aaron; Moessner, Richhild; & Shu, Chang, 2019, "Interest Rate Spillovers from the United States. Expectations, Term Premia, and Macro-Financial Vulnerabilities," BIS working paper, Bank for International Settlements, no. 814.

Meltzer, Alan, 1976, "Monetary and Other Explanations of the Great Depression," *Journal of Monetary Economics,* November.

Mersch, Yves, 2020, "Asset Price Inflation and Monetary Policy," keynote speech at the celebration of INVESTAS' 60th anniversary, Luxembourg, January 27.

Mian, Atif; Straub, Ludwig; & Sufi, Amir, 2019, "Indebted Demand," research paper dated November 2019 (accessed on Mian's website, January 25, 2020).

Micossi, Stefano; D'Onofrio, Alexandra; & Peirce, Fabrizio, 2019, "Herd Behavior in Asset Market Booms and Crashes. The Role of Monetary Policy," *CEPR Policy Insight,* Centre for Economic Policy Research, no. 97.

Miles, David; Panizza, Hugo; Reis, Ricardo; & Ubide, Angel, 2017, *And Yet It Moves: Inflation and the Great Recession,* 19th Geneva Conference on the World Economy, Centre for Economic Policy Research, October.

Miller, Marcus; Weller, Paul; & Zhang, Lei, 2002, "Moral Hazard and the US Stock Market: Analyzing the 'Greenspan Put,'" *Economic Journal,* vol. 112, no. 478.

Minsky, Hyman, 1982, "The Financial Stability Hypothesis: Capitalistic Processes and the Behavior of the Economy," in Kindleberger, Charles & Laffargue, J.P., eds., *Financial Crises: Theory, History, and Policy*, Cambridge, UK, Cambridge University Press.

Miron, Jeffrey, 2015, *Fiscal Imbalance: A Primer*, Washington, DC, The Cato Institute.

Mishkin, Frederic, 2004, "Can Central Bank Transparency Go Too Far?" NBER working paper, National Bureau of Economic Research, no. 10829.

Mody, Ashoka, 2018, *Euro Tragedy: A Drama in Nine Acts*, Oxford, UK, Oxford University Press.

Mojon, Benoit & Ragot, Xavier, 2019, "Can an Ageing Workforce Explain Low Inflation?" BIS working paper, Bank for International Settlements, no. 776.

Montecino, Juan Antonio & Epstein, Gerald, 2015, "Did Quantitative Easing Increase Income Inequality?" NET working paper, Institute for New Economic Thinking, December, no. 28.

-------, 2019, "Draghi's Dangerous Farewell," *Vox*, CEPR's Policy Portal, September 9.

Nelson, Benjamin; Pinter, Gabor; & Theodoridis, Konstantinos, 2015, "Do Contractionary Monetary Policy Shocks Expand Shadow Banking?" Bank of England working paper, London, no. 521.

Nelson, Edward, 2008, "Friedman and Taylor on Monetary Policy Rules: A Comparison," *Federal Reserve Bank of St Louis Review*, March/April.

Niehans, Jürg, 1990, *A History of Economic Theory: Classical Contributions 1720–1980*, Baltimore, The Johns Hopkins University Press.

Nikolsko-Rzhevskyy, Alex & Prodan, Ruxandra, 2019, "The Taylor Principles," *Journal of Macroeconomics*, December.

Norman, Jesse, 2018, *Adam Smith: The Father of Economics*, New York, Basic Books.

Obstfeld, Maurice; Shambaugh, Jay; & Taylor, Alan, 2005, "The Trilemma in History: Tradeoffs Among Exchange Rates, Monetary Policies, and Capital Mobility," *Review of Economics and Statistics*, 87(3).

OECD, 2014, *Effective Public Investment Across Levels of Government: Principles for Action*, Paris, OECD.

-------, 2015, "Can Pension Funds and Life Insurance Companies Keep Their Promises?" Chapter 4 in *OECD Business and Finance Outlook*, Paris, OECD.

Olson, Mancur, 1965, *The Logic of Collective Action: Public Goods and the Theory of Interest Groups*, Cambridge, MA, Harvard University Press.

-------, 1982, *The Rise and Decline of Nations: Economic Growth, Stagnation, and Social Rigidities*, New Haven, CT, Yale University Press.

Papademos, Lucas & Modigliani, Franco, 1990, "The Supply of Money and the Control of National Income," in Friedman, Benjamin & Hahn, Frank, eds., *Handbook of Monetary Economics,* Part I, New York, North-Holland.

Paul, Ron, 2009, *End the Fed,* New York, Grand Central Publishing.

Paulson, Hank Jr., 2010, *On the Brink: Inside the Race to Stop the Collapse of the Global Financial System,* New York, Hachette Book Group.

Peake, Charles, 1995, "Henry Thornton in the History of Economics: Confusions and Contributions," *The Manchester School,* September.

Pettis, Michael, 2019, "Why US Debt Must Continue to Grow," *Carnegie Endowment for International Peace,* Comment, February 7.

Philippon, Thomas & Reshef, Ariell, 2012, "Wages and Human Capital in the US Financial Industry," *Quarterly Journal of Economics,* November.

Pigou, Arthur, 1949, *The Veil of Money,* London, Macmillan.

Plosser, Charles, 2014, "A Limited Central Bank," *Cato Journal,* 34, no. 2.

Posen, Adam, 2013, "The Myth of the Omnipotent Central Banker," *Foreign Affairs,* July/August.

Posner, Eric, 2018, *Last Resort. The Financial Crisis and the Future of Bailouts,* Chicago, The University of Chicago Press.

Powell, Jerome, 2020, "New Economic Challenges and the Fed's Monetary Policy Review" speech given at the 2020 Economic Policy Symposium sponsored by the Federal Reserve Bank of Kansas City, Jackson Hole, Wyoming, August.

Pozsar, Zoltan; Adrian, Tobias; & Ashcroft, Adam, 2013, "Shadow Banking," *FRBNY Economic Policy Review,* Federal Reserve Bank of New York, December 1.

Prins, Nomi, 2018, *Collusion: How Central Banks Rigged the World,* New York, Bold Type Books.

Rajan, Raghuram, 2005, "Has Financial Development Made the World Riskier?" in Fed Kansas City, *The Greenspan Era: Lessons for the Future,* Jackson Hole Symposium, August.

-------, 2009, "The Credit Crisis and Cycle Proof Regulation," The 2009 Homer Jones Lecture, Federal Reserve Bank of St. Louis.

-------, 2010, *Fault Lines: How Hidden Fractures Still Threaten the World Economy,* Princeton, NJ, Princeton University Press.

-------, 2013, "A Step in the Dark: Unconventional Monetary Policy After the Crisis," *Andrew Crockett Memorial Lecture,* Basel, Switzerland, Bank for International Settlements, June 23.

-------, 2014, "Competitive Monetary Easing: Is It Yesterday Once More?" remarks made at the Brookings Institution, Washington, DC, April 10.

Rauchway, Eric, 2015, *The Money Makers: How Roosevelt and Keynes Ended the Depression, Defeated Fascism, and Secured a Prosperous Peace,* New York, Basic Books.

Reinhart, Carmen; Reinhart, Vincent; & Rogoff, Kenneth, 2012, "Public Debt Overhangs: Advanced Economy Episodes Since 1800," *Journal of Economic Perspectives,* Summer.

-------, 2015, "Dealing with Debt," *Journal of International Economics,* July.

Reinhart, Carmen & Rogoff, Kenneth, 2009, *This Time Is Different: Eight Centuries of Financial Folly,* Princeton, NJ, Princeton University Press.

Reinhart, Carmen & Sbrancia, M. Belen, 2015, "The Liquidation of Government Debt," *Economic Policy,* vol. 30, no. 82.

Rey, Hélène, 2013, "Dilemma, Not Trilemma. The Global Financial Cycle and Monetary Independence," in Fed Kansas City, 2013, *Global Dimensions of Unconventional Monetary Policy,* Jackson Hole Symposium, August.

Ricardo, David, 1824, *Plan for the Establishment of a National Bank,* London, John Murray, Albemarle Street.

Roach, Stephen, 2020, "A Return to 1970s Stagflation is only a Broken Supply chain Away," *Financial Times,* May 6.

Rogoff, Kenneth, 2015, "Debt Overhang, Not Secular Stagnation," *Vox,* CEPR's Policy Portal, April 22.

-------, 2019, "Big Tech Has Too Much Monopoly Power: It's Right to Take It On," *The Guardian,* April 2.

Romer, Paul, 2016, "The Trouble with Macroeconomics," Commons Memorial Lecture, Omicron Delta Epsilon Society, delivered January 5 (accessed January 12, 2020).

Rudebusch, Glenn, 2018, "A Review of the Fed's Unconventional Monetary Policy," *FRBSF Economic Letter,* Federal Reserve Bank of San Francisco, 2018-27.

Russell, Bertrand, 1912, *The Problem of Philosophy,* London, Williams and Norgate.

Saiki, Ayako & Frost, Jon, 2019, "Unconventional Monetary Policy and Income Distribution—Is Japan Unique?" Council on Economic Policies working paper, Zurich, Council on Economic Policies, 19/2.

Saint-Etienne, Christian, 1984, *The Great Depression 1929-1938: Lessons for the 1980s,* Stanford University, Palo Alto, CA, Hoover Institution Press.

Samuelson, Paul & Solow, Robert, 1960, "Analytical Aspects of Anti-Inflation Policy," *American Economic Review Papers and Proceedings,* May.

Sanchez, Juan & Sung Kim, Hee, 2018, "Why Is Inflation So Low?" *Regional Economist,* Federal Reserve Bank of St. Louis, first quarter.

Sargent, Thomas, 1982, "The Ends of Four Big Inflations," in HALL, Robert, ed., *Inflation: Causes and Effects,* Chicago, University of Chicago Press.

Sarwat, Jahan, 2018, "Inflation Targeting: Holding the Line," *Finance & Development,* Washington, DC, IMF, June 1.

Saxonhouse, Gary & Stern, Robert, eds., 2004, *Japan's Lost Decade: Origins, Consequences, and Prospects for Recovery,* Oxford, UK, Blackwell Publishing.

Schnabel, Isabelle, 2020, "The Shadow of Fiscal Dominance: Misconceptions, Perceptions, and Perspectives," speech at the Centre for European Reform and the Eurofi Financial Forum, September 11.

Schularick, Moritz & Taylor, Allan, 2012, "Credit Booms Gone Bust: Monetary Policy, Leverage Cycles, and Financial Crises, 1870–2008," *American Economic Review,* April.

Schumpeter, Joseph, 1939, *Business Cycles,* vol. 1, Philadelphia, Pa., Porcupine Press.

Schwartz, Anna, 1989, "A Century of British Market Interest Rates, 1874–1975," in CAPIE, Forrest & WOOD, Geoffrey, eds., *Monetary Economics in the 1980s,* London, Macmillan.

Shiller, Robert, 2016, *Irrational Exuberance,* Princeton, NJ, Princeton University Press, third edition.

Shirai, Sayuri, 2013, "Monetary Policy and Forward Guidance in Japan," speeches at the International Monetary Fund (September 19) and the Board of governors of the Federal Reserve System (September 20), Bank of Japan.

Shlaes, Amity, 2007, *The Forgotten Man: A New History Perspective of the Great Depression,* New York, HarperCollins.

Shleifer, Andrei & Vishny, Robert, 1999, *The Grabbing Hand: Government Pathologies and Their Cures,* Cambridge, MA, Harvard University Press.

Silber, William, 2010, *Volcker: The Triumph of Persistence,* New York, Bloomsbury Press.

Simons, Henry, 1936, "Rules Versus Authorities in Monetary Policy," *Journal of Political Economy,* vol. 44.

Sisson, C.H., 1972, *The Case of Walter Bagehot,* London, Faber.

Skaggs, Neil, 1995, "Henry Thornton and the Development of Classical Monetary Economics," *Canadian Journal of Economics,* November.

Smets, Frank & Wouters, Raf, 2007, "Shocks and Frictions in US Business Cycles: A Bayesian DSGE Approach," *American Economic Review,* 93.

Smith, Adam, 1776, *An Inquiry into the Nature and Causes of the Wealth of Nations,* ed. Edwin Cannan (1976), Chicago, University of Chicago Press.

Snowdon, Brian & Vane, Howard, 2005, *Modern Macroeconomics: Its Origins, Development, and Current State,* Cheltenham, UK, Edward Elgar.

Somary, Felix, 1989, *The Raven of Zurich: The Memoirs of Felix Somary*, London, C. Hurts & Co (transl. Sherman, A.J.).

Song Shin, Hyun, 2009, "Reflections on Northern Rock: The Bank Run that Heralded the Global Financial Crisis," *Journal of Economic Perspectives*, vol. 23, no. 1.

Spence, Michael, 2015, "Why Public Investment?" *Project Syndicate*, February 20.

-------, 2017, "Monetary Policy Challenges Posed by Global Liquidity," paper presented at High-Level Roundtable on Central Banking in Asia, 50th ADB Annual Meeting, Yokohama, May 6.

Steen Knudsen, Jette, 2019, *Visible Hands: Government Regulation and International Business Responsibility*, Cambridge, UK, Cambridge University Press.

Stein, Jeremy, 1989, "Efficient Capital Markets, Inefficient Firms: A Model of Myopic Corporate Behavior," *Quarterly Journal of Economics*, November.

Stiglitz, Joseph, 2010, *Freefall: America, Free Markets, and the Sinking of the World Economy*, New York, W.W. Norton & Company.

Stock, James & Watson, David, 2003, "Has the Business Cycle Changed? Evidence and Explanations," in Fed Kansas City, 2003.

Svensson, Lars, 2014, "Forward Guidance," NBER working paper, National Bureau of Economic Research, no. 20796.

Sylla, Richard & Cowen, David, 2018, *Alexander Hamilton on Finance, Credit, and Debt*, New York, Columbia University Press.

Syverson, Chad, 2019, "Macroeconomics and Market Power: Context, Implications, and Open Questions," *Journal of Economic Perspectives*, Summer.

Taleb, Nassim Nicholas, 2007, *The Black Swan: The Impact of the Highly Improbable*, New York, Random House.

Taylor, John, 1993, "Discretion Versus Policy Rules in Practice," Carnegie-Rochester Conference Series on Public Policy, 39.

-------, 2009, *Getting Off Track: How Government Actions and Interventions Caused, Prolonged, and Worsened the Financial Crisis*, Stanford University, Palo Alto, CA, Hoover Institution Press.

-------, 2012, "Monetary Policy Rules Work and Discretion Doesn't: A Tale of Two Eras," *Journal of Money, Credit, and Banking*, 44(6).

-------, 2015, "A Monetary Policy for the Future," *Economics One*, April 16.

-------, 2018, "Rules Versus Discretion: Assessing the Debate Over the Conduct of Monetary Policy," Hoover Institution Economics working paper, Stanford University, Palo Alto, CA, 18102.

Taylor, John & Wieland, Volker, 2016, "Finding the Equilibrium Real Interest Rate in a Fog of Policy Deviations," *Business Economics*, July.

Temin, Peter, 1989, *Lessons from the Great Depression,* Cambridge, MA, The MIT Press.

Teryoshin, Yevgeni, 2017, "Historical Performance of Rule-Like Monetary Policy," Stanford Institute for Economic Policy Research working paper, Stanford University, CA, 17/005.

The Economist, 2015, "Why the World Is Addicted to Debt," May 18.

-------, 2018, "The Centenary of the Twentieth Century's Worst Catastrophe," September 29.

Thornton, Henry, 1802, *An Enquiry into the Nature and Effects of the Paper Credit of Great Britain,* New York, Reinhart and Co. (1939 edition with introduction by F.A. von Hayek).

Tirole, Jean, 2017, *Economics for the Common Good,* Princeton, NJ, Princeton University Press.

Tooze, Adam, 2020, "The Death of the Central Bank Myth," *Foreign Policy,* foreignpolicy.com, May 13 (accessed October 10, 2020).

Trichet, Jean-Claude, 2009, "The ECB's Enhanced Credit Support," speech delivered at the University of Munich, July 13.

Tucker, Paul, 2018, *Unelected Power: The Quest for Legitimacy in Central Banking and the Regulatory State,* Princeton, NJ, Princeton University Press.

Turner, Adair, 2016, *Between Debt and the Devil: Money, Credit, and Fixing Global Finance,* Princeton, NJ, Princeton University Press.

Ugolini, Stefano, 2017, *The Evolution of Central Banking: Theory and History,* London, Palgrave Macmillan.

-------, 2018, "The Historical Evolution of Central Banking," in Battilossi, Stefano *et al.*, *Handbook of the History of Money and Currency,* London, Springer Nature.

Van Overtveldt, Johan, 2007, *The Chicago School: How the University of Chicago Assembled the Thinkers Who Revolutionized Economics and Business,* Chicago, Agate Publishing.

-------, 2009, *Bernanke's Test: Ben Bernanke, Alan Greenspan, and the Drama of the Central Banker,* Chicago, Agate Publishing.

-------, 2011, *The End of the Euro: The Uneasy Future of the European Union,* Chicago, Agate Publishing.

Viner, Jacob, 1936, "Recent Legislation and the Banking Situation," *American Economic Review,* March.

Volcker, Paul, 1990, "The Triumph of Central Banking?" *Per Jacobsson* Lecture, Per Jacobssen Foundation.

Volcker, Paul & Harper, Christine, 2018, *Keeping at It: The Quest for Sound Money and Good Government,* New York, Public Affairs.

Wallison, Peter, 2010, "Government Housing Policy and the Financial Crisis," *Cato Journal,* Spring/Summer.

Walton, Gary & Rockoff, Hugh, 2005, *History of the American Economy,* Mason, Ohio, South-Western.

Weidmann, Jens, 2020, "Too Close for Comfort? The Relationship Between Monetary and Fiscal Policy," speech at the OMFIF Virtual Panel, London, November 5.

Welch, Finnis, 1999, "In Defense of Inequality," *AEA Papers and Proceedings,* American Economic Association, May.

Wheeler, Mark, ed., 1998, *The Economics of the Great Depression,* Kalamazoo, MI, W.E. Upjohn Institute for Employment Research.

White, William, 2006, "Is Price Stability Enough?" BIS working paper, Bank for International Settlements, no. 205.

-------, 2009, "Should Monetary Policy 'Lean or Clean'?" Fed Dallas Globalization and Monetary Policy Institute working paper, no. 34.

-------, 2013, "Is Monetary Policy a Science? The Interaction of Theory and Practice Over the Last 50 Years?" Fed Dallas Globalization and Monetary Policy Institute working paper, no. 155.

-------, 2019(a), "Are Fears of a Global Currency War Justified?" The Market NZZ, November 5 (accessed January 23, 2020).

-------, 2019(b), "The Effects of Ultra Low Interest Rates on the Banks and the Economy," remarks made at the Imperial College Business School, London, December 12-13 (accessed February 12, 2020).

-------, 2020, "Why Central Bankers Should Be Humble," *The International Economy,* Winter.

Wicksell, Knut, 1898, *Interest and Prices,* London, Macmillan (translation R.F. Kahn).

Wilmarth, Arthur, 2014, "Citigroup: A Case study in Managerial and Regulatory Failures," *Indiana Law Review,* vol. 46, 69.

Wilson, Woodrow, 1895, "A Literary Politician," *Atlantic Monthly,* November.

Wood, John, 2005, *A History of Central Banking in Great Britain and the United States,* Cambridge, UK, Cambridge University Press.

Woodford, Michael, 2012, "Methods of Policy Accommodation at the Interest Rate Lower Bound," in Fed Kansas City, The Challenging Policy Landscape, Economic Policy Symposium, Jackson Hole, Wyoming, August.

Woodward, Bob, 2000, *Maestro: Greenspan's Fed and the American Boom,* New York, Simon & Schuster.

Wooldridge, Adrian, 2012, "The Visible Hand," *The Economist*, special report, January 21.

Yellen, Janet, 2009, "A Minsky Moment: Lessons for Central Bankers," *FRBSF Economic Letter,* Federal Reserve Bank of San Francisco, 2009–15.

Zabala, Jose & Prats, Maria, 2019, "The Unconventional Monetary Policies of the European Central Bank: Effectiveness and Transmission Analysis," *The World Economy,* Wiley, special issue article, October 17.

Zervas, Georgios; Prosperio, Davide; & Byers, John, 2017, "The Rise of the Sharing Economy: Estimating the Impact of Airbnb on the Hotel Industry," *Journal of Marketing Research,* vol. 54, no. 5.

Zingales, Luigi, 2015, "Does Finance Benefit Society?" NBER working paper, National Bureau of Economic Research, no. 20894.

Endnotes

Front Matter

1 Rogers as quoted in Giannini, 2011.
2 Greenspan as quoted in the *Wall Street Journal*, September 22, 1987.
3 Schnabel in the European Parliament, December 3, 2019.

Introduction

1 Although I published a book entitled *The End of the Euro* (Van Overtveldt, 2011), I have always been convinced that a unified currency for the European Union is a good idea, if properly organized. That was certainly not the case in 2011. In the wake of the euro crisis, important steps were taken to improve the setup (for example, the creation of a not-yet-fully-finalized banking union). But the simple truth is and remains that without a real political union, a monetary union will always be a dilapidated structure at risk of implosion. If a real political union isn't the objective, or if the probability of getting a political union is close to zero, a monetary union isn't a good idea. The chances of reaching a real political union were small in Europe when the adventure started, and now, in the third decade of the twenty-first century, those chances are even more remote. Thus, I have no compelling reason to rewrite my 2011 book; its basic thesis remains intact.
2 Rajan, 2013, p. 16.
3 See, for example, Epstein, 2005 and Paul, 2009.
4 Basu, 2013.
5 Bernanke, 2020. An article on Bernanke's speech in the January 11, 2020 issue of *The Economist* was entitled "Why Ben Bernanke Is Wrong" (p. 8). This was remarkable, as *The Economist* had always been a staunch defender of QE policies.
6 For critical comments on these issues, see, for example, former Fed official Charles Plosser in Plosser, 2014.
7 James Gruber in *Forbes Asia*, May 26, 2013.
8 Smith was not the first to form this argument. Traces of it appear in the writings of ancient Greeks. The French economists Pierre de Boisguilbert and Vincent de Gournay and the Anglo-Dutch philosopher Bernard de Mandeville also wrote of the idea before Smith. For more detail on the pedigree of the invisible hand argument, see Hirschman, 1977. Bereft of any mention of the invisible hand *per se*, the first treatise that dealt with the concepts of self-interest, competition, and social welfare in detail was Richard Cantillon's *Essai sur la Nature du Commerce en General*. Little is known about the life of Cantillon, a French economist; he died in 1734, but his year of birth, as well as the year of the *Essai's* publication, are unknown.
9 Smith, 1776, vol. 1, p. 477, 478.

10   Norman, 2018, p. 171.

11   The "great enrichment" is a common theme in McCloskey's *Bourgeois* trilogy: McClo-
     skey, 2006, 2010, & 2016.

12   Referred to in Norman, 2018, p. 193.

13   To see this reality in full, one must read both *The Wealth of Nations* and Smith's other
     major book, *The Theory of Moral Sentiments* (1759). Smith considered the latter to be
     his most important treatise.

14   Dellemotte, 2009.

15   Chandler, 1977, p. 1.

16   *Ibid.,* p. 3.

17   *Ibid.,* p. 3.

18   *Ibid.,* p. 6.

19   Wooldridge, 2012 and Kurlantzick, 2016.

20   Shleifer & Vishny, 1999.

21   Irwin, 2013, p. 8.

22   Tucker, 2018, p. xiv, 3.

23   King, 2016, p. 1.

24   Davies, 2017.

25   https://www.dictionary.com/browse/mystique?s=t

26   https://www.thesaurus.com/browse/mystic

27   King, 2016.

28   Irwin, 2013.

29   Brunner, 1981, p. 5.

30   Posen, 2013.

31   White, 2013, p. 16.

32   Davies, 2017.

33   Tucker, 2018, p. 419.

34   Both quotes are taken from Martin, 2000, p. 207.

35   Greider, 1989.

36   Schnabel during the session in the Committee on Economic and Monetary Affairs in
     the European Parliament, December 3, 2019.

37   Ahamed, 2010.

38   Tucker, 2018, p. 4.

39   On this trilemma, see Obstfeld *et al.,* 2005. This trilemma is the unescapable fact
     that of three desirable effects of central banking objectives—capital mobility, a fixed
     exchange rate, and an independent monetary policy—only two are possible simul-
     taneously. If you opt for capital mobility and a fixed exchange rate, there can be no
     independent monetary policy. If you choose a fixed change rate and an independent
     monetary policy, there can be no capital mobility. Opting for capital mobility and
     an independent monetary policy means that the exchange rate has to be free to move
     around.

40   Alesina & Summers, 1993.

41   Tucker, 2018, p. 9, 402.

42   For a more general overview of central banking and its evolution over time, see Hart-
     mann *et al.*, 2018.

43 Mehrling argued that their actions to fight the global financial crisis of 2007–2009 transformed central banks from *lenders* of last resort to *dealers* of last resort (Mehrling, 2011).
44 Bernanke, 2015(a), p. 208.
45 Mehrling, 2011, p. 17.
46 Posner, 2018, p. 2.
47 Bernanke, 2015(a), p. 243.
48 Hawtrey, 1933, p. 116.
49 Hall & Ferguson, 1999.

Chapter 1

1   Bernanke, 2002(a), p. 9.

2   See his memoirs, Bernanke, 2015(a), and Bernanke *et al.*, 2019.

3   Hildebrand in Blanchard & Summers, 2019, p. 61.

4   Friedman & Schwartz, 1963.

5   Bernanke, 2000. In 1995, Bernanke described understanding the Great Depression as "the Holy Grail of Macroeconomics" (Bernanke, 2000, p. 5). This is similar to Robert Margo's claim, "The Great Depression is to economics what the Big Bang is to physics" (Margo, 1993, p. 41).

6   Bernanke, 2002(a), p. 1.

7   Currie served as Hawtrey's teaching assistant during the latter's time at Harvard, 1928-29.

8   Hawtrey, 1933, p. 213.

9   *Ibid.*, p. 81.

10   Currie, 1934, p. 145.

11   Keynes, 1936.

12   Pigou, 1949.

13   Arrow & Debreu, 1954, and Debreu, 1959.

14   Ahamed, 2010, p. 6.

15   There were exceptions to this general rule. A rare voice warning others of the coming storm was that of Swedish economist Gustav Cassel, discussed in greater detail later in the chapter.

16   Hoover as quoted in Snowdon & Vane, 2005, p. 11.

17   Data taken from Snowdon & Vane, 2005.

18   Data taken from Saint-Etienne, 1984.

19   Data taken from Saint-Etienne, 1984.

20   Fisher, 1933.

21   Shlaes, 2007, p. 5.

22   There is an important distinction between "good" and "bad" deflation. *Good* deflation refers to price declines due to productivity growth, innovation, and technological advancement. *Bad* deflation is a decline in general price levels due to a persistent fall in aggregate demand.

23   An interesting and concise overview of different theories explaining the Great Depression can be found in Bernstein, Michael, "The Great Depression as Historical Problem," the third chapter in Wheeler, 1998. See also Meltzer, 1976.

24   The Dow Jones index of the stock market increased by 145 percent between early 1926 and September 1929. On the link between the stock market boom and the credit boom, see Eichengreen & Mitchener, 2003.

25   For a vivid description of this crash, see Galbraith, 1954.

26   Jones, 1934.

27   James, 2009, p. 23.

28   In the mid-1920s, Cassel warned repeatedly about "a prolonged and worldwide depression." For specifics on several Cassel quotes to this effect, see Irwin, 2014.

29   Eichengreen, 1992 is an excellent book on the gold standard. See also Eichengreen, 2015.

30 *The Economist*, 2018.

31 Keynes, 1924, p. 172.

32 Cassel, 1920, p. 413. See also Cassel, 1928.

33 Carr, 1939, p. 234.

34 Divine, 1967.

35 Kindleberger, 1973, p. 11.

36 McCullough, 1992, p. 234.

37 This asymmetry is emphasized in, for example, Temin, 1989.

38 Technically, the central banks of the surplus countries sterilized the impact of the inflow of gold by selling government bonds and securities from their balance sheet. These actions reduced the money supply, effectively countering the increase in the money supply caused by the inflow of gold.

39 Hall & Ferguson, 1998, p. 87.

40 Eichengreen & Michener, 2003.

41 Among the first to point out these additional difficulties for the gold standard were Frank Knight of the University of Chicago and Otmar Emminger, a young German economist who would later become president of the Bundesbank. See Knight, 1941, and Emminger, 1934.

42 See Bernanke & James, "The Gold Standard, Deflation, and Financial Crisis in the Great Depression," chapter 3 in Bernanke, 2000.

43 Viner, 1936.

44 Friedman and Schwartz attributed a crucial role in these developments to the October 1928 death of Benjamin Strong, the forceful and influential president of the New York Fed. Friedman and Schwartz believed that Strong probably would have been able to impose policies favored by the New York Fed. Friedman & Schwartz, 1963, p. 417.

45 Haberler, 1976, p. 9.

46 Hall & Ferguson, 1998, p. 119, 121.

47 Somary, 1989.

48 For the full story on Credit-Anstalt, see Aguado, 2001.

49 In Germany, Chancellor Heinrich Brüning's desperate attempts during this period to deal with the country's foreign debts through brutal spending cuts paved the way for Adolf Hitler's rise.

50 Hall & Ferguson, 1998, p. 104.

51 Mellon as quoted in Hoover, 1952, p. 30.

52 Rauchway, 2015.

53 By February 14, the state of Michigan had declared a statewide bank holiday. By the day of Roosevelt's inauguration, twenty-eight of the then forty-eight US states had enforced bank holidays.

54 A sharp recession followed in 1937 and 1938 due to the combined tightening of monetary and fiscal policy. See Eichengreen, 2015. Friedman and Schwartz attributed the recession to the imposition of substantially higher reserve requirements for the banks. Friedman & Schwartz, 1963.

55 Niehans, 1990, p. 105.

56 Humphrey, 2014, p. 4.

57 Goodhart, 1999, p. 340.

58 Hetzel, 1987.

59   It remains unclear whether Hamilton was born in 1755 or 1757. He died from a gunshot wound on July 12, 1804, after a duel with a challenger, the sitting US Vice President Aaron Burr. See Chernow, 2004.

60   Cowen, Sylla & Wright, 2009. See also Sylla & Cowen, 2018.

61   Cowen, Sylla & Wright, 2009, p. 61.

62   For more on these historical precedents, see Ugolini, 2017, and especially Ugolini, 2018.

63   Ugolini, 2018, p. 6.

64   *Ibid.,* p. 8.

65   Crowe & Meade, 2007.

66   Wood, 2005.

67   During the first part of the nineteenth century, central banks were created in the Scandinavian countries, Belgium, the Netherlands, Spain, Portugal, and Indonesia. In the last quarter of the nineteenth century, Germany, Japan, Romania, and a few others followed. The Swiss central bank was established in 1907 and the American Federal Reserve System in 1913.

68   Smith, 1776, vol. 1, p. 209.

69   Laidler, 1981.

70   Smith, 1776, vol. 2, p. 340.

71   Ricardo, 1824.

72   For Leeson's own version of this debacle, see Leeson, 2016.

73   Baring, 1797, p. 6.

74   Baring, 1797, p. 22.

75   Biographical data are mostly taken from Friedrich von Hayek's 1939 introduction to Thornton's book.

76   This discussion is often referred to as the "Bullionist Controversy," placing those in favor of a return to gold convertibility against those opposing it.

77   Schwartz, 1989, p. 41.

78   Papademos & Modigliani, 1990, p. 405-406.

79   This statement does injustice to the central bankers who remained keenly aware of the interactions between the real and the financial sphere and of the potentially very destructive macroeconomic impact of financial crises. The late Paul Volcker was foremost among them.

80   Skaggs, 1995, p. 1218.

81   Harman as quoted in Hawtrey, 1933, p. 122.

82   Schumpeter as quoted in Humphrey, 1989, p. 9.

83   Thornton, 1802, p. 259.

84   Thornton, 1802, p. 188.

85   King, 2016, p. 94.

86   St John-Stevas in Bagehot, 1965-1986, Vol. I, p.29.

87   Quoted in Kimball, 1998. Not everyone shares the same enthusiasm for Bagehot's achievements. For a more critical approach of Bagehot and his work, see Sisson, 1972.

88   Quoted in Kimball, 1998.

89   Wilson, 1895.

90   Quoted in Kimball, 1998.

91   Bagehot, 1965-1986, vol. V, p. 226.

92 Bagehot, 1873, p. 20.

93 Sayer in Bagehot, 1965-86, vol. IX, p. 43.

94 Peter Bernstein in the foreword to Bagehot, 1873, p. vi.

95 Goodhart, 1999, p. 340.

96 Bagehot, 1873, p. 71.

97 Bagehot, 1873, p. 158, 159.

98 Confucius as quoted in King, 2016, p. 10.

99 Bagehot, 1873, p. 197, 198.

100 Charles Goodhart develops this argument in full in Goodhart, 1999.

101 Bagehot, 1873, p. 206.

102 It's intriguing to consider why the history has gone this way. Several reasons have been suggested—for example, the fact that Thornton's writing was much more dense and "difficult" than that of Bagehot—but the question remains open. See Peake, 1995. On this issue, I tend to agree with Frank Fetter, who claimed in his reference work on the British Monetary Orthodoxy that Bagehot was more a popularizer than a creator of original ideas: "Bagehot may not have said more than Francis Baring and Henry Thornton had said over sixty years before, but he said it in a way that carried conviction to a wider audience and to a new generation who no longer accepted all the premises from which Thornton's and Baring's conclusions had sprung" (Fetter, 1965, p. 274).

103 King, 2016, p. 163.

104 Humphrey, 1989, p. 8.

105 Significant amounts of time passed before the Chinese authorities began to supply other nations with what they had already learned about the virus. By late December 2019, Beijing was well aware of what was transpiring in Wuhan. Between December 30, 2019, and January 22, 2020, 11,000 people traveled from Wuhan to Thailand; 11,000 more traveled from Wuhan to Singapore; 9,000 left Wuhan for Japan; and 7,000 others traveled from Wuhan to Hong Kong. Data taken from *South China Morning Post*, January 27, 2020.

106 As quoted in the *Financial Times*, April 4, 2020.

107 Wolf in the *Financial Times*, April 15, 2020.

108 As quoted in the *Financial Times*, April 17, 2020.

109 As quoted in the *Financial Times*, May 15, 2020.

110 BoE as quoted in the *Financial Times*, May 8, 2020.

111 Reinhart in The Development Podcast, World Bank, September 16, 2020.

112 *Financial Times*, April 8, 2020.

113 As quoted in the *Financial Times*, June 11, 2020.

114 *Financial Times*, September 24, 2020.

115 Draghi in the *Financial Times*, March 23, 2020.

116 As quoted in the *Financial Times*, March 24, 2020.

117 Borio, 2020, p. 3.

Chapter 2

1   All quotes are from the introduction, p. 1-5 in Bernanke, *et al.*, 2019.
2   Bernanke, 2015(a), p. 336.
3   King, 2016, p. 1.
4   IMF, Global Financial Stability Report, April 2006, p. 51.
5   IMF, World Economic Outlook, April 2007, p. xv.
6   Turner, 2016, p. xi.
7   In January 2007, Rajan left his position as chief economist of the IMF.
8   Roubini predicted a huge crisis as a consequence of an enormous dollar collapse. The huge crisis came, but not as a consequence of a dollar collapse.
9   See, for example, Rajan, 2005, Shiller, 2005, and Borio & White, 2003.
10 During the 2005 Jackson Hole Symposium, former US Secretary of the Treasury Larry Summers attacked Rajan quite aggressively for voicing opinions about the coming turbulence in financial markets.
11 In April 2007, New Century Financial Corporation, a major US subprime mortgage lender, filed for bankruptcy.
12 Many excellent books have been written on the 2007–2009 global financial crisis. See especially Eichengreen, 2015; King, 2016; Bayoumi, 2017; and Bernanke *et al.*, 2019. I dare also mention Van Overtveldt, 2009.
13 Irwin, 2013, p. 2.
14 The four others at that time were Goldman Sachs, Morgan Stanley, Merrill Lynch, and Lehman Brothers.
15 Prince as quoted in the *Financial Times*, July 9, 2007.
16 *The Economist*, June 18, 2005.
17 Bernanke, 2015, p. 106.
18 Reinhart & Rogoff, 2009.
19 Both administrations pursued this strategy as part of a broader strategy to fight rising income inequality in the United States. For more on this, see Rajan, 2010.
20 Wallison, 2010.
21 Bernanke *et al.*, 2019, p. 56.
22 Calomiris, 2009, p. 69.
23 Acharya, *et al.*, 2011, p. 179, 180.
24 Bernanke, 2005.
25 Bernanke *et al.*, 2019, p. 11.
26 According to BIS statistics.
27 *Ibid.*
28 See, for example, Greenspan, 2003. During an interview at MIT's Department of Economics in the winter of 1998, Olivier Blanchard, chief economist at the IMF from September 2008 to September 2015, expressed the same conviction.
29 Bernanke, 2015(a), p. 143. During the financial crisis, it became clear that much of the securitized paper created by Bank X ended up on other banks' balance sheets, making the exercise in risk diversification rather pointless for the banking sector.
30 Bernanke, 2015, p. 99.
31 Keys *et al.*, 2010.
32 Yellen, 2009, p. 4.

33 See, for example, emails quoted in Dowd, 2009, p. 145. See also Eisinger, 2007. As minister of finance of Belgium from 2014 to 2018, I experienced firsthand how these rating agencies doubled down on their efforts to show that they were really serious this time around and had discarded their bad habits.

34 Tirole, 2017, p. 331.

35 See Rajan, 2005, and also the contribution of Clementi *et al.* in Acharya & Richardson, 2009.

36 In 1989, Jeremy Stein outlined the "attractiveness" of such strategies as detrimental to longer-term performance. See Stein, 1989.

37 Derman, 2004.

38 For more on the shortcomings of these quantitative models, see Estrada, 2008 and 2009.

39 Taleb, 2007.

40 Haldane, 2009, p. 1.

41 King, 2016, p. 110.

42 Data taken from Dobbs *et al.*, 2015, p. 1.

43 See also Chapter 5: "The Michael Jackson Syndrome."

44 Rule of thumb suggested in Turner, 2016, p. 7.

45 Data taken from Buttiglione *et al.*, 2014, p. 37 and 48.

46 Data taken from Dobbs *et al.*, 2015, p. 10.

47 That tendency reversed dramatically during and after the financial crisis, as the leverage of the Chinese corporate sector exploded from 72 percent of GDP at the end of 2007 to 125 percent of GDP by the end of 2014. See Dobbs *et al.*, 2015, p. 10.

48 Friedman, 1997.

49 Eichengreen, 2011.

50 Quote from ipe.com (October 2007), accessed on November 1, 2019.

51 See, for example, Merkel as quoted in the *Financial Times*, December 16, 2012.

52 If you consider the eventual tax deductibility of the interest paid, the net return is even higher.

53 Although the epicenter of the financial crisis was in the United States, the degree of leverage among major financial institutions was higher in Europe than in the United States. For more background on this, see Bayoumi, 2017.

54 Most of these rules were negotiated at the Bank for International Settlements (BIS), the central banks' bank, which is located in the Swiss city of Basel—thus, "Basel rules."

55 For more details on the Basel rules and their problems, see Admati & Hellweg, 2013, and Bayoumi, 2017.

56 Greenwood & Scharfstein, 2013.

57 Abundant evidence for this argument can be found in Philippon & Reshef, 2012; Greenwood & Scharfstein, 2013; and Cecchetti & Kharroubi, 2012, 2015, and 2018.

58 Zingales, 2015, p. 2.

59 See, for example, Philippon & Reshef, 2012.

60 Turner, 2016, p. 28.

61 Schumpeter, 1939, p. 223.

62 Reinhart & Rogoff, 2009, p. 292.

63 Mehrling, p. 92.

64   Bernanke *et al.*, 2019, p. 21.
65   The reference work *par excellence* on this issue is Reinhart & Rogoff, 2009; see also Cecchetti *et al.*, 2011; Gourinchas & Obstfeld, 2012; Reinhart *et al.*, 2012; Reinhart *et al.*, 2015; Lo & Rogoff, 2015, and Rogoff, 2015.
66   Mackay, 1841.
67   As in the Federal Reserve Reform Act of 1977.
68   As stipulated in Article 2 of the ECB's Statute.
69   See, for example, Friedman, 1960. Friedman's arguments in favor of a fixed monetary growth rule were similar to those of his teacher at the University of Chicago, Henry Simons. For more on this, see Van Overtveldt, 2007, Chapter 5.
70   The seminal article was Kydland & Prescott, 1977.
71   See, for example, Taylor, 1993; Asso *et al.*, 2010; Koenig *et al.*, 2012; Hoffman & Bogdanova, 2013; Taylor, 2018, and Nikolsko-Rzhevskyy & Prodan, 2019.
72   Asso *et al.*, 2010, p. 1.
73   Holston, Laubach & Williams, 2017.
74   Board of Governors of the Federal Reserve System, "FOMC Projections Materials," June 19, 2019.
75   Taylor & Wieland, 2016.
76   Song Shin, 2017.
77   The same conclusion is reached in Kliesen, 2019, which only covers the United States.
78   Ahrend, 2010, and Teryoshin, 2017.
79   Rey, 2013, and Chen *et al.*, 2015.
80   Borio, 2019 (a), p. 3. This theme will return in Chapter 5.
81   Mehrota *et al.*, 2019.
82   Saxonhouse & Stern, 2004; Hoshi & Kashyap, 2004 & Koo, 2009.
83   Bernanke, 2002 (b).
84   A clear and concise exposition of this approach is to be found in Greenspan, 2003.
85   LTCM refers to Long Term Capital Management, the mammoth New York hedge fund that imploded in the autumn of 1998.
86   Greenspan, 2007, p. 201.
87   King, 2016, p. 192.
88   White, 2009.
89   Yardeni quoted in the *Financial Times*, December 8, 2000.
90   See "Pavlov's Dog" in Chapter 6.
91   For evidence on this evolution, see Miller, Weller, & Zhang, 2002.
92   See, for example, Greenspan, 2007, p. 229.
93   A typical example of this kind of model is Smets & Wouters, 2007. For a thorough critique of these models, see Romer, 2016.
94   King, 2012, p. 5.
95   See, for example, White, 2009; Taylor, 2009; Stiglitz, 2010; Schularick & Taylor, 2012; Micossi *et al.*, 2019; and Filardo *et al.*, 2019.
96   Micossi *et al.*, 2019, p. 2.
97   Minsky, 1982.
98   Rajan, 2009, p. 4 and 5.
99   Reinhart & Rogoff, 2009, p. 292.

100 See, for example, Mackay, 1841; Galbraith, 1990; Garber, 2000; and Kindleberger & Aliber, 2005.

101 Tulip mania will be mentioned again in Chapter 5 in "The Semper Augustus Syndrome."

102 Newton as quoted in Kindleberger & Aliber, 2005, p. 41.

103 Russell, 1912.

104 Gennaioli *et al.*, 2015. See also Kahneman, 2011.

105 Bernanke *et al.*, 2019, p. 3.

106 Galbraith, 1954, p. 99.

107 Shiller, 2008, p. 41.

108 The original notion of the Great Moderation came from Stock & Watson, 2003.

109 Blanchard, 2008.

110 A point forcefully made in Kaufman, 2009.

111 Yellen, 2009, p. 2.

112 See several of the contributions in Fed Kansas City, 2005. Ben Bernanke describes his arrival at the Fed in Washington as his joining of "the Maestro's Orchestra," Bernanke, 2015(a), p. 66. See also Woodward, 2000.

113 Quoted by CBS News, October 5, 2007.

114 Borio, 2019(b), p. 1.

Chapter 3

1   MIT economist Daron Acemoglu convincingly argued that popular outcry about greed being the main cause of the financial crisis doesn't hold water if carefully analyzed. Acemoglu, 2009.

2   Turner, 2016, p. 2.

3   Yellen, 2009, p. 5, 6.

4   LIBOR stands for London Interbank Offered Rate.

5   Song Shin, 2009.

6   James, 2009, p. 104. See also Kelly, 2009.

7   To a large extent, Bear Stearns financed itself in the "repo market," where investment banks and other financial firms arrange short-term financing transactions among themselves. Bernanke feared that a failure of Bear Stearns might lead to a total breakdown of the repo market, with major consequences not only for financial markets but for the economy as a whole. See Bernanke, 2015(a), p. 216.

8   At the end of the day, JP Morgan Chase paid $1.5 billion for Bear Stearns. Bear Stearns' New York headquarters on Madison Avenue was estimated to be worth at least $1.4 billion.

9   Bernanke at al., 2019, p. 47.

10 Rogoff in the *New York Times*, August 20, 2008.

11 For the full story on Lehman Brothers, see McDonald & Robinson, 2009.

12 Trichet as quoted in Bernanke, 2015(a), p. 266.

13 The final deficit left by Lehman's collapse is estimated at $200 billion.

14 Bernanke, 2015(a), p. 268, 269.

15 Bernanke, 2015(a), p. 262.

16 Bernanke in his testimony before the Committee on Banking, Housing, and Urban Affairs of the US Senate on September 23, 2008.

17 Ball, 2018 also argues extensively that the legal obstacle argument does not hold.

18 Paulson, 2010.

19 Bernanke *et al.,* 2019, p. 58.

20 *Ibid.,* p. 71.

21 Bernanke, 2015(a), p. xi.

22 See, for example, Reuters, September 17, 2008.

23 Bernanke, 2015(a), p. 286.

24 It was called—fasten your seatbelt—the Asset-Backed Commercial Paper Money Market Mutual Fund Liquidity Facility (AMLF).

25 Noyer quoted in *The Economist*, October 4, 2008.

26 Steinbrück quoted in the *Financial Times*, September 26, 2008.

27 Iceland ranked third on the United Nations' 2009 Human Development Index.

28 *The Economist*, December 11, 2008. For more details on the Icelandic crisis, see Boyes, 2009, and Bagus & Howden, 2011.

29 At one point, the European central banking system had given around €100 billion in emergency financing to Fortis and Dexia.

30 Banks in France and in the Scandinavian countries sailed through the financial crisis with rather limited damage, as did Japanese banks. This was partially because they

benefited substantially from the bailout of AIG by American taxpayers. See Tirole, 2017, p. 327.

31 Donovan & Murphy, 2013.

32 Bernanke, 2015(a), p. 334.

33 The hemorrhaging finance departments of car companies General Motors and Chrysler, and the carmakers themselves, received a total of $80 billion in TARP funds.

34 The amount of the fraud, at least $65 billion, was staggering. See Henriques, 2011. It was a remarkable sign of the times that Madoff could hoodwink not only a large number of individual investors but also reputable outfits, such as Banco Santander, AXA, BNP Paribas, Nomura Holdings, HSBC, and many others.

35 Wilmarth, 2014.

36 Sheila Bair, the chairman of the Federal Deposit Insurance Corporation, pleaded strongly for putting Citigroup in liquidation. The giant corporation mobilized enough support in Washington to get this proposal of the table. See Bair, 2012.

37 All data are from IMF, World Economic Outlook.

38 Bernanke, 2015(a), p. 397.

39 In February 2009, the incoming Obama administration launched a $787 billion fiscal stimulus program.

40 Buti, 2020.

41 The reunification of Germany in 1990 was another reason several politicians—especially French president François Mitterrand—pushed hard for the creation of the monetary union. Mitterrand and others feared that a unified Germany would come to dominate Europe completely. They saw the monetary union as a way to limit German power. For more on this, see Van Overtveldt, 2011.

42 King, 2016, p. 218.

43 For more on the structural handicaps of the euro area and the evolution of the crisis, see Brunnermeier *et al.*, 2016; James, 2012; Mody, 2018; and Van Overtveldt, 2011.

44 All quotes from Draghi in this paragraph are from his speech at the Global Investment Conference in London, July 26, 2012 (available on the website of the ECB).

Chapter 4

1   Jeremiah Harman, governor of the Bank of England from 1794 to 1827, as quoted in King, 2016, p. 189.

2   Huskisson as quoted in Coggan, 2020, p. 255. This echoes an address made by Ben Bernanke in late September 2008 to Congressional leadership. If these leaders did not decide to take decisive action, Bernanke claimed, "We may not have an economy on Monday." Bernanke as quoted in the *New York Times,* October 1, 2008.

3   Bagehot, 1873, p. 173, 205.

4   Bernanke, *et al.,* 2019, p. 8.

5   Bagehot, 1873, p. 185, 186.

6   Borio, 2019(b), p. 1.

7   Bernanke, 2015(a), p. 164.

8   Borio, 2019(b), p. 2.

9   Powell as quoted in the *Financial Times,* August 1, 2019.

10 For details on this turbulence, see the *Financial Times,* July 10, 2020.

11 The exact definition of the ECB's target rate of inflation is "below but close to 2 percent."

12 Lonergan & Greene, 2020. See also the ECB's press release of March 12, 2020.

13 Saxonhouse & Stern, 2004; Hoshi & Kashyap, 2004; and Koo, 2009.

14 Hoshi & Kashyap, 2015, and Kirkegaard, 2019.

15 Hayami quoted in the *Japan Times,* July 4, 2019.

16 Pozsar, *et al.,* 2013.

17 The shadow banking system is discussed in more detail in Chapter 5.

18 Again, the obvious contradiction: if Bear Stearns had to be saved because it was too interconnected to fail, then Lehman should have been saved, too, as it was even more interconnected than Bear.

19 Bernanke, 2015(a), p. 208.

20 Bernanke, 2015(a), p. 209.

21 Haircuts are the reductions applied by central banks in order to make up for the risk involved in certain assets. An asset nominally worth one hundred dollars would be refinanced for ninety dollars by the central bank if the asset is judged to be risky. A haircut of 10 percent is applied in this example.

22 The Fed tried to address this problem by making companies that wanted to access the CPFF pay an upfront fee that was taken in reserve by the Fed against possible losses. Also, the amount of paper one company could offer at the CPFF was capped.

23 Bernanke, 2015(a), p. 358.

24 Geithner, the former president of the New York Fed, had succeeded Hank Paulson as Secretary of the Treasury for the Obama administration.

25 Bernanke, 2015(a), p. 468.

26 The Fed's AMFL program was helpful in stabilizing the money market funds industry.

27 McNamara, 2016.

28 Posner, 2018, discusses the legality of these and other crisis interventions.

29 Quoted in the *Financial Times,* May 29, 2020.

30 *Financial Times,* April 17, 2020.

31 These differences involve highly technical aspects. However, Neil Irwin's claim that for the different QE programs, it is foremost about "a distinction without a difference" (Irwin, 2013, p. 255) has some merit.

32 See, for example, Bauer & Rudebusch, 2016, and Del Negro *et al.,* 2018. Borio *et al.,* 2017 stresses monetary factors as the main drivers of the decline in long-term interest rates.

33 Bernanke, 2002(b).

34 There is extensive literature on QE. See Bernanke, 2015(a), and King, 2016, as well as Borio & Disyatat, 2010; Rajan, 2013; Dell'Ariccia *et al.,* 2018; Gagnon & Sack, 2018; Kuttner, 2018; and Rudebusch, 2018.

35 Bernanke never felt at ease with QE terminology. He always preferred to talk about *credit easing* because QE suggested that the purpose of the operations was to increase the money supply, while in the United States, the objective was solely to bring down long-term interest rates.

36 During the policy deliberations inside the Fed, the research department presented simulations that, given the circumstances of that moment, the federal funds rate had to be at -6 percent! Massive QE interventions were considered to be an alternative to lowering policy rates to a completely unrealistic level.

37 Bernanke, 2015(a), p. 491.

38 Quoted in *National Review Online*, November 7, 2010.

39 Corker quoted in Bernanke, 2015(a), p. 553.

40 On November 15, 2010, twenty-three reputable economists published a letter arguing against QE in the *Wall Street Journal*. The best known of these economists were Niall Ferguson of Harvard University and Michael Boskin and John Taylor of Stanford University.

41 As quoted in *Der Spiegel,* November 8, 2010.

42 As quoted in the *Financial Times*, September 27, 2010.

43 As quoted by the Associated Press, November 8, 2010.

44 The Fed countered the international criticism by arguing that the Fed's actions reinforced the American economic expansion, which contributed to growth elsewhere. See Fisher, 2016.

45 Kevin Warsh, a Fed governor generally considered to be close to Bernanke, published an op-ed in the *Wall Street Journal* on November 8, 2010 that was quite critical about the policies being pushed by Bernanke.

46 *Financial Times*, September 18, 2013.

47 Bernanke, 2015(a), p. 557.

48 *Bloomberg*, January 15, 2020.

49 *Financial Times*, March 25, 2020.

50 *Financial Times*, April 3, 2020.

51 Trichet, 2009.

52 Cour-Thimann & Winkler, 2013.

53 Weber resigned from the ECB in April 2011, a year before his term in office at the ECB was set to expire.

54 Handelsblatt, September 17, 2020.

55 This was not the first time the GCC had dealt with ECB policies. The ECB's Outright Monetary Transactions (OMT) program, which was prompted by Draghi's

"whatever it takes" speech, was challenged by several German plaintiffs. In 2015, the GCC rather unenthusiastically ruled these OMTs to be acceptable.

56   Hutchinson & Smets, 2017.

57   At the same time, the deposit rate the ECB applied was reduced to -0.50 percent.

58   ECB press release, September 12, 2019.

59   *Financial Times,* October 4, 2019.

60   Interest rates didn't really remain unchanged, as the ECB had initiated a dual rate system that allowed banks to borrow money *below* the -0.5 percent deposit rate.

61   See the earlier discussion on the dual interest rate structure in this chapter under the heading "Stubbornly Negative."

62   Quoted in the *Financial Times,* April 23, 2020.

63   Quoted in the *Financial Times,* June 5, 2020.

64   Lagarde as quoted in the *Financial Times,* December 11, 2020.

65   For more on forward guidance, see den Haan, 2013; Svensson, 2014; McKay *et al.,* 2016; and Ehrmann *et al.,* 2019. See also Mishkin, 2004, on the risks involved in forward guidance.

66   Chapter 5 discusses the "stealing" aspect of these policies in the section "The Butch Cassidy Syndrome."

67   All quotes in this paragraph are taken from Shirai, 2013.

68   Press release from Bank of Japan, October 31, 2019.

69   The quotes in this paragraph are all taken from "Review of Monetary Policy Strategy, Tools, and Communications," available on the website of the Federal Reserve Board.

70   All quotes on the ECB taken from different press releases of the ECB.

71   Michael Woodford of Columbia University, a prominent monetary economist, sees forward guidance as very important in its own right and even more decisive than the actual asset purchases done by the Fed. See Woodford, 2012.

72   Adrian & Shin, 2008.

Chapter 5

1   FDIC stands for Federal Deposit Insurance Corporation.

2   Draghi as quoted in the *Financial Times*, September 13, 2019. As a matter of fact, in June 2015 Draghi admitted that "a long period, a protracted period of very low interest rates causes a series of problems," also for financial stability. However, he went on to argue that this observation should not distract the central bank from the main goals the unconventional monetary toolbox was aiming at. Draghi as quoted in *Marketwatch*, June 24, 2015.

3   Testimony of Lagarde before the European Parliament on February 11, 2020.

4   Keynes in *New Statesman and Nation*, July 10, 1937.

5   For this positive twist to the whole story of unconventional monetary policies, see, for example, Ball *et al.,* 2016 and Eichengreen, 2019.

6   It is possible that in some cases, very low interest rates inspire people to increase their savings effort even more, because they feel the growth rate of their saving stock will be too low. In those cases, there's not really any stealing from the future, but there's also no positive impact on spending now. When low interest rates lead to more saving, the policy of trying to stimulate current spending fails. The drain on present consumption and investment can intensify when, given a rise in overall debt levels, people become worried about the availability of sufficient resources to maintain pension obligations. Former OECD chair and BIS economist William White referred in this context to rising "levels of unease among both households and corporations." (White, 2019(b), p. 4).

7   As Belgium's minister of finance from 2014 to 2018, I tried very hard to take advantage of the very low long-term interest rates on government bonds. Given Belgium's debt-to-GDP ratio that had surpassed 100 percent, securing long-term cheap financing was an obvious strategy. Doing so meant forgoing the relatively small advantage of opting for shorter-term financing, as short-term interest rates were below longer-term rates. In several budget meetings, I had to struggle to maintain this strategy, because some colleagues were much more interested in the short-term advantages of slightly lower interest rates than in the longer-term beneficial effects of securing attractive long-term financing. Taking advantage of lower short-term rates and forgetting about the longer term would have permitted us to slow efforts to reduce the deficit in the short run.

8   Ian Heslop, head of global equities at Merian Global Investors, as quoted in the *Financial Times*, September 13, 2019.

9   Claudio Borio as quoted in *The Telegraph*, June 4, 2014.

10   White, 2020, p. 31.

11   Mian *et al.,* 2019, p. 1.

12   As a matter of fact, all countercyclical policies try to bring consumption and investment forward in order to avoid a feared recession. What makes the unconventional monetary policies of the last decade so extraordinary is how long they have been consistently applied.

13   See, for example, Hesse, Hofman & Weber, 2017; Dell Ariccia *et al.,* 2018; Filardo & Nakajima, 2018; Mian *et al.,* 2019; and Zabala & Prats, 2019. These papers contain many references to other relevant research work on this topic.

14   Smithers, 2019 and Acharya & Plantin, 2019.

15   For further reflections on such issues, see White, 2019(a).

16   See, for example, Gern *et al.,* 2015 and the references in that paper.

17   See, for example, Chen *et al.,* 2017 and De Guindos, 2019.

18   Rajan, 2014.

19   Many other celebrities were proven to be also impressive debt addicts. See *Business Insider*, August 8, 2019.

20   CNN Business, January 14, 2020.

21   IFF, 2020(b).

22   *Washington Post*, July 16, 2018.

23   *Financial Times*, May 25, 2020.

24   *Financial Times*, September 25, 2019.

25   Turner, 2016, p. 7, 12.

26   Caruna, 2014.

27   David Malpass as quoted in a World Bank press release, December 19, 2019.

28   For the very long-term history of debt, see Graeber, 2011.

29   Data taken from BIS, Annual Report, 2018, p. 13.

30   Kose *et al.,* 2019.

31   IIF, 2020(a).

32   IIF, 2020(b).

33   Georgieva, 2019.

34   IMF, Global Financial Stability Report, October 2019.

35   Tobias Adrian and Fabio Natalucci as quoted in *The Guardian*, October 16, 2019.

36   Mikkelsen as quoted in the *Financial Times*, August 8, 2020.

37   Powell as quoted in the *Financial Times*, May 2, 2020.

38   *Financial Times*, January 31, 2020.

39   *Financial Times*, August 8, 2020.

40   Symposium held on January 16, 1976.

41   Sayuri Shirai in *The Japan Times,* May 14, 2019.

42   Georgieva, 2019.

43   De Larosière, 2020.

44   *Forbes*, April 22, 2006.

45   The damage to real savings was somewhat contained in Belgium by the fact that the law imposes a minimum annual interest rate on savings accounts of 0.11 percent.

46   See also the section "Savior-Turned-Bully Syndrome" in this chapter.

47   *Bild*, September 13, 2019.

48   *Der Spiegel*, November 8, 2019.

49   Karen Petrou in the *Financial Times*, August 19, 2019.

50   See also the section "The 26 = 3.8 Billion Syndrome" in this chapter.

51   Allan Sloan in the *Washington Post*, July 27, 2019.

52   Chis Mortenson in the *Wall Street Journal*, October 22, 2014.

53   The last two quotes in this paragraph are taken from the *Financial Times*, October 4, 2019.

54   Wolfgang Schäuble as quoted in a Dow Jones newswire, April 2016.

55   See Goldgar, 2008 and 2018.

56   This search for yield is linked to the "portfolio rebalancing effect" that central bankers hope to achieve with their unconventional policies.

57 Initial Public Offerings.
58 *Barron's*, July 23, 2019.
59 Shiller, 2016.
60 Robert Shiller as quoted in *Investor's Business Daily*, October 25, 2019.
61 *Financial Times*, January 31, 2020.
62 In early January 2020, the Shiller P/E ratio (CAPE) stood at 31, which is close to twice the historical median value of 16.
63 *Forbes,* October 20, 2019.
64 *Financial Times,* December 11, 2020.
65 IMF, Global Financial Stability Report, October 2020, p. ix.
66 IMF, Global Financial Stability Report, October 2019, p. ix, x.
67 IMF, Global Financial Stability Report, October 2020, p. xi.
68 *Financial Times*, September 25, 2020.
69 See, for example, Jimenez *et al.,* 2014; Becker & Ivashina, 2015; Heider *et al.,* 2019; and ECB, 2019.
70 Robert Kaplan as quoted in Bloomberg, January 15, 2020.
71 Mersch, 2020.
72 Bloomberg News, December 10, 2020.
73 Grant as quoted in the *New York Post*, July 28, 2019.
74 The hedge fund manager came to see me regarding some technical issues about regulation of Central Counterparties in the derivative markets. He also urged me to be less critical of the unconventional monetary policy stance taken by major central banks.
75 JP Morgan Asset Management, Investment Outlook 2020, December 2019.
76 Barnaby as quoted in the *Financial Times*, August 14, 2020.
77 Jim Reid as quoted in the *Financial Times*, September 25, 2019.
78 *Financial Times*, January 31, 2020.
79 King as quoted in the *Financial Times*, September 17, 2020.
80 The term "shadow banking" was first used in 2007 by Paul McCulley, the executive director of Pacific Investment Management Company.
81 Bernanke, 2013.
82 *The Economist*, October 20, 2020, p. 62.
83 FSB, 2019.
84 White, 2020, p. 33.
85 For an overview of the risks associated with shadow banking, see Claessens *et al.,* 2012 and FitchRatings, 2019.
86 Adrian as quoted in the *Financial Times*, April 14, 2020.
87 Sobel as quoted in the *Financial Times*, April 14, 2020.
88 In traditional bank runs, the public rushed to their bank to get their money out. Modern bank runs are mostly electronic, as substantial amounts of bank funding can be withdrawn with a click of the mouse.
89 Kirti, 2017.
90 See, for example, Fiedler & Gern, 2020 and Hartwell, 2020. These arguments are rather unconvincingly rebuffed in Blot *et al.,* 2020. In this last paper, the possible impact of the increased riskiness of financial institutions' assets is completely ignored.
91 OECD, 2015, p. 112.
92 *Ibid.*, p. 142.

93 This conclusion was also reached in the IMF's Global Financial Stability Report, October 2019.

94 Rick Rieder as quoted in Bloomberg, August 4, 2019.

95 Bill Gross as quoted in Financial News, February 6, 2017.

96 This is what the British economist Douglas McWilliams has labeled the "inequality paradox." McWilliams, 2018.

97 For an excellent overview of the different arguments and the accompanying evidence, see Kanbur, 2020.

98 Darvas, 2018 and Lakner, 2019.

99 See also Colciago, Samarina, & De Haan, 2019.

100 See, for example, the article "It's a Matter of Fairness" in the *Financial Times,* July 8, 2020.

101 Based on an Oxfam analysis extensively reported in *The Guardian,* January 20, 2019.

102 Collins & Hoxie, 2018.

103 For a thoughtful defense of inequality, see Welch, 1999.

104 Helpman, 2018 gives an excellent overview.

105 See, for example, the data in OECD, 2018, Wealth Distribution Data, Paris, OECD.

106 Data taken from ECB, 2016, The Household and Consumer Survey. See also the arguments developed in the "David Copperfield Syndrome" section in this chapter.

107 Bernanke, 2015(b) and Lenza & Slacalek, 2018.

108 Montecino & Epstein, 2015; Cui & Sterk, 2018 and Saiki & Frost, 2019.

109 A most interesting and very nuanced narrative can be found in Honohan, 2019.

110 In these topics, see, for example, Hayek, 1976.

111 Krugman first made this claim in his book *The Age of Diminished Expectations* (MIT Press, 1990).

112 *The Economist,* September 26, 2020, p. 61.

113 Goldin *et al.,* 2019, p. 6.

114 See, for example, Adalet McGowan *et al.,* 2017; Banerjee & Hofmann, 2018 and 2020; Acharya, 2019; and Andrews & Petroulakis, 2019.

115 Caballero *et al.,* 2008.

116 This is measured by the ratio comparing the market value of the assets held by the companies to their replacement value (Tobin's q). Growth potential is considered to be meager if this ratio is below the median in the sector of the company considered.

117 All data in this paragraph are from Banerjee & Hofmann, 2018 and 2020.

118 IMF, Global Financial Stability Report, October 2019.

119 *Financial Times,* June 25, 2020.

120 *Ibid.*

121 European Commission, 2019, Fourth Progress Report on the Reduction of Non-Performing Loans and Further Risk Reduction in the Banking Union. One of the main authors of this analysis confided me that the Commission's estimate gives "most probably an optimistic picture of the status of the non-performing loans in the EU."

122 *Financial Times,* December 3, 2020.

123 Liu *et al.,* 2019.

124 On the rise in concentration and market power, see De Loecker & Eeckhout, 2018 and Syverson, 2019.

125 See, for example, Khan, 2017.

126 *The Economist*, September 26, 2020, p. 12.

127 Banerjee & Hofmann, 2020, p. 23.

128 The moral hazard issue becomes quite pronounced when QE policies increase the profits of central banks, as they in fact do. These profits invariably lead to higher dividends paid out by central banks. Higher dividends enter into national budgets as government revenue. When central banks buy more government bonds, governments face fewer budget constraints.

129 John Cochrane on his blog The Grumpy Economist, September 4, 2020.

Chapter 6

1   Some commentators perceive the relationship between central bankers and financial powers-to-be as a conspiracy to create a new world order that will benefit only a happy few. See Prins, 2018.

2   El-Erian, 2020(a).

3   El-Erian, 2020(b).

4   Wood as quoted in the *Financial Times*, September 27, 2020.

5   Cieslak & Vissing-Jorgenson, 2018 contains strong evidence on these causal links.

6   See, for example, Friedman, 1948 and Reinhart & Sbrancia, 2015. In the mid-1990s, Mervyn King, who later became governor of the Bank of England, noted that "central bankers are often accused of being obsessed with inflation. This is untrue. If they are obsessed with anything, it is with fiscal policy." King as quoted in Weidmann, 2020, p. 5.

7   Schnabel, 2020.

8   For an introduction to the real size of the fiscal imbalances that had already become enormous before the COVID-19 pandemic arrived, see Miron, 2015.

9   Remember the remark Benoit Coeuré half-jokingly made that about the limit of QE policies being reached when the entire euro economy is on the balance sheet of the ECB (see the introduction).

10   Weidmann as quoted in the *Financial Times*, October 1, 2020.

11   Tucker, 2018, p. 16, 17.

12   Tooze, 2020, p. 5.

13   Mallaby, 2020.

14   Borio, 2019(b), p. 8.

15   Lagarde in the *Financial Times*, March 30, 2020.

16   Powell, 2020.

17   For critical voices on this issue, see Issing, 2020 and Gros, 2020.

18   This is reminiscent of the words of the British poet and essayist W.H. Auden, who wrote: "What fascinates and terrifies us about the Roman Empire is not that it finally went smash ... (but rather that) ... it managed to last for four centuries without creativity, warmth, or hope." Auden as quoted in Douthat, 2020, p. 13.

19   We leave aside here considerations of the different definitions of "inflation" that can be used. There are, for example, the GDP deflator, the index of consumption prices, and the core index of consumption prices (the former cleared of food and energy prices). We also do not include the disconnect between official inflation data and consumers' experiences related to the COVID-19 pandemic. Sectors that were hit hardest by the pandemic (air traffic, fuel consumption, hotels, restaurants, and so on) experienced steep falls in demand, so an unchanged weight of these sectors in the consumer demand basket led to an enhancement of these sectors' negative contribution to inflation.

20   Data taken from the *Financial Times*, June 2, 2021.

21   The Phillips curve-inspired trade-off between inflation as celebrated in, for example, Samuelson & Solow, 1960 increasingly proved to be elusive or even nonexistent, since higher and higher degrees of inflation were needed to stimulate employment. See Friedman, 1968.

22   Keynes, 1924.

23   Volcker & Harper, 2018, p. 222. Volcker immediately added that he thought it was "a pretty good reputation."

24   This debt-deflation nexus goes back to Fisher, 1933.

25   Borio, 2017, p. 1.

26   Schnabel, 2020.

27   See Hammond, 2011 and Sarwat, 2018.

28   Powell, 2020.

29   Data taken from *The Economist*, November 28, 2020, p. 80.

30   During an exchange of views with former ECB president Jean-Claude Trichet on December 2, 2020 in the European Parliament, I asked Trichet this question. His answer came in two parts. First, he remarked, "Practically all the major central banks are pursuing this 2 percent target. There seems to be a high degree of consensus." Second, Trichet emphasized the need for further refinements and examinations in order to better understand the inflation process.

31   See, for example, Beckworth, 2014 and Brown, 2018.

32   Jorda *et al.,* 2019.

33   Freeman, 2007.

34   See, for example, ECB, 2017; de Soyres & Franco, 2019; and Forbes, 2019.

35   For evidence of and extensive reference to research material on this topic, see the 2019 Annual Report of the Bank for International Settlements, p. 9, 10.

36   Cavallo, 2018.

37   Juselius & Takats, 2018.

38   Sanchez & Sung Kim, 2018. See also Gajewski, 2015.

39   Awazu Pereira da Silva, 2019.

40   Mojon & Ragot, 2019.

41   Zervas at al., 2017.

42   On its December 12, 2020 cover, *The Economist* raised the question "will inflation return?" Recognizing that a temporary burst of inflation might be in the cards, the magazine concluded that "the odds of a more sustained period of inflation remain low," but added that "the COVID-19 pandemic has shown the value of preparing for rare but devastating events. The return of inflation should be no exception." (p. 13).

43   Goodhart & Pradhan, 2020.

44   Greenspan as quoted in Volcker & Harper, 2018, p. 225.

45   Feldstein, 1997.

46   These memoirs (Volcker & Harper, 2018) were published a little more than a year before Volcker passed away at the age of ninety-two on December 8, 2019.

47   Volcker & Harper, 2018, p. 224.

48   Frenkel, 2019.

49   Volcker & Harper, 2018, p. 226, 227.

50   Volcker & Harper, 2018, p. 227.

51   *Financial Times*, March 27, 2015.

52   Rajan made this remark during the "Rethinking Macro Policy III: Progress or Confusion?" panel discussion at the IMF Conference. The panel discussion took place on April 16, 2015 at the Jack Morton Auditorium of George Washington University in Washington, DC. A video of this panel discussion is available on the IMF's website (accessed on November 4, 2020).

53   Gros, 2016.

54   Borio, Erdem, Fillardo, & Hofmann, 2015, p. 48. See also Borio & Filardo, 2005.

55   A fast-growing body of evidence substantiates this chain of events. See, for example, Jorda, Schularick, & Taylor, 2015; Brunnermaier & Schnabel, "Bubbles and Central Bankers: Historical Perspectives" in Bordo, Eitrheim, Flandreau, & Qvigstad, 2016; Drehman et al., 2017 and Filardo *et al.,* 2019.

56   The concept of the financial cycle was mainly developed by economists working in the research department of the BIS. See especially Borio & Lowe, 2002; Borio, 2014; and Juselius *et al.,* 2016. See also the annual reports of the BIS from the last few years.

57   Volcker & Harper, 2018, p. 227.

58   In 2006, William White posed the question: "Is Price Stability Enough?" (White, 2006). His answer: a firm no. For an historical overview of how and why monetary policy objectives have changed over the very long run, see Davies, 2002.

59   See the section "Too Low for Too Long" in Chapter 2.

60   Borio, 2019(b), p. 11.

61   Weidmann, 2020, p. 9.

62   See, for example, Reinhart & Rogoff, 2009 and Goodhart, 1988.

63   Powell, 2020. This new target generated a new acronym: FAIT, short for "flexible average (2 percent) inflation target."

64   For more extensive critical remarks, see, for example, Angeloni, 2020; Issing, 2020; and Levy & Plosser, 2020.

65   Lagarde, 2020.

66   This is, of course, a reference to the monetarist episodes in central bank policies.

67   Issing, 2013, p. 284.

68   M1 is basically cash money in circulation and its equivalents; M2 is M1 plus short-term time deposits and certain money market funds; and M3 is M2 plus long-term deposits. The Fed no longer reports M3.

69   See, for example, Borio & Lowe, 2020; Alessi & Detken, 2018; and Jokipil *et al.,* 2020.

70   Calculation of intrinsic values of equities and real estate is a very difficult job, but there are normally enough reference points to determine when the market value of an asset is out of line with fundamentals. Some deviation is not really noteworthy, but major deviations are, and those are usually well recognizable.

71   Quite a bit of research at the BIS has focused on this topic. The annual reports of the BIS contain many references to more specific research results in this field. See also Jorda, Schularick, & Taylor, 2011 and 2016.

72   White, 2013, p. 16.

73   Kuhn, 1962.

74   Eichengreen, 2014.

75   *Ibid.*

76   *Wall Street Journal,* May 2, 2015.

77   Taylor, 2012, p. 1018.

78   Taylor, 2015, p. 5.

79   Taylor, 2018, p. 35, 36.

80   Friedman, 1960. Another major statement of Friedman's views on monetary policy is Friedman, 1968.

81   These substantial changes in Friedman's thinking are extensively argued in Nelson,
     2008. I can corroborate this story, since Friedman made similar remarks in the last
     conversation I had with him in August 2006, three months before he died. See also
     the interview with Milton Friedman in the *Financial Times*, June 29, 2003.
82   Bernanke, 2003.
83   Felstein in ECB, 2006, p. 167.

Epilogue

1   For the complicated issues involved in prudential and regulatory policies, see Barwell, 2013.

2   Ferguson, Schaab, & Schularick, 2014; Bordo, 2014 and Bordo *et al.*, 2016.

3   Nakaso as quoted in the *Financial Times*, November 24, 2020.

4   Hyperinflations are caused by large and long-lasting fiscal deficits and can only be stopped when fiscal holes are sufficiently plugged. See Sargent, 1982.

5   Bloomberg, December 1, 2019.

6   There's a wealth of research and literature on this topic. See, for example, Cecchetti, Moharty, & Zapolli, 2011; *The Economist*, 2015; and Pettis, 2019. For a comprehensive overview of the research on debt and growth, see de Rugy & Salmon, 2020. For emerging countries, an additional risk is that large amounts of corporate debt are in dollars. This creates not only exchange rate risks but also liquidity risks, if at some point maturing loans are no longer easy to roll over into in dollars.

7   See the section "Michael Jackson Syndrome" in Chapter 5.

8   See, for example, Kurz, 2018 and Rogoff, 2019.

9   See, for example, OECD, 2014; Spence, 2015; and ECB, 2016.

10 Olson, 1965 remains the classic work on organized interest groups and their impact.

11 This is the theme of another Mancur Olson classic. Olson, 1982.

12 de Rugy & Salmon, 2020, p. 10.

Index

Note: page numbers followed by n and nn indicate notes.